C000176666

Stalking Deer
in Great Britain

I. C. N. Alcock

Illustrated by Diana E. Brown

SWAN HILL
PRESS

Copyright © 1993 by I. C. N. Alcock (text) and Diana E. Brown (drawings)

First published in the UK in 1993
by Swan Hill Press, an imprint of Airlife Publishing Ltd
Reprinted 1996

British Library Cataloguing in Publication Data
A catalogue record for this book
is available from the British Library

ISBN 1 85310 250 4

All rights reserved. No part of this book may be reproduced or transmitted
in any form or by any means, electronic or mechanical including photocopying,
recording or by any information storage and retrieval system, without
permission from the Publisher in writing.

Printed in England by Livesey Ltd., Shrewsbury.

Swan Hill Press
an imprint of Airlife Publishing Ltd
101 Longden Road, Shrewsbury SY3 9EB, England

Contents

Foreword

Of all field sports, pastimes, call them what you will, stalking is the one in which atavistic instincts come most to the fore and play a vital role in successful outcome. It is also the one most justifiable in this modern world with its increasingly urban population unfamiliar with the countryside and the realities of natural life and food production and procurement. That deer have to be controlled by man is becoming more apparent to the conservationists, as well as to gardeners, farmers and foresters. The control of deer in a humane manner requires a degree of skill – in the choice of animals to be culled, the circumstances in which this is to be done, the accuracy of the shot and the subsequent utilisation of the carcase. Man was designed with an omnivore's dental equipment and digestive system, and has hunted animals from the earliest times. His instinct to hunt and to feed himself is as natural as his sexual proclivities. The unconstrained indulgence of the latter world-wide, as well as urban existence, has dulled the former and reduced its opportunities. These days the vast majority of people would deny the hunter-gatherer instinct and have no conception of the origin of the food that they buy in the shops. Although the emphasis in communication media is on disappearing populations of creatures and plants of many kinds, there is a latent awareness of the dangers of uncontrolled populations that have no predators. Most people know of the dramatic rabbit population problems in Australia prior to myxomatosis. Occasionally there are reports of locust plagues that bring home, temporarily, the horror of population explosions. The awareness of famine in many areas of the world is beginning to bring home the message of the devastation and the inevitable disaster resulting from uncontrolled population growth even in humans.

The rise in deer populations is not restricted to this country. Significant increases in numbers have taken place in continental Europe and USA too, partly as a result of conservation measures, and partly because of changes in environment, including new afforestation reaching growth stages of optimum habitat. In this country the expanding woodlands, and the general encouragement to plant more, particularly hardwoods, will further enhance suitable deer habitat. Concern is being expressed by even well known conservationists at the increase in the red deer population, particularly in the north-east of Scotland. It has been shown that population assessment of deer in woodland is notoriously difficult, and guesstimates of deer numbers of all species in woodland are likely to be lower than the reality. The remarkable spread of deer, particularly roe and muntjac in southern England, suggests the speed with which their population is increasing. Thus the opportunities for stalking and the necessity for control are appearing in areas that previously contained few deer.

Although opportunities for stalking, and the richness of game and wildlife population, in Britain are to be envied by people in most other countries, we lack the hunting traditions of continental Europe, and indeed only in the last thirty years have woodland deer become regarded as other than vermin. In Scotland they were so regarded, and killed by shotgun drives much more recently. Red deer stalking on recognized deer forests was practised from Victorian times with social implications that differed completely from the hunting of the deer in the past. As with grouse shooting, and other driven game shooting, the cachet involved in Highland red deer stalking has provided the funds to allow deer forests to be maintained. I would not decry the thrill of the stalk, the exhilaration of wonderful scenery and the satisfaction experienced subsequently of enduring tiring and uncomfortable conditions, enjoyed by those taken out by professional stalkers on the hill, but, having always been somewhat of a 'loner', I am glad that I had the opportunity of learning for myself by my own experience. Under such circumstances the atavistic instincts come to the fore, and the awareness of the environment is not only apparent but a vital requirement to achieve success. Deer movement or restlessness on the hill may presage a change in the wind. A jay calling at the end of the wood may mean a walker disturbing deer. Such recognition becomes second nature to the stalker who has to depend on his own wits to achieve success.

I believe that being a stockfarmer, with sheep and cattle, for the past twenty years, has heightened my awareness of animals and their habits. I have been fortunate enough to see deer on virtually a daily basis for many years, but the necessity of detailed observation of cattle and sheep, to the extent that it becomes second nature, in order to manage them properly, has inevitably led to comparisons with other animals both from behavioural aspects and from a management viewpoint. It has also led to numerous questions arising relating to deer, to many of which answers are not easily apparent. Deer in different areas can have varying behaviour, and even appearance, and frequently the dogma of the traditions of continental Europe is not applicable to deer in Britain. One of the fascinations of deer stalking is that there is so much to learn about deer and their environment and each sortie offers the opportunity to see and learn something new.

Chapter 1
The First Roe

What stalking experience I have has been learned largely on my own. I did not have the benefit of being taken out by an experienced stalker to be shown the ways of deer, nor did I suffer the disadvantage of absorbing set ideas from such a mentor. From a very early age I spent much of my free time roaming the woods and fields. At the age of twelve I acquired a .410 shotgun and my wandering about the countryside had a hunting purpose. The success of bringing home an occasional pigeon or rabbit, or the triumph of returning with a pheasant, was ample reward.

I was aware of deer from quite an early age, for there were fallow deer that occasionally passed through my territory and I saw their tracks from time to time. When I discovered these they caused great excitement, akin perhaps to Crusoe finding the footprints in the sand. The deer remained elusive, however, and I never saw them. At one stage I actually went hunting for deer on an estate managed by a friend of my father, armed with a little Browning repeating .22 rimfire rifle lent to me. Mercifully I never saw any of these deer, despite finding plentiful slots and other signs. At that time it would have been legal to shoot a deer with a .22 rimfire, but in retrospect I am horrified to consider the prospects of a clean kill, or indeed a kill at all.

Although shooting and fishing remained a strong interest in my life, as they have always done, I had no further contact with deer for some years. Circumstances involved my reluctantly living in London for a time, and my forays from the horrors of urban life to fish or shoot at weekends or on holidays did not take me into country where I might come across deer. Finally there came a time when I could tolerate living in London no longer, and circumstances permitted my moving out into the country. Because I had to continue to work in London, and commuting was an important part of my life, I was restricted in the areas in which I could live. I had no wish to live in Surrey, and indeed I regarded it as rather an unattractive idea to live in what was described as the 'stockbroker belt', but it so happened that in 1966 I came across a cottage on the North Downs that seemed ideal and I was able to purchase it. Only subsequently did I learn that Surrey is actually one of the most wooded counties of England. From the situation of my cottage this was not difficult to believe, since it lay half a mile off the road down a rough flint track in the middle of a wood, or rather, surrounded by several thousand acres of woodland. The owner of some adjacent woodland told me later that he had always known my new home as 'the enchanted cottage'. I did not know at the time that there were deer in Surrey, let alone that it was thickly populated with roe that were steadily extending their range of territory.

My little cottage was set in a tiny valley in about three acres of deciduous woodland. There was a small open space of perhaps quarter of an acre in front of the house where my predecessors had started to make a garden. I fell in love with the setting at first sight. The main problem with the cottage was its access. The local farmer who owned the rough flint track that led to the cottage maintained that there was no legal right of access over it. The sellers had necessarily to warn me of this situation and they had been trying to establish an alternative route by which to reach the property through a parallel strip of woodland.

However, they had set about it in a way that had caused a certain amount of disquiet to a neighbour, through whose property the proposed route might have run. My enquiries revealed that the Forestry Commission, who controlled a large area of woodland that ran close up to the back of my house, actually had the lease of the six acres of yew wood that ran in a strip between my property and the road, although they made no use of it. I approached the Forestry Commission to try to acquire their lease of this small block of woodland, and I was told that they might be prepared to part with the lease but that I would be best advised to approach the owner of the freehold to see if she would be prepared to sell this. They gave me her address and I wrote off accordingly. The reply, from solicitors, eventually came that the freeholder would not be interested in selling the right to the small strip of woodland but would be prepared to consider selling the entire freehold of the area leased to the Forestry Commission, amounting to 467 acres. This freehold was not particularly valuable since the Forestry Commission had an extremely long lease and the rent involved was hardly generous. The lady who owned the freehold had merely inherited it with other property in the past and had no interest in it otherwise.

Soon after I arrived at my new cottage I discovered that a small syndicate rented the shooting on the ground leased to the Forestry Commission as well as an adjoining area of a couple of hundred acres of mixed deciduous woodland and farmland. In that part of Surrey pheasants were rare in any case, and the Forestry Commission area, having been planted with trees a year or two previously, was becoming gradually impossible to walk through for a rough shoot. Naturally I was eager to participate in a syndicate operating literally on my doorstep and I was able to join the shoot. They were pleased to have me, since by that time I had acquired two labradors and there was a shortage of dogs on the shoot, and I lived on site.

Having agreed to purchase the freehold of this area of land, for a sum that was comparatively modest in terms of securing the access to my house on a legal basis, I discovered that I had become the owner of the shooting rights of most of the ground shot over by our syndicate. This was an added attraction to the purchase. After the deal had gone through and I finally received the appropriate plans and papers I discovered too that included in the purchase were a few odd plots of land that were not subject to Forestry Commission lease and therefore belonged to me freehold without encumbrance. I managed to sell a couple of these to adjoining owners of property and recoup the cost of the purchase of the whole. Thus I ended up with two alternative access routes to my house, a small area of extra freehold land, the shooting rights on 467 acres of conifer woodland and a modest rent from the Forestry Commission.

In the course of the next year or two the Forestry Commission's plantations grew up, so shooting became rather hopeless as a syndicated rough shoot and this packed up. In practice this suited me admirably since it meant that what shooting there was became entirely my own. Moreover I was able to approach the owner of the adjoining woodland and rent the shooting on this for a peppercorn rent and the promise to keep an eye on a picnic hut that he had built in one of the woods and used once or twice a year in summer.

Over these first couple of years I had become aware that there were roe deer in the area, but I had not paid them a great deal of attention. I had had a good deal of work to do in trying to continue the making of a garden and in clearing some of the scrub woodland in front of the house to give rather more of a view. In addition I had been training my two young labradors. I had also devoted quite a lot of time to trying to reduce the enormous population of grey squirrels, jays and magpies. When the syndicate shoot ceased I was able to spend more time prowling about the woods on my own and I gradually became more and more aware of the deer. The prospect of actually stalking and shooting one had not really occurred to me, since at that time I had no idea of the substantial population.

One summer afternoon I was walking along a ride at the back of my house when I heard loud barking in the woodland down a slope below me. I thought that it was a large dog, but then I became aware that it was moving slowly nearer and was clearly not a dog. It dawned upon me that it must be a roe deer. For some reason I generally carried a couple of heavy shot cartridges in my pocket when out with a gun, and I slipped an SG into the right barrel of my 12-bore. I had just passed what was obviously a deer path that came up the slope and on to the ride along which I was walking, and it occurred to me that perhaps the deer would come up this path. I waited hidden at the edge of the ride in ambush about ten yards from the path. The barking ceased, but after waiting a minute or two I heard movement in the undergrowth and suddenly the front part of a roebuck emerged on to the ride. Before he could turn to look at me he received the charge of shot in his shoulder and fell dead instantly. It was as if he had been struck by a handful of 9 mm bullets simultaneously. I do not know now why I shot the buck, but I suppose that it was some atavistic hunting instinct caused me to do so, and I am glad that I did, for this was undoubtedly the start of my interest in stalking and deer.

I dragged the beast back to the house two or three hundred yards away and realised that I would have to gralloch it. I had paunched countless rabbits and quite a few hares, and was familiar with cleaning birds, but I had never tackled anything as large as a roe deer before and was unsure how to set about it. The first thing was to find a knife. The only knife that I had, other than a kitchen knife and a massive sheath knife that I had carried on expeditions to Canada and Lapland in my younger days, which was totally unsuitable for gralloching, was my late father's ex Argyll & Sutherland Highlanders dress skeandhu. It was perhaps fitting that my first deer should be gralloched with a silver-mounted knife with a cairngorm on top of the hilt! Anyway it was sharp and did the job and I succeeded in eviscerating the animal without mishap and hung him in an outbuilding.

My first contact with a deer made me very much more aware of their presence: I took a great deal more interest in looking for their sign as I walked about the woods, and started deliberately to try to see deer. My interest in roe and the prospect of stalking them increased noticeably. However, I realised that if I was to try to shoot another deer clearly I had to obtain a suitable rifle. Despite having killed my first deer with one, I did not favour the use of a shotgun for this purpose and even then regarded it as an improper way to try to kill deer except at extreme close range. The then manager of Churchill, Atkin, Grant & Lang, as it then was, had been a member of the shooting syndicate and so I decided to pay a visit to his shop and make enquiries about rifles. I do not know if I had any views on calibres then, or whether he influenced me, but I am glad that somehow I settled on .243 as the most suitable rifle for roe, with the possibility of being able to use it on red deer in the future should the chance arise. He showed me several of the usual makes of rifle from which to choose, and then brought out a weapon that had apparently been made by Churchill in an attempt to break into the luxury American market. It was nicely stocked with a horn tipped fore-end front, and had a Redfield mounted telescopic sight without any open sights. There was no comparison in the quality of this rifle to the others in my mind, and it seemed so much nicer in looks and feel that I had no difficulty in deciding to buy it. Subsequently I learned that in fact Churchills had made the rifle seven years earlier and had been unable to sell it because the price was rather high. I believe that I paid £250 for it, which then was expensive even for a one-off rifle, though compared with present prices the purchase appears in a better light. I have never regretted it.

I had little difficulty in obtaining the necessary firearm certificate, having the shooting over quite a large area of land, and I soon had the rifle home, sighted in and ready for action. Repeated sorties in the woods frustratingly produced nothing more than barks in the undergrowth or the glimpse of pale bottoms disappearing.

I had noticed that the path running along the edge of the forestry plantation at the back of the house, about a hundred yards from my back door, showed signs of a lot of deer movement. So I decided to build a high seat in one of the maple trees overlooking my back gate and this ride. I nailed a few bits of wood to the tree as a ladder and made a reasonably comfortable plank seat. The first fine free evening that I had I resolved to sit up there and see what transpired. My field of view was confined to about fifty yards in either direction, so figuring that there might not be much to look at unless a deer actually came along below me, I took a book with me up the seat as well as the rifle. Half an hour later I was reading away when I heard footsteps below me, and looking down saw a roebuck passing underneath the tree along the ride. I think that he must have heard me shut the book, because as I grabbed the rifle he looked slightly alarmed and turned to move off the ride. As he did so I shot him through the shoulder. He ran about ten yards under the branches of a large yew tree and I heard him fall.

I had acquired a small book on deer stalking to try to learn something about it, and in this I found reference to the length of roe antlers. It seemed to me that this buck, my first with a rifle, had antlers as long as I had seen on occasional glimpses of deer in the area and so when I had dragged him home I measured them. Unfortunately they were not perfectly symmetrical, the right-hand one being slightly shorter and with a longer back point. The left hand antler was twelve inches long and according to the book this appeared to be unusually long. By this time I had acquired a proper knife for gralloching and skinning deer and so I was able to complete the job rather more quickly, with the experience of having already cleaned one animal before. The subsequent eating of the venison confirmed the opinion that I had formed after eating my first roe, which was that it was absolutely first class meat and a highly desirable addition to the menu.

Chapter 2
Roe in the Woods

My stalking interest was now beginning in earnest and gradually I was starting to find that I was learning to spot deer before they saw me. I got to know likely places and I began to learn to look for tell-tale signs, such as tiny movements or horizontal lines amongst trees where there should be none, or glimpses of unusual shapes and so on. The dogs were learning, too, and would often wind deer and let me know of their presence by their reactions. As I became a little more competent, and more successful, I also started to appreciate the high population of roe deer that existed on the ground. The forestry plantation of various stages of growth provided ideal cover and feeding. In the process of trying to tidy up the woodland immediately around the house I decided to clear fell a couple of small areas of perhaps half an acre each and replant with young trees, for various reasons, including that of attracting roe so that I could see and watch them from the house. For the felling and sale of some of the mature hardwoods I contacted a commercial forestry company, and it was arranged that the proceeds of the timber sold would cover the cost of replanting.

During the course of talking to the manager of this forestry company I learned that they controlled an area of a thousand acres of woodland, managed for their clients, immediately adjoining my own shooting, and moreover he was concerned about the deer damage that was taking place there. He was quite pleased when I offered to take over the control of the deer in the area for him. This extended my area of stalking to some 1700 acres of woodland surrounding my house and within walking distance of it. It also put upon me a certain amount of pressure to shoot deer, because whereas I was under no obligation to shoot any on my own ground, having taken over control of the commercial forestry area I had undertaken to kill a sufficient number of deer to keep damage to a minimum. This new ground varied from newly planted areas to mature trees, and all ranges of growth in between. There were some hardwoods, but most of the ground was softwood plantation. The roe deer population was very high.

I was fortunate enough to have the stalking on this area for a number of years until we moved north, and during that time, despite my repeatedly offering venison to the manager and his colleagues, they showed little interest in the meat, or in the deer other than from the viewpoint of having them shot, with the result that the annual cull of twenty-plus bucks, and a suitable number of does, from the ground, kept both myself and my dogs, and a good few friends, plentifully supplied with venison, indeed to the extent that we ate little else. Other than on one occasion, when I sold a few carcases to help a friend who was handling them on a commercial basis, I have never sold deer, nor indeed game of any kind, except for red deer carcases in the far north of Scotland where there was no other satisfactory means of disposal. I have always felt that the introduction of commercial value to deer or game of any kind insinuates a distasteful element to what one might describe as a sporting pastime or a manifestation of one's primitive hunting instincts, and I have long believed that one should eat what one shoots, within reason, or give the spoil to someone else to do so. Surprisingly, despite eating venison perhaps five days a week before I was married, and very frequently afterwards, we have never tired of it.

Although I subsequently became a member of the local Deer Control Society and one of their stalkers, and indeed served on their committee, the fact that I had a significant area of stalking of my own, meant that my involvements were largely helping them on winter exercises to move does, or friendly stalks with other enthusiasts to see their ground or merely accompany them. In those days roe stalking had little commercial value attached to it and indeed it was almost regarded as a form of pest control, so that many of the early keen stalkers were able to obtain free stalking of first-class quality bucks, roe and fallow, and often free venison too.

In order to take the twenty bucks or so that I decided to cull annually from the commercial forestry ground, I had to stalk it regularly. In the early stages stalking can be rather frustrating, when one makes silly mistakes, like not checking suspicious looking objects with binoculars, or moving a little too quickly, or not pausing to examine thoroughly areas were deer are likely to be seen feeding. However, at least those frustrating early times taught me a few lessons in woodland stalking – tactics that have been valuable subsequently. The quality of binoculars is very important for woodland stalking, especially when one needs to use them in poor light either around dawn or dusk, or even in gloomy light under trees. It is essential that the binoculars have good light gathering power. I believe that the best combination is 7 x 50 but 8 x 56 is also good. The size of the binoculars is significant, because one does not want a huge pair getting in the way of shooting. Rubber-covered binoculars have the great advantage that they do not clunk metallically if accidentally banged against the rifle, and a cover that can be put over the eye-piece in rain is very useful. An alternative is to cover the binoculars with soft leather, such as tanned deerskin, with a flap that can be put over the eye-piece in wet weather. Years ago I had the opportunity of buying a pair of binoculars on a trip to Hong Kong, where a contact owned a shop selling them and offered a liberal discount. I was delighted with these cheap Japanese glasses and wondered why anyone was so stupid as to spend a lot of money on an expensive pair. I discovered the reason why on the second occasion that I dropped them, when they became useless. As a result of this I bought a pair of rubber covered 7 x 50 Carl Zeiss binoculars. They were expensive, although the price that I paid over twenty-five years ago does not appear so now, but I have never regretted it. Their depth of field is so great that I never need to focus them, at whatever distance the object, and they are so clear that even on the open hill after red deer they can be preferable to a telescope in poor light conditions.

The area on the chalk downs where I stalked mostly had a significant number of large ancient yew trees dotted around which had been left uncut. These served as excellent high seats for most of the productive clearings and newly planted areas, the old yews being easy to climb, with many branches, and easy seat construction with minimum pruning. I soon learned that the best, and most successful, procedure was the one that I believe is most adopted on the continent – stalking on foot in the mornings and sitting up high seats in the evenings. The latter generally helps to give one a substantially better picture of what deer are in the area. In the evenings, emerging from cover or from a period of resting up, deer tend to be more wary, and getting to a high seat or vantage point in good time can give one the advantage by waiting still and silent for deer to appear. In the mornings, when deer will have been out and about feeding undisturbed for a while, they are often more easily approached on foot.

When the summer days lengthened I was able to rise early in the mornings and get in a couple of hours stalking before getting back to the cottage to wash and change into a city suit and have breakfast preparatory to commuting to my office in London. In the evenings I tended to have a snack and change and be off into the woods up a high seat until dark whenever there was the opportunity, which was frequently. I generally stalked two or three mornings each week at least, and four or five evenings, either on my own ground or with friends, or on some Deer Control Society errand. It often used to afford me amusement to sit in the London-bound train in the mornings observing my fellow commuters and wondering what they might think did they but know that I had already been up for several hours that morning, out stalking, and had shot a buck now hanging at home in my larder. I remember one morning in particular when I had just got home from a successful stalk, and had been dealing with the heart, lungs, liver and kidneys that I had brought home as usual in a plastic bag. My hands were all bloody still when the postman came, and I went to answer the door and take the mail. I saw him stare with what appeared to be a mixture of amazement and horror at my bloody hands, and he looked somewhat incredulous when I said with a rather sickly grin 'Its all right, I have just been having a fight with the wife!' (I think that he was probably aware that I was not married.)

With abundant stalking opportunities, I decided early on to leave the area in the vicinity of my house as a sort of sanctuary. The ground that I had cleared and replanted I stocked with a variety of trees which I thought might be attractive to roe; I even bought a number of roses, from a stalking friend who owned a nursery, and planted these outside the garden fence specifically for the deer. Needless to say, they always preferred the flowers actually in the garden to the ones that I provided for them outside. Other patches of the cleared area had thick growth of wild raspberries and also rosebay willowherb, both much favoured by roe, and I used to see deer constantly from the house. It was interesting to observe how quickly the deer got used to the normal noises from the house, and when the postman came in the mornings they scarcely took any notice of the noise of his van arriving, nor of our voices as we exchanged conversation. The sound of the radio or even of the dogs barking seemed to bother them little, and one was able to watch them going about their feeding, or resting, without disturbance.

Those early morning stalks, with the dogs at heel, on warm sunny mornings, gave me the necessary invigoration to face the grime of suburban trains and a day in a London office constantly on the telephone. I remember many of those lovely mornings. On one day I had decided to take a walk through an open wood of large oaks close to the house. It was a lovely spring morning and the traditional bluebell wood was a carpet of blue. Halfway through the wood I spotted a badger shambling along a path towards me. I could see that he would pass me at a distance of only a few yards if undisturbed, so I hissed at the dogs, which was their signal to sit quietly, and stood stock still. The wind was favourable and we watched the badger shuffle past, the dogs with their eyes almost out on stalks. When immediately opposite us he must have sensed something, as he stopped still for a second or two, questioning, before ambling on reassured.

On another morning, walking along a path at the bottom of a steep little valley, I watched a parrot fly overhead. I wondered how long this presumed escapee would survive in the wild. On hot summer mornings I refreshed myself with wild strawberries, which grew in profusion in a couple of areas of my stalking territory.

In the middle of a hazel coppice, one morning out stalking with a friend on his ground, I watched a pair of little black water shrews chasing each other in a tiny stream, and marvelled at these comparatively rare creatures, perhaps the fiercest of our mammals in proportion to their size. There was always something to see on these outings, the bee and fly orchids that grew at the edge of one of my rides, the masses of sweet-smelling butterfly orchids that grew in some newly planted areas but are probably now long swamped by conifers, and occasionally a slow-worm, that snake-like legless lizard. I saw badgers quite often, for there was a big set in the oak wood, and foxes frequently, though I rarely had a chance of a shot at them. In the evenings as I returned home along the rides at dusk I was enchanted by the strange little luminous lights of glow-worms twinkling on the grass or on bushes, hoping to attract their mates.

Chapter 3
Deer Control Society and Roe Sign

Involvement with a Deer Control Society as a so-called accredited Society stalker carried a few responsibilities to help people with deer problems. This meant visits to garden owners and so on, most of whom could have avoided having deer eating their roses by a little judicious fencing or even keeping gates shut. Occasionally the problem led to the acquisition of the stalking on adjacent local council-owned woodland, or farmland where the farmer did not shoot or had no rifle, which opportunity was readily taken up by those anxious for more stalking opportunity. Part of the public relations programme was the offer to the police to try to sort out road damage problems, and I volunteered to allow my name to be given if it was required for someone to go out to deal with deer struck by vehicles. Almost invariably the infrequent calls were at night, and whilst one was happy to assist, mostly they were tiresome and often fruitless problems. The police appeared soon to learn that a carcase contained a certain amount of good meat, and the evidence disappeared. On a number of occasions I drove out to the poorly described area of an accident, and after eventually finding hair or whatever and identifying the precise spot, and a subsequent extensive search, concluded that either someone had removed the carcase, or the unfortunate animal had gone off to die elsewhere. From those carcases that I took home, to try to salvage meat, if only for the dogs, the massive nature of the internal damage, usually far from obvious externally, taught me that a deer hit by a motor vehicle with any degree of impact, and certainly a beast that did not immediately vanish into adjacent cover or countryside, was almost certainly critically injured internally and unlikely to survive. More often than not the extent of the damage and broken bones rendered the carcase unfit even for the trouble of removing some dog meat. We, ourselves, conscious of this and of the frequency of roe colliding with cars in the area, were always very cautious driving round Surrey lanes, fearful that a deer might leap across the road without warning, especially at night.

However, the only occasion that I ever had this happen to me actually took place quite recently in Aberdeenshire, close to the edge of my own land. Fortunately I was in my old Land-Rover, which has on it the largest size tyres

to give it maximum clearance. I had been flighting ducks with a friend and was returning home an hour or so after dark when a roebuck jumped out of a patch of young larch trees on to the road immediately in front of the vehicle, with no chance at all for me to react. I stopped immediately, already well past the beast, and went back up the road with a torch. He appeared to have hit the bumper and the underneath of the vehicle, so perhaps the impact had knocked him over and then he had bounced on the underside. A low-slung car might well have found the beast jammed underneath, and suffered a lot of damage to the front or wings, but the Land-Rover showed no sign of harm. The blow, or blows, had broken off both antlers at the pedicle; I found one of these lying in the road a few yards away, but despite a search next day in daylight as well I never found the other, which must have catapulted into the undergrowth with the force of the impact. When I came to cut up the carcase none of the meat was fit for the table because of massive bruising and contusion, and the shoulders were too full of splintered bone to be used as dog meat.

Two night-time call-outs to road casualties I remember particularly. The first was to the middle of a common only a couple of miles from our house. When I arrived there was a car parked at the roadside and a young couple standing looking at a roe lying on the verge, breathing heavily and clearly in a bad way. I explained to them that there was no possibility of the animal being other than extremely badly damaged internally, for it would never have lain there all that time otherwise, and from the look of it the poor brute was near death, so the kindest thing was to put it out of pain. When they asked what I would do, I told them that I would cut its throat. Whereupon I was called an unfeeling swine and other pleasantries, and they drove off without any appreciation of the fact that I had climbed out of bed and driven to assist them, and was doing what my experience indicated was the kindest action. Subsequent post-mortem on the carcase revealed that the roe was just a mangled mess inside, and I was surprised that it had actually lived so long. I suppose that in these days of ignorant and misguided 'animal rights' supporters such an attempt to be as humane as possible, as well as practical, would meet with even more hostile criticism and I am glad to be no longer involved.

The other incident also called us out of bed in the middle of the night. Diana came with me on this occasion. It turned out to be one of those circumstances when one felt that the requirement for humane killers to be on a Firearm Certificate was ludicrous. Often I have felt that, quite to the contrary, a humane killer ought to be a regular piece of stalking equipment and a required item for stock farmers. We were told that a roe had been hit by a car and was now in someone's garage where it had been carried after being knocked down. Diana and I arrived at the house to be taken to the adjacent garage, where, when the light was put on, we saw a groggy and, although still very much alive, clearly badly injured roebuck, which had apparently recovered consciousness after being taken there. It was a typical semi-suburban smart clean garage, and the buck was standing in the middle of the empty concrete floor, looking terrified and bleeding from its mouth. I had visions of awful internal damage, subsequently proved correct. I said to the garage owner that I felt that it was badly damaged and that it would be best and kindest if I put the animal down as quickly as possible, and fortunately he agreed. The problem was how to do it, for I did not think that using a .256 Mannlicher in a small enclosed garage was appropriate, and I had visions not only of being deafened and waking the neighbourhood, but of the bullet ricochetting off the nicely painted walls in a dangerous manner. The buck was clearly still mobile and I did not fancy wrestling with it in front of an audience.

I recalled that a good many years earlier I had been staying with a friend in Kenya and we had gone to shoot a Thomson's gazelle on a big ranch belonging to somebody that he knew. My friend had made an unfortunate shot and had broken both front legs of a buck, which remained very mobile, if slower than normal. Our host had a large hunting knife, and he hid behind a bush and told us to drive the buck past him. We succeeded in doing so, and he leaped out and with one stroke cut the animal's throat and finished the affair. I now saw this as the solution to my problem. I explained to the owner and told him that his garage would get bloody, but he did not mind this, being anxious to see the matter settled. I reckoned that if I failed with the first attempt I should have a more difficult task with a mobile, bleeding, injured deer. Fortunately my first lunge was successful and put the deer out of further pain, though leaving the garage owner with somewhat of a mess. He did not want the carcase and was glad to see it removed, so we bundled it into a plastic bag and made our way back to bed.

Usually, when I shot deer in someone's garden or on their property I offered them the venison, or most of it, butchered and in plastic bags ready for their freezer, since at that time we had so much of our own and gave away a lot, because I always had this disdain for selling it. Mostly they were delighted at the offer, but only accepted a little, although there were some who seemed horrified at the idea of eating the deer. This sort of deer control was rather a chore and mainly hard work rather than interesting, since shooting deer in a garden, however large, is not my idea of sport. It was necessarily an early morning excercise, to be around when the deer were, before people were out of their beds and moving about. I, too, had to get home, changed and on to the London train after the hunt. However, in some ways this somewhat unusual facet of stalking added to experience. One had to look carefully for deer sign, examine droppings to determine if a buck or doe, or both, were the culprits, and look for evidence of where the deer entered the property and so forth. One also had to determine whether a safe shot was possible if the opportunity arose, and very often this was not the case and I had to tell the garden owner this.

Checking for deer sign is the first thing any stalker has to do when entering new territory. After a while it becomes almost automatic. Bitten off twigs, bramble shoots and willow-herb, slots and droppings all help to give a picture of the possible deer activity in the area.

Slots, or footprints, are very often not as obvious as one might expect. I always used to look forward to the few days of snow sprinkling that we might have on the North Downs, hoping to see all the tracks in the early morning, but I was always disappointed. Fox tracks were evident, but the roe seemed to stay put in the thick cover and their tracks were scarce in relation to what I expected from the population level there. I used to see more sign in the wet grass on dewy mornings. Inside the cover beds and scrapes show the level of activity, and frequent scrapes suggest an agitated buck delineating his territory in the face of interference from interlopers. Does scrape, of course, especially when about to lie down, but bucks fray too, and combined scrapes and fraying are sure signs of a buck marking out his territory, especially later in summer when the deer are in hard horn and no longer cleaning their antlers of velvet.

The droppings of roe deer can be difficult to distinguish, unlike those of red deer where the stag's 'fewmets' are usually bigger than those of a hind, pointed at one end and flatter than the hind's at the other though still with a concave end. Sometimes those of a roe doe are oval and symmetrical at both ends, whereas those of a buck can be pointed at one end and concave at the other, with an overall slightly squarer appearance, according to that authority Ferdinand von Raesfeld. Much depends on what the deer have been feeding on, of course, and in spring after lush food the droppings can be quite soft and coagulated.

Having spent some time examining the completely fresh droppings of roe, red deer and sheep on the same morning close to each other, I have formed the view that firstly a great deal depends on what the animal has eaten, and secondly that it is extremely difficult to distinguish between all three at times. Large sheep produce pellets the same size as those of hinds and small stags, and small sheep, hoggs and lambs produce droppings the size of roe faeces. Moreover, examination of fresh sheep droppings in fields of which one contained only females and the other only males showed that ewes do produce pellets with tails at one end and a concave end at the other where the next pellet end fits, as well as more symmetrical-shaped cylindrical ones. Certainly one finds roe droppings where the whole pile consists of symmetrical, round ended, oblong pellets, and other piles where all are of a square-shape with a pointed 'tail' at one end and a concave depression at the other, both types easily distinguishable; this was especially so in southern England.

There was no doubt in my mind then that the latter type, with the pointed 'tail', were those from a buck and the others produced by a doe. It may be that I was mistaken or it may be that the difference in food is significant, or it may simply be some difference in varied population characteristics, just as roe in the north have pale rumps in summer as well as white ones in winter, whereas in southern England the summer roe do not have pale backsides until they flare their rump patches in anxiety.

Hair is another sign for which to look, or 'pins' as the old venery term had it. In early summer when the deer's coat changes from the thick winter pelage to

the fine red summer shade, the thick winter hairs shed, and one can find tufts of these where deer have been lying and where they have crept through fences. All deer seem to far prefer crawling under fences or through holes in these to jumping over them, if they can avoid the latter, however much within their capability it may be. Deer hair on or below fences is a sign for which to watch out, and often is the tell-tale indication of areas that deer frequent. The observant stalker will note all these points and build up a picture of the woods and their inhabitants. There is so much to see and hear, and the true stalker and woodsman will take note of, and interest in, all that goes on round him. The fellow who goes out into the countryside solely interested in killing a deer not only misses so much of the beauties of nature, but undoubtedly overlooks too the many deer signs that the keen watcher notes.

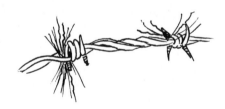

Chapter 4
Diana

My interest in roe stalking had developed to a degree that must almost have reached the point of eccentricity. The bulk of my spare time was taken up with stalking in one way and another, and in addition I collected avidly both books on deer and stalking, and paintings of deer, and indeed anything relating to deer. My little house was festooned with deer items and antlers to the point where it was difficult to see the wallpaper. This was perhaps just as well since I had never redecorated the house when I took over, and I suspect that my predecessors might not have redecorated the sitting room when they took over either and that the wallpaper was rather ancient.

Stalking new ground always attracted me and it was interesting seeing different habitat, and even different deer. Antlers of bucks in Dorset, for instance, vary quite considerably from those in Surrey, the latter tending to be more heavily pearled but narrower and less attractive in shape to my eye.

I had been asked to take over the stalking on a farm in Sussex where there were both roe and fallow deer, though mostly the latter, which the owner found tiresome in her crops. A friend, a fellow stalker, also had some ground that he visited quite close to this farm and we arranged to meet one morning after stalking down there. Discussing the area, my friend told me that he knew of a woman living close by, a wildlife artist specialising in deer, who spent a lot of time watching these animals in that area, and he thought that this included watching them on the farm on which I was now stalking. It seemed to be diplomatic that perhaps I should be introduced to her. Thus when we met up after our respective stalking outings he suggested that we went over to this artist's cottage to say hello.

Diana welcomed us and offered us facilities for washing and then breakfast. She had been out that morning in the woods and had picked some chanterelles, and offered these to us fried with bacon. I had never tasted chanterelles before, and indeed I believe that I had never heard of them then. We have always jokingly considered the idea that they must have had some magical effect because Diana is now my wife!

Diana was having some paintings in an exhibition not far away soon afterwards and, intrigued that there would be some deer paintings there, and certainly hers, I decided to go and arranged to meet her there. During this meeting I discovered that she intended to go to the World Hunting Exhibition in Budapest due to be held that summer, and I had already decided that I was going to go there, too. That we had mutual interests led to further meetings, and after what we calculated later was being with her for a total of eight hours I asked her if she would marry me. There may well have been other people whose lives were so involved with deer as mine was then, but there can not be many couples where the same could be said for both spouses. Diana had been interested in deer for considerably longer than I had, and was more knowledgeable, though from perhaps a slightly different aspect.

We decided that she would move from her small cottage in Sussex, and the fallow deer that she used to watch daily, and move to my marginally bigger cottage in the middle of the Surrey woods and roe country. There were roe in her area of Sussex, of course, but not perhaps in quite the quantity as in my area of the North Downs, though fallow are absent there.

The first time that Diana came out stalking with me I was filled with trepidation because I knew that she was highly concerned at the prospect of a deer being wounded and not killed outright. She did not object to the shooting of deer as such, realising full well that they had to be controlled in order for numbers to be kept down for the good of the deer themselves quite apart from any other reason. She had seen deer shot before and was not squeamish about this, only anxious that the shooting should be as humane as possible. Whilst I had no reason to feel nervous or self-conscious, I was aware that if for some awful reason I made a bad shot at a roe it might result in a difficult situation and perhaps spoil Diana's enthusiasm for coming out stalking with me again. We went to a small, quite steep valley and sat against some trees on one side, looking down and across to the other side that had recently been planted with conifers, which had already suffered some fraying damage. At the top of the opposite slope was thick plantation, and this little newly planted valley extended some distance to our right, a good part of it in range of the rifle from where we sat. After a wait of half an hour or so a buck emerged from the thick wood opposite and advanced a little way down the slope towards us. I was able to take a careful sitting shot at a hundred yards, perhaps a little more, and was quite confident.

At the shot, the buck turned and ran off back into the thick wood. My heart jumped a little. Whilst the reaction of the buck was one that I should probably

have regarded as normal for a heart shot, under the circumstances I was
nervous that something might have gone wrong – an unseen twig or plant in
the way, perhaps. Diana and I crossed the little valley, walked up the slope on
the other side and found a spot of blood and a few hairs where the buck had
stood, indicating a hit. Inside the wood there was a thick carpet of pine needles
and trying to follow a trail was extremely difficult. However, I could not see
the buck lying anywhere. Fortunately a brief search showed him lying quite
dead about forty yards into the wood, and so all was well. This helped to build
Diana's confidence in my ability, and future outings with her carried less of a
feeling of apprehension.

Most of our holidays, if not all, since then have involved deer in one way or
another, and our honeymoon trip resulted in our seeing the most roe that I think
that either of us have ever seen in a comparatively short period of a few days,
as well as the best fallow deer that we have seen anywhere, and a few red deer
too. Our holiday was to Denmark, including a visit to the leading Danish
sporting artist, under whom Diana had studied many years before, to the
famous Kalo Game Research Station with its population of heavily studied
marked roe deer. We drove up through northern Germany and whiled away the
journey with an 'I spy' game of counting the roe that we saw out in the fields
in great numbers, totalling figures that I previously would not have believed.
We also saw the only black roe that we have seen, and in Denmark saw the
largest winter party of roe that either of us have seen, amounting to twenty-two
animals in one group. Almost all our subsequent holidays have been taken
stalking in Sutherland and elsewhere.
    From her new home Diana was able to see and draw roe deer from the
comfort of the house if she so wished. We were able to see roe from every
window in the house at one time or another, and could lie in bed watching
them in the early mornings on a clearing at the back of the house, the farthest
end of which was only two hundred yards away from the window. One

summer we had the pleasure of watching a litter of fox cubs on the back clearing every day – these being given sanctuary at Diana's request! On more than one occasion I missed my normal commuting train to London due to dallying too long in bed watching the cubs playing. Frequently we saw roe in the clearing at the same time as the cubs, and often very close to them, and they took comparatively little notice of each other. The roe would come within a few yards of the windows of the house and, being there for a longer part of the day than myself, Diana was soon able to recognise individuals, having the gift of being readily able to distinguish between animals, as can any experienced shepherd or cattleman with his own flock or herd.

It was rather ironic that we encouraged roe into our garden, when the Deer Control Society had requests from garden owners irate at deer eating their flowers and shrubs. Often with the minimum of precautions and effort these people could have kept the roe out of their gardens had they really wished to do so, but most of them would not consider putting up a fence, nor did they appreciate the privilege of being able to watch deer.

In the winter, when stalking does was more difficult, partly because the roe tend to become more nocturnal during the shorter days and partly because one could only stalk at weekends due to having to go to work during daylight hours, the Deer Control Society stalkers often arranged combined operations to achieve a cull of does out of various areas of woodland. This was not always successful, but mostly it produced some satisfactory results, depending on the type of woodland. The operation consisted of placing two or three rifles at strategic points, preferably up high seats, which not only kept the person out of sight of the deer and offered a comfortable shot but with the downward angle meant safer shooting, whilst another two or three members of the party walked slowly through the wood downwind with the object of making the roe move slowly and not particularly alarmed out of that piece of woodland, perhaps crossing a ride or a field to move into adjoining cover. The rifles had the opportunity of taking a shot as the deer paused before crossing open ground. In the winter, roe move around mostly in family parties, and when the bucks have cast their antlers it is necessary to examine the deer carefully before shooting to see there is evidence of a tush underneath or a more circular rump patch to indicate a buck, or an anal tush to identify a doe. These roe-moving manoeuvres in winter can be an excellent way of achieving cull numbers, given the right sort of ground and competent rifles, and the exercise can be carried out with only two or three people if likely deer movements are known. Even a single person walking through an area of woodland downwind so as to disturb the area can cause deer to move out temporarily, and it certainly gives the stalker an insight into the effect that he may have on woodland whilst stalking deer in the summer should he fall foul of the wind.

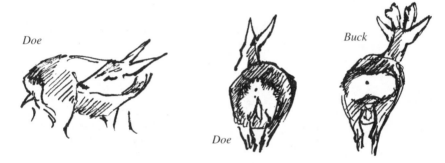

Doe

Buck

Doe

    There is no doubt in my mind that the major factor in determining the quality of roe, other than the obvious one of food supply, is that of disturbance, particularly by other deer. There is abundant evidence that some of the best roe deer from the point of view of both antlers and body weight have come from areas recently colonized by them. Similarly, where the deer are present in large numbers, the quality of the animal necessarily goes down. When I first started to stalk in Surrey I expected all mature bucks to weigh over 50 lb and perhaps as much as 55 lb with head and legs on, but gralloched from end to end. When we left that area and moved to Scotland in 1974, the normal weight of mature bucks had dropped to well below the 50 lb mark and the quality of the antlers seemed to have deteriorated, whilst the number of deer seemed to have increased. In Aberdeenshire, where we now live, the lower weight of a mature roe is very noticeable and a 40 lb buck would be a big one. Although there are some roebucks with quite good antlers in this part of the country, the majority of them are poor compared to the heads of those that would have been regarded as average in Surrey and Sussex say twenty years ago.
    The most impressive roe antler that I ever saw was a cast antler picked up by a keeper in a wood where roe had not been noted before and where the first roe had evidently just crossed the main Guildford to Redhill road. This antler, picked up in 1973, was 12 inches long and weighed 7 ozs – though it was clearly well dried out – and moreover was heavily pearled and of a lovely shape with all long tines. If the antlers were symmetrical the buck's head must

have been singularly impressive. The
heaviest body weight of which I
have had personal knowledge
was of a buck shot in 1971 in
Hampshire, where again the roe

were starting to spread: he weighed over 75 lb as he fell and just over 65 lb
gralloched. He was killed by our good friend the late Christopher Dalgety, one
of the most knowledgeable and accomplished men in all types of field sports
that it has been my privilege to know.

Since the Surrey ground that I stalked mostly had a lush growth of bramble
and willowherb and other food favoured by roe, and this was available all year
round with snow and hard frost comparatively rare, it was clear to me that the
deterioration in roe quality, noticed elsewhere in the vicinity by fellow stalkers,
came with the deer population reaching what seemed to be almost saturation
point. Since twin kids seemed to be the norm then, with occasional triplets and
singles comparatively rare, it can readily be seen that the compounding effect
on the roe population over a few years of this level of reproduction, even
allowing for casualties, would be, and clearly was, dramatic. In Aberdeenshire,
though twins are not infrequent, I believe that there are at least as many roe
does with single kids as there are with twins, and triplets are quite uncommon.
In view of the considerably harder winters and periods when food must be
difficult for the deer to obtain, this is hardly surprising. I have twice shot runt
roebucks of abnormally low weights, one of which I was able to suspend from
one finger when gralloched, and I have been unable to determine whether these
were late kids or simply runts that had failed to grow properly.

When we moved to Scotland we noted several factors that differed between
the resident roe and those that lived in the south of England. The most obvious
of these was that our Scottish roe have pale fawn or off-white rump patches
even in summer, which are quite clearly visible without the deer flaring up its
rump patch. In the south the deer had more evenly coloured backsides except
when alarmed. I recall with embarrassment years ago criticising a painting of
roe in a birch wood in summer by a well-known artist of mostly fishing scenes,
saying that he had the bottoms all wrong because they did not have light-
coloured rump patches in summer. I had fallen into the trap of generalisation,
and demonstrated how a little knowledge can be dangerous, especially when
treated dogmatically. I know now that the painting was of Scottish roe, quite
probably in the north-east, and quite correct.

Presumably as a result of being less disturbed, roe in this area are seen
feeding in daytime much more often than in the south, though this may also be
to do with the long daylight hours in summer and short days in winter when
food is scarcer. Down south deer tended to lie up during the daytime and it was
rarely worthwhile stalking in the middle of the day except perhaps during the
rut, whereas I have quite often shot roe in the middle of the day in
Aberdeenshire, and see them around feeding as I go about the place. There

seems to be a period in this area, in summer, perhaps around early breakfast time, when the roe appear to rest and be less obvious. This could be due to the early daylight causing them to have fed sufficiently by then. Cattle too often rest at this time of day.

In most other parts of the country my impression was of the ratio of bucks to does being about even. This was certainly so in the Surrey woodlands. My initial impression in Aberdeenshire was of a noticeable preponderance of does over bucks. At rutting time I have seen a buck in close proximity to two does, chasing one but with another close by and clearly part of the group, which is something that would have astonished me in the south. Over the past years this substantial excess of does over bucks has appeared to be constant, and has been confirmed to me by keepers on both neighbouring large estates. This could be due to heavy shooting of bucks on a commercial basis with little attention paid to does in winter, but I find this difficult to accept as an explanation in view of the heavy buck cull that I saw taken in the south; this was invariably very disproportionate to the number of does killed. Another factor could be that buck kids are less robust than the females and succumb more readily to winter weather or disease. We invariably find roe remains in early spring, suggesting that winter deaths are significant.

One reads frequently in writings on roe deer references to the territories of bucks. My observations, particularly on my own land here in Aberdeenshire, lead me to believe that it is does that have territories rather than bucks. My land is birch woodland and open hill, as well as fields, almost entirely surrounded by commercial forestry plantations of varying ages. Although roe are present throughout the winter, they are certainly not on the ground in their summer numbers, and it is clear that in winter they move into the conifer woods for shelter. In the spring the does move out again into the more open ground with better feeding and establish territories; at the same time, or a little later, the bucks also move out. Frequently in the spring, at the time when the foliage is growing on the open ground out of the shelter of the woods, there seems to be an influx of bucks

moving around, many never seen again on the same area. Consequently I suspect that the dogma about leaving master bucks to hold territories to avoid tree damage is even less applicable in this part of the world than it might be elsewhere.

The does establish their territories where they intend to have their kids, and stay in roughly the same area throughout the summer, chasing off other does. Bucks are attracted in during the rut. These bucks have more opportunity for polygamy than in other parts of the country, I suspect, and this may contribute to a more itinerant, or less sedentary, buck lifestyle. If there were several does to a buck in the area it would stand to reason that he would be inclined to move around. In fact I never subscribed wholeheartedly to the master buck theory put about by dogmatic theorists, even when I stalked regularly in areas that clearly had equally balanced sex populations. I recall going to stay in Belgium with a stalker well known to many in this country, at his chateau in the Ardennes. I went out one morning, at his direction, to a high seat overlooking a small meadow in the woodland area, and after a short wait shot a buck there. It was quite a nice head, but by no means remarkable by our standards at home. On my return to the chateau my host exclaimed, 'Oh! That's our big buck!' I was embarrassed that I should have shot one of his best bucks, but he assured me that it was quite in order and that he was delighted. 'Anyway,' he assured me, 'another buck will soon come into that doe's territory. ' I am sure that there are master bucks that guard certain areas, especially so at rutting time, but I am equally sure that much depends both on the nature of the area and of the habitat, and on the population level of the deer in the vicinity, and that to be dogmatic on this subject is as mistaken as it is inclined to be with most things concerning animals and the workings of nature.

Although I have watched roebucks running does many times in various parts of the country, I have only actually seen them mating on two occasions. On neither of these occasions did it take place on a rutting ring. The first time I was actually working in a field greasing and carrying out maintenance on a combine harvester when I noticed a buck chasing a doe in an adjoining turnip field. He chased her briefly and then they stopped and he mounted her. This was in the middle of the morning. The other time was in an evening when I was sitting up a high seat with a substantial view of an open hill and some old fields perhaps a quarter of a mile away. With binoculars I watched a buck running a doe in these fields, and again I saw him mount her.

I have only once watched roebucks fighting, though I have been told accounts of them doing so quite viciously and one of them being found dead subsequently with gore wounds. I was sitting up a favourite high seat that overlooked an area of new conifer plantation of about twenty acres surrounded by mature woodland when I saw and heard a buck emerge at some speed from the woodland behind me and about fifty yards to my right, followed closely by another buck. They ran well out into the open area and chased in a somewhat half-hearted manner. They then paused a while and the bucks faced each other. I am not sure now if one attacked the other, but I rather think that they both advanced at the same time, and there was a brief head on encounter two or three times, perhaps more, before the apparently younger buck decided to give in and ran off. He was no longer chased by the older looking buck, who eventually returned back into the wood whence he had come, without offering me the opportunity of a shot. However, the excitement and interest of seeing the brief fight was much more rewarding so far as I was concerned.

Needless to say, when we took the decision to leave the south and move to Scotland the presence of roe was part of the consideration that decided us to move here. That part of our hill is a rutting area for red deer, and that a few red deer hinds spend much of the summer on the farm is an added bonus.

Chapter 5
Buck Fever and Misses

I imagine that most people who have stalked deer and shot them have, at one time or another, had 'buck fever' to some degree, whether it just be an attack of nerves and a slight shake of the rifle, or a full-scale experience of trembling, shaking and sweating, rendering shooting temporarily impossible. I would go so far as to say that anyone with substantial stalking experience and who has shot a lot of deer, who has never had buck fever, must be an insensitive person. However, what brings on an attack is rather a mystery. If it occurred when the shooter was faced with a particularly superb buck, or a beast that he finally had the opportunity to shoot after days of effort, then it would be more understandable, but sometimes it seems to happen at unlikely moments and without apparent reason. I recall one of the most impressive and knowledgeable stalkers that it has been my privilege to meet, a professional shooting well into three figures of deer each year, telling me that every now and again, perhaps once a year and for no reason so far as he could tell, he would get an attack of buck fever. Then he would shake and simply have to put the rifle down and wait until it passed over.

I have read strange stories in American hunting magazines of clients taken out to stalk deer getting attacks of buck fever, manifesting itself in scarcely credible ways. In one incident the guide referred to an occasion on which he and his client approached a party of good bucks. They peered over the top of a knoll to look at the beasts; the hunter decided which to take and instructed the client to shoot, whereupon the latter stood up trembling and rushed forward a couple of steps, ejecting all the rounds from his magazine and yelling, 'Did I get him? Did I get him?' I have only observed this malady once in a companion, though I have been out with people who were clearly very shaky and missed an easy shot. My companion was presented with a comparatively easy shot, and I was quite surprised when he hesitated, for he was a regular stalker of roe, shot a lot of deer and was a very competent target shot, too. I turned to see the reason for the delay in shooting and saw sweat pouring off his face and the rifle unsteady, and then the opportunity of the shot was gone and the incident over.

I have been nervous and unsteady on several occasions, and had to pause to let the adrenalin, or whatever, settle down, but certainly I have had an attack of buck fever at least twice. As it happens, both times I was up a tree. Perhaps this added to the tension somehow. The first time this happened was actually when I was about to shoot the second buck that I had killed. A long narrow path or ride ran from the back of my house through the forestry plantations, close to the boundary of the area of deciduous hardwood adjoining. There was a thin strip of conifer planting interspersed with occasional small areas of beech between this ride and the adjoining oak and hazel wood, and the softwoods were of differing species and ages. One small patch of about half an acre was cypress, where some of the trees were only one to two feet high. These had suffered significant fraying damage, which was hardly surprising, with such a small patch of nicely smelling easily frayed trees amongst an area of much older woods. Along the ride at intervals were several large ancient yew trees and a couple of holm oaks or evergreen oaks (*Quercus ilex*), remnants of the days when the area was part of the estate of a mansion some miles away. These old yews were ideal as high seats, being easy to climb, with many branches, and rather open and flattish at the top. I have often used them as permanent vantage points, and usually only an odd branch needed removal to make a comfortable perch with a good view, whilst the occupant remained reasonably well concealed. One of these old yews stood conveniently at the edge of the middle of this area of young conifers, and it seemed to me, from the amount of deer sign, that all I had to do was go and sit up this tree and sooner or later I must see this buck.

For several evenings in sequence, after getting back from work, I hurriedly changed, took out my rifle and made off to the yew tree, where I spent the evening in anticipation, but without success. On more than one occasion as I sat in the tree I thought that I heard movement in the trees behind me, and I came to the conclusion that perhaps this buck came out of the wood behind and along the ride where I had walked, and that my fresh scent was scaring him away. So I decided to give the vicinity a rest for a few days, and then to approach the tree from a completely different direction. The next time that I went there I walked through the oakwood on the other side of the patch of cypress and in front of my high seat, and crossed the fence directly opposite my tree, heading straight across the area of young trees to the yew. I figured that by the time that the buck came to my scent he should be shootable. It might have been coincidence, of course, but this tactic certainly proved successful. I had been sitting up the tree for three quarters of an hour or so, listening to the birds singing and watching a squirrel foraging, with its quick, impulsive, movements, when I became aware of a roe moving through the slightly taller trees on my right.

It was a buck, and rather a good one too. Quite clearly he was going to walk straight across in front of me. I realised that once he got immediately opposite he would smell my scent where I had crossed earlier, and this might alarm him if it was still sufficiently strong. I got my rifle ready, looked through the telescopic sight at him, and suddenly I began to shake violently. It was not simply a wobbly rifle – I trembled all over and had to lower the rifle in a mixture of astonishment and frustration. I had read about such an experience, and realised that it was nervous excitement, but I was concerned that the moment of failure to control myself would not pass before the buck reached my path. I had no hope of trying for a shot as I was, for the rifle shook as though I suffered from that awful Parkinson's disease. Such moments always seem long and yet in actuality are brief, thankfully; my uncontrolled shaking passed and I became steady again at the precise moment that the buck reached the track I had taken through the planting. He put his nose to the ground and I fired as he did so. He ran about fifteen yards and fell dead. I sat for a few moments a little overcome by the experience of the past few minutes, and the excitement of the achievement of not only successfully shooting my second buck but also having taken the animal damaging this area as I had planned.

The second occasion when I was seized with buck fever occurred a couple of years later. I had found a considerable amount of fresh fraying in some young conifers at the far end of my ground, where it was rather overgrown and the young trees had not been weeded, so there was quite a heavy growth of birch saplings and so on. There was really no open space offering the opportunity of a clear shot and the only chance that I could see was a well used deer path running through one side of the planting; it had one or two clearer patches that might allow enough gap for a shot. A couple of large yew trees stood at the edge of this area, and climbing one of these I could see that the deer path ran right up to it, giving several gaps, so that if one spotted a deer coming down the path and identified it one could be ready when he passed the next gap, perhaps fifty or sixty yards from the tree, with another two short opportunities subsequently. I cleared a couple of small branches to give me a better view from where I found a big branch that gave me a comfortable seat with a footrest on another below.

A couple of evenings later, having given the area time to settle down after my wandering around looking at it, I went off to see if I could see a buck there. In view of the thick cover, and the almost certain problem of finding a buck that was shot and did not drop in its tracks, I decided to take my dogs with me. We approached from behind the planted area and I left the dogs lying at the foot of the other large yew tree, just behind the one in which I sat myself. It was quite a pleasant, warm, sunny evening, but the view was somewhat restricted, and I had little option but to concentrate on the narrow deer path in front of me, or what I could see of it. I had been waiting about half an hour when I glimpsed a red shape and then saw a deer at the furthest point of the path in my sight.

I kept the glasses on this and a few moments later, as he passed another opening, identified him as a buck. To my delight he appeared to be walking straight down the path towards me. I got the rifle ready and decided to try for a shot if he paused at the next spot where I had a clear view. The next moment I felt myself shaking violently. I had to hang hard on to the tree, and I felt that this was shaking so much and noisily that I was terrified that the buck would see or hear me. Fortunately at that point he chose to stop and fray a tree and then scrape aggressively at the base of it. I suppose that my shakes only lasted a minute or so in reality, but it seemed much longer at the time and I remember wondering whether I was going to be able to get back into control of myself before the buck came actually under the tree. He continued walking towards me as my self control returned and I was able to raise the rifle again and sight it on where I could see parts of him approaching. At about twenty yards I got the opportunity of a clear threequarters-on shot as he paused for a moment and took this, aiming to allow for the angle. At the shot he dashed down the path towards me, straight past the tree and apparently almost over the dogs, and I heard a crash in the undergrowth beyond. I quickly climbed down out of the tree, and was delighted and surprised to find the dogs sat up and alert but still where I had left them. I sent them to find the buck and they rushed about ten yards into the birch thicket to where he lay quite dead.

I do not recall having such a violent attack of buck fever again, but of course there have been many times when I have been distinctly nervous and wobbly when trying to take a shot initially. Generally this wears off if one is given the chance to take it easy and wait until one is calmer, as is usually the case, but if a quick shot is necessary there is mostly no time to develop nervous shakes. I believe that to experience moments of nervousness when getting prepared to take a shot is quite normal, and no one need be afraid to admit this. I understand that many, if not most, well known public performers, speakers, politicians, actors and so on suffer from excited nerves prior to delivering a speech or a performance, and some have said that they believe this to be a healthy sign. I believe the same to be the case when one sees an animal that one respects and admires and one is anxious for a clean kill. I do not recall being nervous when shooting at rats, and the only occasion when I have had almost a slight version of 'buck fever' when shooting a fox was when I was desperately anxious to kill it and felt that I should not get another opportunity;

moreover I had been watching the animal for some minutes in a spotlight beam. This fox had killed about twenty of my lambs, one night leaving a dozen dead in the field in pools of blood, some with their stomachs eaten and some only with their heads crushed. My shepherd and I sat up in a Land-Rover with spotlights and shotgun and rifle, prepared with thermos flasks and sandwiches to sit there in the lambing field all night if necessary. At about 11 p.m. we detected fast moving eyes at the end of the field and saw ewes hurriedly standing up and staring at them. Unhappily the fox heard the Land-Rover door creak as I got out, unable to shoot from the window at that angle, and I thought that the desperately important opportunity was gone as he fled over the stone dyke again. However he was soon back, and came towards the vehicle clear of the flock; kneeling on the ground beside the Land-Rover I took aim with the .222, nervous and unsteady with tension. He stopped and stared in our direction at one hundred yards and the bullet hit him in the centre of his chest. I have never wanted to kill a fox so desperately! (As a matter of interest, he had a broken canine tooth, and the small one next to it; I believe that the nerve was exposed and that he was probably in great pain, which might explain why he chose to kill soft bellied lambs instead of the ubiquitous rabbits.)

Thus it seems that buck fever, or its equivalent, is brought on by anxiety that the shot will not be successful. In the case of rats or rabbits and such like where perhaps one is not so concerned about the result of the shot for some reason the problem is less likely to arise, and when a quick shot is required and there is little time to think about it and only to shoot instinctively one is less likely to show nervous reaction. A good few years ago now, at a time when perhaps my eyesight was keener and I was shooting deer more regularly, I was sitting up a high seat in Hampshire overlooking a long plantation of conifers that had been created about three years earlier. The strip of trees was perhaps 150 yards wide and three or four hundred yards long, divided from a similar strip of mature hardwood trees by a grass track. Quite early in the evening I spotted a roebuck and doe appear in the plantation away to my left, and I spent a while watching them and occasionally looking through the telescopic sight of my .243 wondering if the buck might wander my way; I judged him to be two hundred yards away, too far for a shot, and I could only see his neck and the top of his back above the trees.

Frustratingly, both he and the doe stayed around in the same spot, apparently quite content with whatever they were eating. I watched them for half an hour or so and was beginning to wonder if I should get down out of the seat and stalk closer to see if I could get a clear shot. My experience is that impatience causing one to get out of a seat and go for a stalk is almost invariably unwise.

It is rather like trying to kill two creatures with one shot; it usually fails to be as successful as hoped. Nevertheless a long, unfruitful wait in a seat can tempt one to come down when one can actually see deer out of range.

Fortunately I resisted the temptation, for had I got down and stalked up the track I should have looked back and seen the classic situation of a buck then standing right in front of the seat! A young buck came from behind me to my right and walked straight across thirty yards in front of where I was sitting. He paused to nibble a leaf, offering an easy shot. I fired, and then without thinking I chambered another round and put my sight on the distant buck, who was standing looking in my direction with head up, but only head and neck visible. The shot that I had refused all evening I took without any further thought or concern and he fell where he stood. I can remember the incident very clearly, and even now I am surprised to think how I took this shot with such confidence – but there we are! I was well pleased to take these two beasts off this new area, and so was the owner that had asked me to deal with them.

In retrospect I believe that, though actually successful, this shot was probably unwise, because a two hundred yard neck shot at a roe is too far. I suppose that we all make unwise shots at some time, and perhaps reflection on these is no bad thing, for it may warn others and possibly save somebody else from similar action. Any stalker who has done a lot of shooting of deer who claims never to have taken a shot that upon reflection should not have been taken, or who claims never to have missed, would incur my suspicion.

One stupid shot that I took, and regretted subsequently, occurred early in my stalking career when a friend took me to a farm where he shot a lot of roe. It was quite a small farm, surrounded by hardwoods, mostly hazel and oak. One field in particular yielded an amazing number of roe. I never discovered what was special in its attraction, but it had obviously been reclaimed from woodland at some stage, since there were still tree stump remains to be seen, and a certain number of wild flowers and so on. We arrived at the field and peered through the hedge beside the high seat that he had overlooking the area towards the wood, and spotted two young bucks feeding together. My friend told me to take one, and both if I could. As they were close together I conceived the silly idea that the 105-grain bullet from my .243 would go through the animal, so I might take both with one shot. I waited until they lined up in a couple of paces, one only perhaps ten yards behind the other, and fired. The nearer beast ran a couple of steps and fell, but to my horror the other ran off into the wood behind. Bitterly regretting my irresponsibility I waited to see what happened and saw the wounded buck lie down about five yards into the wood, more or less on the edge. As we could see the beast, clearly very sick, we decided to wait for a few minutes. It was too far and too difficult a target for me to try another shot from where we were. We decided that my friend would stalk round to the edge of the wood and come along the side until he could see the wounded buck, while I stayed where I was, keeping it under observation. All went to plan and he shot the animal from close range. It was clearly badly wounded, but the quicker it was put out of any suffering the better. My bullet had apparently been slightly deflected by the first beast, or else perhaps it was impossible to gauge properly the correct point of aim for the one behind, but whatever the situation it was a salutary lesson learned and we were lucky that it ended no worse.

I think it as well that errors and faults are imprinted in memory to provide a lesson learned for oneself, and perhaps hopefully to save others from a similar experience.

I can remember misses clearly too, though relating these is perhaps likely only to comfort others to know that they are not alone, rather than to obviate such occasional eventuality unless the circumstances caused the result. One miss that I remember clearly I never explained, though subsequent experience with a thistle raised my suspicion.

The evening was memorable also for me because I watched a badger climbing a fence, which I have not seen again since. On part of the ground where I stalked roe was a young plantation that was now thick and high enough to make a shot at a deer amongst the trees impossible, but a firebreak or track ran through the middle along the contour of the slope. I had never been able to take a buck on this part of the ground, which was surrounded by thick woodland on three sides, two of which were over the boundary. I decided to try sitting looking along this ride one evening, so I positioned myself on the fourth side inside a rather younger clearing of a considerable size. Sitting on a slight bank above an old overgrown chalkpit I had a good view along the firebreak as far as I could shoot. During the evening I heard movement in the undergrowth below me and a badger emerged. He shuffled off purposefully away from me and over to the rabbit fence at the edge of the clearing, and then proceeded to climb up this and down the other side in an obviously familiar way. I saw badgers from time to time, and there was a large well-used sett in the bluebell wood on the other side of my house, but I was always thrilled and enchanted to see them. Sitting thinking about this and wondering how far he had gone, and at the same time listening to the churring of a grasshopper warbler on the clearing behind, I became aware that a buck had come out on to the firebreak in front and was standing eating some plant threequarters on to me facing away. I took aim and fired and the buck looked round in surprise, loped off up the firebreak for ten yards and then turned into the trees and disappeared.

I was nonplussed, since he appeared to be totally unharmed. I looked through the scope sight again to check and mark where he had been standing, and also to see if anything had got in the way of the bullet. I had read of bullets blowing up on grass and leaves and failing to reach their destination, but I did not believe that the hundred-grain Norma ammunition that I was using then in my .243 would do that. In any case I could see nothing in the sight in the way of the slightest obstacle. Having searched for a while where the buck had stood, and where I judged that he had gone back into cover and found absolutely no trace of blood nor even a hair, I concluded that it must just have been a miss, though I could not see how. Next day, of course, I sat down on my range at the house and fired a magazine full of shots at the life-sized roe cut-out target that I kept there, and there appeared to be nothing wrong with the rifle. The incident remains one of those mysteries, where one cannot quite bring oneself to believe that one could have just plain missed, especially without reason.

It was the following year before I had the experience of a bullet blowing up on a thistle and apparently not even fragments reaching the deer a few yards behind. This time it was with a slightly faster and much lighter bullet from my .222. I could not actually believe that it had happened until I found the evidence. The buck was an easy shot, broadside at sixty yards or so, in an open part of a young plantation, and I was sitting comfortably up a metal high seat with an arm rest. I was astounded when the buck just skipped off and hopped over the rabbit fence, apparently quite unconcerned and certainly unharmed. Only next day, sitting up the same seat and continually looking at that spot with binoculars, trying to understand what could have happened, did I spot the headless thistle. I got straight out of the seat and went to look, and was then in no doubt that the thistle head had been blown off; being in the line of fire as I judged it, it must have been the cause of the otherwise inexplicable miss.

One winter some of my Deer Control Society friends asked me to join them on a doe-culling operation. The farm was a mixture of hardwoods and fields divided by shaws, largely of hazel, with a few oaks and other hardwoods scattered about. The plan was to have three people walking quietly downwind through the woods to move deer slowly across the fields into other woods and shaws where three of us were stationed with rifles. When the probability was that shots would be under one hundred yards, and perhaps not stationary, I generally took a .256 Mannlicher, partly because I liked its shallow rear open hunting sight, and partly since I believed that its slower heavy bullet would be less likely to be deflected by unseen foliage. Indeed I had once shot a roebuck through a sapling behind which it was standing, without any problem.

I was stationed in a shaw overlooking an obvious deer path, well marked in the clay ground, through the hazel scrub. I positioned myself beside a large oak tree where I had a clear shot of the path in the middle of the shaw, where it dipped down to a little stream and gave me a safe background towards which I could fire, at the same time giving me a view of the field in front across which it was hoped that roe might come. Sure enough, after a time a doe and her well-grown kid came running briskly across the field and into the shaw opposite me. There they paused to check the situation. They then walked quite fast down the path to the stream and paused again, whereupon I fired at the doe. It was not a difficult shot by any means, and I was astonished that instead of her falling dead they both rushed off up the other side and away across the next field. No more came to me during that part of the operation, and when it was over I went forward to try to determine what had happened. Before I reached the place where the deer had stood I saw the reason for the miss, which was a great splintered gouge out of the side of a hazel about the diameter of my arm. Concentrating on the deer I simply had not seen this narrow tree several yards nearer to me. Had the bullet hit it centrally it might well have gone clean through and killed the beast, but glancing from the side the wood had clearly deflected the bullet well off course.

A year or two ago I was stalking in a wood at the far end of the farm at roe rutting time, in the middle of the afternoon. I was actually more on a reconnoitring outing than on a stalk, but I had my rifle with me. In a thick part of the wood I heard crashing close to me, and saw a buck chasing a doe about forty yards away. Then they turned and I realised that they were coming straight for me. The doe was running directly at me, with the buck about ten yards behind her; clearly at some stage she would see me and jink and scare the buck, too. I do not know how close she might have come, doubtless with her concentration fully on the pursuing buck, but when she was very close, having my rifle already up and pointing, I got the buck's chest in my sight and fired. He was very close, perhaps twenty yards or less, and coming straight towards me. To my surprise he and the doe both veered off at the shot, and halted thirty yards to my left, at the top of a steep bank, no doubt wondering what the bang was. They did not pause long enough for another shot before they disappeared down the bank and I could hear crashing and barking into the distance, but they stood quite long enough for me to realise that the buck was completely unharmed. I had not moved, so I put up the rifle again to where I had fired, and all seemed clear. When I lowered the rifle again, still looking in the direction of the shot I saw a small branch in front of me with a clear, fresh bullet mark. The line of sight through the telescope had been clear, but the line from the rather lower rifle barrel had not!

This same problem (or rather I should say fault, because it is a fault of which shooters should beware!) occurred one day when I was out on the west coast of Sutherland with a companion after a hind. I had, in fact, killed a hind, and my host had told me to take her calf as well. What had transpired was that we had come across the two of them lying in long heather and my host had instructed me to take the right-hand beast, which he judged to be a poor hind by its coat colour and appearance. I had expressed the view that the hind was on the left and the animal on the right was her calf. However, he insisted and I deferred to his authority. It was a longish shot for a beast lying down in long heather, at two hundred yards, but I managed to kill the right hand deer outright. The other got to her feet and was clearly a hind, so having been told to shoot her too, I reloaded and took aim. She did not react to the shot, and moved off before I could try another. My host then told me that he had seen a piece of heather move in front of my rifle barrel as I fired, and sure enough there was a broken twig. My telescopic sight had been clear of vegetation, but my rifle barrel had not. No great harm had been done since I had not wounded the second beast, and it was not desperately needed. Moving forward to the dead deer we discovered it to be the calf, as I had known, and my host apologised and called up the stalker with the pony to take it home.

It is extremely important always to check that the line of trajectory from the rifle as well as that from a high mounted telescopic sight is unobstructed, since there are circumstances, such as rocky ground for instance, where a bullet striking a close object could be positively dangerous.

In the case of longer shots, which should only ever be undertaken by someone with complete confidence and considerable familiarity with his rifle and his ability with it, two other factors can lead to problems in more open country, particularly in steep ground – shooting across a valley, for instance. These are faulty range judging and wind. From time to time I have seen distance judging competitions by people interested in deer, mostly stalkers, and their level of competence at this has not been impressive. One fellow I spoke to, who had made a hopeless guess at the range of a life-sized roe target, told me that he used his telescopic sight and the reticule normally to measure distance. The incentive to judge distance is not assisted by the capability of the modern high velocity rifle to shoot more or less flat to over two hundred yards, at which range a roe is a small target and even a red deer not large. Estimating range over undulating or steep ground is much less straightforward than across flat terrain. Distances across a steep gulley or valley can be quite deceptive, and the difference of fifty yards at long range could mean a misplaced bullet. A person used to shooting with a shotgun has a useful yardstick for short ranges if he estimates what might be a long shot with a shotgun. Someone habitually using a .22 rimfire for shooting rabbits soon begins to pay attention to ranges, for the trajectory of a .22 rimfire bullet is almost arc-like in comparison to that of a .243, and for longer shots the sights have to be adjusted or allowance made in sighting by holding high on the target, and consciousness of range is soon evident. Misjudging of range is most prevalent on the open hill, of course, not only with the longer distances and contours, but because very often the assessment is made lying prone on the ground. These circumstances can make estimating very difficult for a tyro unused to the terrain. However I have also seen errors of judgement across fields in woodland stalking territory, and stalkers should practise estimating ranges and pacing these out for confirmation, until they become reasonably confident. Relying on instruments to do this seems quite unacceptable to me.

Wind drift is less likely to be a problem to the woodland stalker, although it should by no means be ignored. But it can be a very real factor on the open hill where not only are substantially stronger winds experienced, especially on the high tops, but wind eddies can also affect bullet flight. This is particularly the case in shooting across a valley down which a strong wind is being channelled, especially if one is shooting from a sheltered spot across this to another sheltered place where deer are out of the wind. Having myself experienced wind drift that previously I would not have believed possible with a modern high-velocity rifle under such circumstances – it deflected the bullet in feet rather than inches, on a day when I had to tie my deerstalker hat to my head with string to keep it on my head – I now respect the possibilities that might occur to result in an unfortunate shot. I have seen at least three other people make poor shots due to wind drifting the bullet to one side, though thankfully on all these occasions the beast was killed with a quick second bullet. A small, fast bullet is affected more by wind than a heavier, slower projectile, and for instance a .308 or a .256 would probably be blown off course less than a .243, or especially a .222, though this would depend to some extent on range, wind angle and so on. The actual degree of deflection under differing conditions and with different calibres is something that can only be learned by experience, for though theoretical calculation is possible, in practice the wind speed and exact range cannot be measured at the time of the shot! It is worthwhile for a conscientious stalker to go to the trouble of trying out a few shots at a target on a stormy day with strong cross winds, to get some idea of the effect at differing ranges.

Chapter 6
Targets and Practice

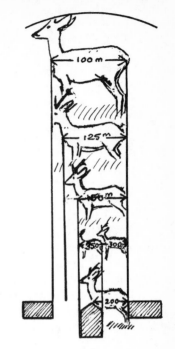

I have never been a keen competitive target
shooter, that is to say on shooting ranges. At
school I never managed better than vacillating
between the top of the second team and the
bottom of the first. I never achieved impressive
groups and I was always intensely irritated by
one plump boy who consistently scored almost
possibles in his group shooting, yet apparently
had no interest whatsoever in shooting outside
the range. I was best at rapids and snaps, and I always used to enjoy shooting
off my rapid as quickly as possible, trying to finish before the others. We were
not allowed to get up while shooting was in progress, let alone leave the firing
point, but I used to put my rifle down and shuffle about rather ostentatiously,
advertising the fact that I had completed my ten shots, trying to panic others
into thinking that they had little enough time to finish their shots. As a small
boy I must have fired thousands and thousands of airgun pellets at targets, but
these were seldom printed paper targets – mostly things like matchsticks,
which I used to be able to hit at twenty yards or so. These days I could not
even see a matchstick at twenty yards.

When I progressed to centrefire rifles, similarly I spent a great deal of time
practising. Once my rifles were sighted in, and I had settled on the particular
type of ammunition that I intended to use, there was no necessity to resight the
rifles again, except in the case of an accidental knock, perhaps. When I first
acquired my .243 I obtained a variety of ammunition for it, but I found that the
difference at a hundred yards between a hundred-grain and seventy-five-grain
bullets was something like three inches vertically and two inches horizontally
in this particular rifle. This meant that it was utterly unsuitable to use both sorts
of ammunition, and though I started off with seventy-five-grain bullets to give
the higher velocity, I came to the conclusion that they made too much mess of
a roe. Accordingly I settled on hundred-grain bullets and sighted the rifle in for
these. Subsequently, on a visit to Germany, I obtained some 105-grain DWM
ammunition, which shot exactly the same as the hundred-grain Norma, but I
became convinced that these marginally heavier bullets knocked roe, and red

deer, down better than the others. Accordingly I bought in a supply of these and since then have never used any other. I have never had cause to alter the sights on this rifle since. Indeed I have not had to alter the sights of any of my rifles for twenty years at least.

On one occasion a good few years ago I took the .243 on a trip to Hungary. I carried the rifle in a solid case so danger of sight damage was small, but one likes to be sure when a weapon has been handled by others. A couple of sighting shots at the Hungarian hunting lodge revealed that it was shooting slightly to one side – I forget in which direction now – but a companion found much the same with his rifle and we concluded that it must be something to do with either the low temperature or the light conditions. I decided that as i had taken limited ammunition over there and did not wish to waste a lot of resighting shots, I would aim off for the comparatively few shots that I expected on that trip. I shot roe and red deer successfully, and on my return home retested the rifle to find that its sighting was perfect again, so I was glad of my decision.

There seem to be two types of shooter, with rifle or shotgun, and I have stalked and shot with both. On the one hand there is the person who has been brought up with a gun of one sort or another ever since childhood. He, or she, will have progressed from an air rifle at a very early age, with which automatic safety and more or less instinctive shooting should have been instilled, to perhaps a .410 shotgun or .22 rimfire later on before handling a centrefire rifle or a heavier shotgun. The other type of shooter is the person introduced to rifle shooting later in life, perhaps in the armed services, attracted either by competitive target shooting or the prospect of stalking deer, the former often leading on to the latter.

Those who do a lot of shooting of all kinds, with both shotgun and rifle, tend not only to have a rather different approach to taking a shot than the target shooter, but can suffer a disadvantage. Living in Surrey, where feathered game is not plentiful and there are far more deer than pheasants, my rifle shooting far exceeded my use of a shotgun. When we moved north to an area of abundant game I used a shotgun regularly throughout the season. However, these two forms of shooting differ completely, the one requiring a steady, unmoving aim, and the other a flowing swing. Having used a shotgun since I was a small boy I was aware of my standard of ability, and that first season in Aberdeenshire brought home to me just how damaging to shotgun shooting continuous use of a rifle can be. My performance was so bad that I contemplated resigning from the local syndicate. However, by the following season I had regained my standard to an acceptable level, not by a noticeable reduction in rifle shooting (for, if anything, this probably increased with frequent use of a rimfire rifle at rabbits) but by this being continually matched with shotgun use. The reverse does not appear to be the case, or certainly not to the same extent. The shotgun shooter can perform more easily with a rifle than the rifle shooter can with a shotgun, and may possibly shoot more instinctively and quicker, and have fewer problems with offhand shots and situations where no satisfactory rifle rest is available.

There is a world of difference between shooting at an inanimate target and at a live creature. The most obvious is that the live target does not have a point of aim painted on it. Consequently the rifle shooter has to judge first of all where a vital organ may lie, depending on the position of his quarry, and then try to place a bullet in that spot. Moreover, most often the time factor is critical, because the live target is unlikely to wait around motionless like a piece of paper, and the first shot has to be regarded as the only shot and must be successful. An adage well worth bearing in mind by all stalkers and would-be stalkers is 'Accuracy is fine, but an accurate first shot is final. '

Those who believe that because they can produce one-inch groups at one hundred yards, or tight groups at two-hundred-and-fifty yards on a rifle range under ideal conditions, they are ready for any shot out stalking, are deluding themselves. Many other factors are involved in addition to the ability merely to deliver tight groups on a paper target. It is essential to establish confidence that the rifle is capable of consistent accuracy, and also that the user is able to perform consistently with the weapon. When that stage has been reached, one should be able to regard the actual taking of the shot with confidence. When one is stalking red deer on the open hill, most shots are likely to be taken from a prone, or occasionally sitting, position. Shooting from a high seat generally involves a comfortable sitting shot with adequate opportunity to rest the rifle. However, most woodland stalking on foot involves standing shots, very often with no rest available for the rifle, except perhaps the shooter's stick. For this reason I believe that anyone regularly indulging in woodland stalking must familiarise himself with standing shots, and preferably with offhand shots. A person who can walk to the firing point and shoot, either standing or sitting on the ground, and consistently hit a beer can at one hundred yards, but particularly with that vital first shot, is potentially a far better hunting shot than the fellow who can produce impressively tight groups on a target from a bench rest.

Personally, vital as that first shot is, I like to satisfy myself that the first sighting shot was not a fluke, whether it be myself doing the shooting or a companion, by seeing at least three shots fired, the last two being consistent with the first. Years ago I was on a hunting trip with a friend in Australia, in pursuit of sambar. My friend had lent me one of his rifles. I forget the calibre but recall that it was quite heavy. He put a beer can on a tree at deer height at what he regarded as a suitable range and told me to shoot it. Fortunately my shot went through the middle of the can. My friend was satisfied and did not wish to waste more ammunition, since the rifle was sighted in perfectly for him and I appeared to have similar eyesight and to be able to hold it properly. Although all went well on the trip, I always remember wondering if shots number two and three with the strange rifle would have been just as accurate! In fact a beer can is quite a small target in comparison to the vital area of a sambar stag, and quick shooting of an acceptable standard was more important than a one-inch group at one hundred yards on a beer can.

I have always felt that the best practice target for stalking, as opposed to a target for sighting in a rifle when a specific small point of aim is required, is a life sized silhouette of the real quarry, be it rabbit, roe deer or red deer. We have had a life sized roe deer cut from half inch steel, standing on a slope providing a safe background, for many years, and sufficiently realistic that many people have pointed at it and exclaimed, 'Oh! Look, a deer!' Indeed, one day in the middle of the roe rut Diana and I watched fascinated as a roebuck came down the hill, presumably having seen the artificial deer, and proceeded to circle this, presenting an aggressive shoulder towards it for what seemed like several minutes. We fully expected that when he was confronted with the head on view and his 'rival' subsequently vanished he would lose interest, but not so – he circled the target at a range of a dozen paces or so a number of times before finally retiring back up the hill.

This roe target is particularly advantageous over a more conventional paper target for a number of reasons. Most friends who see it or prepare to take a shot at it comment that the buck has no legs, but of course these are sunk into the grass as would be those of a real buck. Some tyros ask where to aim, but this emphasises the reality of a shot at a live beast that has no mark painted on it. The person taking the shot has to judge where to try to place the bullet as well as then to endeavour to hit that chosen spot, and subsequently to decide if that bullet would have killed the animal cleanly. Moreover the life sized target also presents the shooter with the opportunity of judging range and deciding the extent of his or her capability with regard to confident, accurate shooting. A naturally coloured target set in a natural background is better experience for the real thing than even a similar target set up on a shooting range. Paper silhouette targets are available, and these can be used as outlines for cutting out more permanent targets from hardboard or plywood, or better still half-inch steel.

We also have a supply of life-sized rabbit targets, some of tin plate, which are destroyed after some use of rimfire practice, and some cut from half-inch steel which register only lead marks from hits by rimfire bullets. Tyros soon find that killing shots on the head or heart areas are less easy on these standing in grass at fifty yards than a nice group on a black bull on a white paper target.

In the past a number of my friends were members of a local rifle shooting club with a small outdoor range, of which they were able to obtain the use from time to time to invite members of our local Deer Control Society to come and have a friendly practice or sight in their rifles. One of the more interesting tests, of great practical value to stalkers, was for the marker in the pit at the target end of the range, who checked and changed the targets, to run along in the pit holding above him at target level a life-sized roe cut-out mounted on a pole, which simulated a deer running along at ground level as seen from the firing point. This practice at moving deer, at varying speeds, gave a very useful lesson, essential to anyone likely to participate in continental deer or boar drives, but equally important to any stalker of deer, for inevitably during a stalking career one will be faced at some time with the requirement to shoot a moving beast, whether a wounded animal or one where unusual circumstances dictate the necessity of a shot at the deer on the move. There is no substitute for practical experience, and conditions vary according to the range and the speed at which the animal is travelling, but mostly if the deer is not running at great speed and the range is reasonably close the speed of the bullet dictates impact at point of aim provided one swings with the sights on the required spot. The rifle accustomed to the use of a shotgun has an advantage in this respect.

There are some, mostly those principally involved in target shooting, who deprecate the idea of shooting at any moving deer. As a general rule I would not disagree with this view, but there are circumstances where taking a moving shot is not only acceptable but actually essential. On three occasions I have shot a red deer stag at full gallop. The first was not of necessity, but I did so instinctively at close range. I was stalking with two friends in Argyll, one of whom owned the estate, and we were in rather hillocky ground with some areas of bracken. In one clump of bracken we spied what at first sight appeared to be a dead, stunted tree, but examination through binoculars revealed this to be the antlers of a large stag. Our host suggested that he and our companion remain where they could observe, while I stalked in as close as I could to the stag, and if he remained hidden in the bracken they would make a noise to encourage him to rise. The stalk was quite easy since there was plenty of dead ground amongst the hillocks, and I made my way quickly down to beyond where the stag lay, on the basis that he would run away from my companions if they had to disturb him. I was moving up a small depression in the ground that I anticipated would take me to some eighty yards below where the stag lay, when I heard hooves and saw the stag running at full speed on the small ridge slightly above me about thirty yards away. I swung the telescopic sight on to his shoulder and fired; he bowled over like a shot rabbit and lay still. At some stage a gust of contrary wind must have carried up one of the undulations in the ground and scared him, for my watching companions saw him leap to his feet and dash off before ever I came in view and thought the opportunity lost.

On a different occasion, the three of us were stalking the same ground, and we had spied a stag with hinds in broken ground on top of a hill on the far side of a large valley and decided to stalk him. We did not see the deer again during our approach, but confirmed the location by his roaring. When we were clearly very close, anticipating the deer to be just over a small rise, we decided that my host would take the shot and I would accompany him as a back-up, since we all three carried rifles, while the third member of the party would remain some hundred yards behind. My host crawled up the rise while I moved slightly to the right where I had a longer view but could not see over the top where the deer seemed to be. My host slid over the top on his stomach, took sight and fired. Suddenly the stag galloped past me, as some hinds ran off away from us. Assuming that something had gone wrong, I fired at the beast at thirty yards or less range, and again he went over like a shot bolting rabbit. I do not now remember where my host had hit him, but recall clearly his somersaulting head over heels at my shot, and the rather memorable experience that the three of us had subsequently lowering the dead beast down a very steep slope into the valley below.

The third occasion was more traumatic, and an instance of where the ability to shoot a moving deer is imperative. I had taken a friend out after a stag on our own ground in the north of Sutherland. We had found a stag with a few hinds in a small area of 'greens' by a burn and after a stalk had reached a suitable firing position a hundred yards or so from the beast. Unfortunately my friend, a normally competent shot, but more used to stalking fallow than red deer, made a bad shot and the stag ran off straight away from us apparently with a broken front leg. It was always my rule that if a beast was wounded every effort should be made to kill it, irrespective of the number of shots or disturbing the ground, and for this reason generally two of us carried rifles, since I had no professional stalker and we did our own stalking. In this case I carried my rifle and, seeing the stag run off, my rifle being already uncased and ready as a back-up, I opened fire. A stag running directly away at almost full speed is not an easy target, especially in a moment of anxiety, and I fired three rapid shots at him before I felt him to be out of range. At least one of these hit him hard. We watched him go a short distance and then lie down in a peat hag, but with his head still up. I told my friend, and our respective wives who were with us, to remain where they were, to keep a good watch on the stag and signal to me if he moved, while I took a detour round to stalk up to him from dead ground slightly beyond him. I got to within twenty or thirty yards of the spot that I had marked as being where he lay, though I was unable to see him yet. I stalked forward very slowly and cautiously when suddenly he sprang out of the peat hag and rushed away past me, offering a broadside shot. It was with great relief that I brought him down and finished the unsatisfactory episode.

I have shot moving fallow on a couple of occasions, taking part in drives, or more correctly deer-moving operations where the object was to move the beasts slowly through woodland past waiting rifles, and on one occasion a sika stag. We used to carry out deer-moving operations through woodland in winter for culling roe does quite successfully, and while mostly one hoped for the deer to pause at the edge of a ride or cleared area to enable a stationary shot to be taken, sometimes it was a question of taking animals moving slowly down a deer path or through a hedge at close range. On these occasions I used an open-sighted .256 (6. 5 mm) Mannlicher with shallow rear hunting sights – much more satisfactory for quick shots than a telescopic sight – and which fired a big, heavy, slower bullet that was less likely to be deflected by a twig or foliage. The practice at the moving roe target on the range was invaluable for this.

An example of the importance of having some degree of practice at quick moving shots so that one can be taken if absolutely necessary is illustrated by one occasion when I allowed a friend of mine to take an acquaintance of his to try for a roebuck on a large clearing over which I had two high seats on opposite sides. As it happened it was my friend, who did a great deal of stalking, who had an opportunity at a buck and not his companion, who had little opportunity but considered himself to be an experienced roe stalker. My friend's shot was a bad one. I suppose that he had tried for a neck shot but

succeeded only in blowing off the unfortunate animal's lower jaw. The deer ran across the clearing and stood briefly in shot of the other high seat, but to my subsequent anger the other fellow, for all his boasting of being fully experienced at roe stalking, took so long to get ready for the shot, despite seeing that the animal was wounded, that it moved off, and he commented that of course he could not shoot when it was moving. That buck moved into a huge area of thick woodland and we never found him, although I searched with dogs by torchlight well into the night.

I believe that constant use of a rifle of any type at odd targets is a considerable help to quick and confident shooting. For this purpose an air rifle or a .22 rimfire is as good as a centrefire rifle, and perhaps even better. I understand that wealthier German hunters of an earlier period had weapons called *zimmerstutzen,* or room rifle, often made as identical to their larger calibre hunting rifles except that these fired 4 mm cap and ball ammunition, with which they could practise. Constant rabbit shooting with an air rifle or a rimfire is excellent practice both for stalking up to the quarry and for taking shots in hunting situations and positions of many varieties. I expend large numbers of airgun pellets not only at rabbits, on which I find them extremely effective and really the most satisfactory way to shoot rabbits up to forty yards or so, but at an infinite variety of frivolous targets such as sticks, stones, fenceposts and the like, it being difficult to unload most air rifles in any case. This constant use of rifles of all sorts helps ensure confidence when confronted with an opportunity for a shot at larger game.

I was fortunate that in front of our Surrey house, which was situated in a little valley, there was a clearing that I had made, in order to see roe, about two hundred yards in length and ending in a high bank, which made an ideal small rifle range. Many stalkers are not so fortunate as to have a suitable site at home where they can fire rifles at will and practise whenever they wish to do so. Indeed, most stalkers probably have no other form of practising with their rifle beyond shooting at recognised rifle ranges. This means that many of them never have the experience of shooting in other than a prone or sitting position, and I feel that this is unfortunate and places them at a strong disadvantage in the field. I read in a South African hunting magazine an account of a man whom the author regarded as one of the finest hunting shots that he had known. This man had always disdained shooting at paper targets or trying to achieve groups, but he did an awful lot of what Americans call 'plinking', whether with a .22 rimfire at small stones or marks, or with hunting rifles at rocks or tree stumps or whatever object took his fancy. Regardless of calibre, distance, size of target or anything else, only two shots mattered to him – hits and misses.

Although it may be difficult to find a site where one can practise with a high powered and noisy hunting rifle, and even a silenced .22 rimfire may present danger problems (though the use of BB caps rather than long rifle ammunition helps considerably in this connection), it is far easier to find somewhere that one can 'plink' away with an air rifle and simulate all stalking shots on a miniature scale. Good air rifles are often available at comparatively small cost, and some pre-war models are to be had second-hand quite inexpensively. Most of these are fully capable of effective action against rabbits and other vermin in addition to valuable rifle practise, and, in my opinion, they are generally nicer to handle and shoot than modern versions in the same way that older shotguns appeal more than most modern ones.

As well as being able to hit a desired spot on a beast one has to be able to judge the spot required for a clean kill in the first place. Many stalkers of deer of all species never actually gralloch the deer themselves, let alone skin and butcher the carcase. As an artist without the knowledge of an animal's anatomy cannot hope to paint those animals in realistic pose, so the stalker cannot instinctively envisage the placing of an animal's internal organs in differing positions without an intimate knowledge of that creature's anatomical layout. It is not sufficient merely to be able to kill deer consistently without knowing how they have been killed: a worthwhile stalker, even if taken out by a professional who does all the dirty work for him, will take a close interest in the gralloch, if not asking to do it himself, to take note of the precise bullet route and damage, as well as the relative position of vital organs.

With the handling and butchering of many carcases one becomes familiar not only with the position of internal organs and the location of the spine in the neck, but with differing blood colour and bone structure from which one can often identify the probable area of a bullet strike when examining evidence at the site of a shot. Through skinning animals one becomes familiar with differing hair length and coloration from different parts of the body, which can give important information to the stalker, especially in woodland situations. Most stalkers will know that pink frothy blood indicates a lung shot and dark blood probably means a heart shot, while a messy sort of blood with apparent bits in it probably indicates a gut shot. Lighter coloured hair might indicate a shot lower down on the body, very short hair might come from a leg and dark, thicker hair from higher up the animal. The old venery terms for blood and hair are 'paint' and 'pins' respectively.

Stalkers have to learn these things, and often this can only be achieved by experience. The reaction of deer when hit by a bullet in different places and under different circumstances is not always the same, and it is impossible to be pedantic about this and lay down rules, since even with a rifle of the same calibre and type of ammunition a particular beast may react in a slightly different way from another. There is no telling how far a deer may run when shot through the heart and clinically dead. Generally it will only be perhaps thirty to sixty yards, but there are instances of deer shot perfectly through the heart running considerably further than this before falling dead, and deer with quite horrible injuries can travel a surprising distance. Undoubtedly a certain amount of the reaction will depend on whether the beast is alarmed or excited before the shot and thus with a strong flow of adrenalin in its body. Rutting animals, particularly red deer stags and fallow bucks, are often more difficult to kill instantaneously with what would normally be a lethal shot.

Deer shot through the heart will mostly run very fast straight ahead, or in a half circle, for a short distance before falling dead. This action very often makes tyros believe that they have missed. Sometimes the animal will give a little jump or other reaction on the bullet strike. Deer shot through the lungs tend to react in the same sort of way but may run further. A beast shot through the large blood vessels immediately above the heart will very often drop in its tracks, as will one shot through the spine. A liver shot will have much the same effect. Beasts shot through the spinal column in the neck will also drop instantly, but one should always regard with great caution any deer that drops on the spot to the shot, for a bullet that is too high and creases the spine or neck can have the effect of knocking the deer down temporarily, before it gets up and runs off at speed, suffering only from a flesh wound and a sore neck or back.

No responsible stalker would consider shooting a deer through the head, in my opinion, other than in exceptional circumstances. This is because unless the bullet hits the beast cleanly in the brain it is quite capable of inflicting the most horrible damage to the creature without actually killing it. The brains of different animals lie in slightly different positions, and anyone who has investigated the heads of domestic animals of different types, or has had to kill sheep, cattle and pigs, for instance, will know that the brains of these animals are of different sizes and in different locations and that one has to place a bullet in a slightly different place for each animal for a clean kill. One summer I carried out an experiment with the shooting of rabbits with air rifles, recording the effects of different powered weapons, using different pellets, and all four airgun calibres. In the process of this I extracted pellets from over 150 rabbits in order to record the track and location of the pellet and the damage done to both the rabbit and the pellet, where this remained in the body (which was not more than half the specimens recorded) compared to the reaction of the shot rabbit. I came to the conclusion that the head shot was actually far from satisfactory from the viewpoint of a humane kill, since where the projectile did not enter the comparatively small brain area the rabbit was not always dead despite massive skull damage. Unfortunately with rabbits a heart or lung shot most often enables a rabbit to run into its hole or cover and many are lost. If one has the opportunity to shoot rabbits in open ground away from holes, so that they can be watched for a while after a shot, most rabbits so hit will fall quite dead after running some distance.

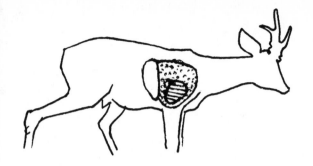
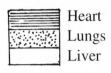

Heart
Lungs
Liver

A deer, or a rabbit for that matter, that is gut shot hunches up, and may stand looking extremely sick and in pain or may run off. Frequently the sound of a bullet strike in the gut area is obvious, and generally a second and more effective shot as a rapid follow-up to put the animal out of pain as soon as possible is desirable. It is difficult to describe the sound of bullet strikes on animals, and this has to be learned by experience, although those who have shot a lot of rabbits with .22 rimfire rifles will be familiar with the different sound of a bullet striking the head or the stomach or the heart and lung area.

Personally, I have always favoured a high heart shot as the most sensible and satisfactory for deer of all sorts, taking a line up the back of the foreleg to behind the shoulder, at a point somewhere between halfway and two thirds of the way down from the top of the back. The heart lies low in the chest cavity so that if the bullet should happen to go low from the point of aim it will pierce the heart; if too far back it will be a lung shot and if too high it will either still be an effective high heart shot or hit the spine. If too far forward the bullet should then strike the base of the neck and fell the animal. Neck shots are very satisfactory because they spoil the minimum of the carcase and kill the animal instantly if the vertebrae are shattered. However, the actual target is small and the vertebrae do not follow a line along the middle of the entire neck as viewed from broadside; one therefore has to know where these lie and be sure not to shoot too high or too low, either of which might have the result of knocking down the deer but not killing it and risking losing it.

I do not have great knowledge of, nor indeed interest in, ballistics. I have never been able to raise enthusiasm for home loading ammunition, and it has always appeared to me, judging by the activities of friends who load their own, that any savings in cost that might be made by so doing are frittered away by having to try out batches of home loaded ammunition to check that it is performing satisfactorily. I have never been conscious of any inadequacies in factory produced ammunition, but perhaps this is because I have never been attracted to the idea of achieving minuscule groups on paper targets. It could be, but I would not know, that factory ammunition tolerances do not permit the achievement of the tightest of groups, but so far as I am concerned they do permit quite satisfactory one shot kills of live quarry. My views on suitable calibres for different purposes are based on the wish to kill the animal as cleanly and humanely as possible, with the minimum of damage to the carcase and wastage of meat. I can see that the stalker who is going to only have one rifle for a possible variety of purposes has to allow for these. This may well mean using a much heavier rifle than necessary for smaller deer if the opportunity for stalking larger deer also occurs. Personally I have a variety of rifles for different purposes and am not restricted to one calibre, which has advantages, although on rare occasions it has disadvantages too when one finds that one has taken the wrong rifle for the circumstances. For instance, in thick woodland I favour one of my .256 Mannlichers with open sights. I enjoy using these weapons: they are nice to handle and I find them more satisfactory for close work in thick cover, with less likelihood of problems from a higher velocity bullet hitting a leaf or some such. It has happened on more than one occasion that when carrying this rifle I have come across a roe in an open field at a longer range than I am comfortable to shoot at with open sights, and consequently wished that I had taken my .222 or .243 with telescopic sights.

I have seen roe deer killed by a large variety of rifle calibres and I have always found it distasteful to see those shot with heavy rifles with large holes in them, particularly exit holes, with the accompanying waste of meat. Consequently I personally dislike using a calibre heavier than .243 on roe, and I believe that a heavier calibre for these small deer is unnecessary and undesirable. A dead beast cannot be any deader from using a bigger bullet. To my mind a .222 is the ideal roe rifle; it is also perfect for foxes, and it is fortunate that this calibre remains legal in Scotland for roe but illegal in England. Probably the .22-.250 is much the same, but I have no experience of it. However, I would far rather that any beast was killed quickly and humanely with the spoiling of meat, which is only a secondary consideration after all, than otherwise. Therefore I cannot condemn the use of larger calibre rifles, and I appreciate that many stalkers wish to own, or are able to own, only one rifle, so that this must be of sufficient calibre to be suitable for use on all likely quarry.

I have always found my .243 completely adequate for shooting red deer on the open hill, and were I to be restricted to one calibre only, this is the one that I should choose. However, I am not convinced that a .243 is a sufficiently heavy calibre for shooting rutting fallow bucks, or for that matter red deer stags, in woodland. On the open hill it is a different matter, because one can usually see, or follow, the beast, but in woodland failure to knock down the

animal quickly, or to leave an adequate blood trail, can create great problems.

The most important factor is not to get into detailed discussion on ballistics and calibres, but to have a rifle with which one becomes totally familiar and completely confident.

In my early days I used to use a stick as a shooting aid for woodland stalking, rather longer than the walking stick that is a vital part of hill equipment. There is not always a tree available, or convenient, or any other alternative rest from which one can take steady aim. Mostly it is not possible to take a prone shot in woodland stalking as it is on the hill because of undergrowth, and often this precludes the opportunity of a sitting shot, too, unless one is in a high seat. Therefore a stick to give some support with a standing shot is very useful. After a while I found that carrying a stick as well as a rifle and binoculars also had disadvantages, coupled with the fact that one has to be careful not to bang the stick on a stone or tree and make a tell-tale noise. If one wishes to look quickly at some suspicious object with the binoculars one first of all has to get the stick out of the way. Similarly, unslinging the rifle quickly from a shoulder is not facilitated by holding a stick in one hand. Using a stick as a rest certainly improves any vertical wobble with the rifle sight, but it does little to assist a horizontal wobble. I prefer now to have a free rifle and if taking a broadside shot, for example, to follow up the back of the animal's foreleg to a point about

halfway up the body and fire as soon as this point is reached. Different stalkers doubtless have differing ideas and procedures for taking a shot that suits them better, and it is important that the person doing the shooting should follow whatever procedure makes him most comfortable, and be fully prepared not to take the shot at all if he is unhappy with it or with his aim. It is better to leave the shot unfired than to risk losing a wounded beast.

Chapter 7
Roe Deer Management

I have very little experience of Chinese water deer or muntjac and am unable to comment on the question of their management, though I see little justification for shooting either unless they are tiresome in gardens that are unable to exclude them. The latter had only just started to spread their range significantly when I lived in the south of England. Why anybody should glory in the trophies of these is completely beyond me, but I have seen them featured in trophy shows. I presume that the length of the tusks excites some trophy hunters, or the small differences in muntjac antlers.

My experience of fallow deer and sika is insufficient for me to form strong views on their management, since I have never had ground on which these lived and so I have not had to involve myself in the question. Nevertheless, it seems to me that some principles of managing these herding deer may be the same as for red deer, allowing for their woodland existence, but in other respects the woodland deer differ completely from those living on open hill, and those living in low ground woodland again differ from those inhabiting country not adjacent to agricultural land.

To consider the question of the management of any animal one has to establish first of all the reason for doing so. In the case of all deer in this country the principal reasons for managing, or controlling, or interfering with the deer population beyond taking an odd animal for meat can probably best be described as damage limitation, well-being of the animals and commercial cropping. Superimposed on these is stalking for sport, since the objective of stalking may be to encompass any or all of these. To some extent the three reasons are interlinked anyway, but in some circumstances there may be greater emphasis on one aspect or the other. In any case an uncontrolled or unmanaged deer population would lead to much deer damage, which in turn would lead to unfortunate retribution on the deer, and almost certainly to a marked decline in the quality and health of the animals when the population of particular areas reached saturation point. Therefore there is a definite purpose to the control of deer populations as well as the purely commercial aspect.

The commercialisation of woodland deer stalking is comparatively recent compared to red deer on the hill. For practical purposes one can regard the latter as peculiar to the Scottish Highlands, since the overwhelming bulk of open hill red deer stalking occurs there. Although the hunting of these deer is ancient, the deer forest and traditional deer stalking on the hill as we know it now developed in Victorian times. The letting and taking of deer forests, for a season or a period, has taken place since the early 1800s and is not new. The commercialisation of woodland stalking is an altogether different matter: it has developed over the past thirty, and particularly over the past fifteen, years to the point where stalking is a valuable asset. Nowadays the value of the sport far exceeds the value of the venison involved, and this factor has itself affected the whole attitude towards deer and their management, not always beneficially.

Particularly in woodland deer stalking, trophy hunting has become an obsession with many, if not most, stalkers. The preservation and appreciation of trophies is in itself no bad thing, but the motivation of competition introduced a scale of measurement of horns and antlers, and this scale provided commercially minded entrepreneurs with an ideal system for maximising financial returns both for owners of the land and for the many renting agents and sporting organisers that cream off a percentage of these returns as payment for arranging the clients. The valuation of deer antlers not only places the overwhelming financial worth of a deer population on the males, the stags and bucks that carry antlers, both in terms of capital valuation and financial return, but it places a higher value on the animal carrying fine antlers when he is dead rather than alive. No financial value is placed, as such, on the potential offered by superb bucks and stags that are allowed to remain alive on the ground, and in the case of deer forests, where these are valued almost entirely on the number of stags likely to be shot in a season, with figures running to £10,000 and more on a capital basis, while the quality of stags may be mentioned, the actual valuation is based on numbers killed and no value is attributed to breeding stock remaining, however fine. As yet woodland stalking is not valued on this basis, but the emphasis is more on the income side and the charge for trophies actually shot.

The system of charging for trophies in addition to the cost of the stalking expedition has three unsatisfactory aspects. Firstly it introduces the 'shopping choice' to the paying stalking client. The wealthy stalker, for whom money is no obstacle, can feel free to shoot any trophy beast for which the opportunity of a shot is offered, and will probably prefer the prestige value of the more expensive animal, whereas the stalker of more moderate means may have to tailor the beast shot to his purse. The idea that a stalker should be faced with the dilemma as to whether he can afford to shoot a particular beast, like choosing a motor car or box of chocolates, is itself repugnant. It can also lead to absurdly inhumane situations. Some years ago I was sitting up a high seat in Hungary at a cross ride in woodland, with open, thinned hardwood on one side and conifer on the other. My objective was the opportunity of shooting a wild boar. I saw no boar that evening, but as the light was starting to dim I became aware of a small group of red deer moving through the young hardwoods on my left. It was not my intention to shoot red deer or roe on that trip for we saw a lot of roe and, aside from the fact that I had the opportunity for shooting a great many at home without cost, I considered that mine at home were better than any that I saw in that part of Hungary. Some of the woodland red deer were certainly better than mine at home on the open hill, and indeed we saw some veritably monstrous stags, but I had no inclination to shoot them even had they been free, which they were most certainly not. My interest at that time was solely boar.

Nevertheless, I watched these red deer through binoculars with interest. As they moved closer and became more visible I made out seven hinds, older ones and yearlings, and a staggie, whose antlers would have been regarded as decidedly indifferent even on a poor Scottish hill. As I watched them approach I became aware that the staggie was lame, and indeed very much so. He was clearly in a bad way, with at least a broken front leg. A day or two earlier on a boar drive I had shot a roebuck that we saw moving through the trees with a clearly broken front leg, and the keepers had obviously thought that I had done the right thing and were pleased. There was no question of the beast being chalked up on my bill, since my shot was taken in the cause of humane action. Therefore I imagined that the reaction to killing a clearly damaged poor young stag would be the same and I gave this little thought. It had occurred to me that if the beast had been a twelve pointer, or perhaps an eighteen pointer, my decision might have been difficult, since I certainly could not afford the charges exacted for large stags there. With a poor spiker the situation clearly presented no alternative. I felt that I should shoot him. As the first hind reached the edge of the ride she stopped, and so did the line of others, including the staggie; he was well back into the wood, but clear of trees and underbrush, offering the opportunity for a shot. He fell where he stood, and the hinds ran off across the ride into the thick conifers.

I quickly got down out of the high seat, by then full of those silly misgivings and doubts that really one knew were absurd, wondering if he really was as badly injured as all that and if I had done the correct thing. I need not have worried, for the poor animal appeared to have been hit by a vehicle, or involved in a similar accident, for not only were his leg and shoulder smashed, and he had damage to his side with the look of smashed ribs too, but gangrene had set in – he must have been in great agony. I reported the situation to the head keeper on my return to the Lodge; he seemed well pleased, and through the interpreter told me that I had acted correctly and that he would send somebody to fetch the beast first thing in the morning – it was extremely cold there at the time so no fear about the carcase being left out at night. I had gralloched it, of course.

We returned to Budapest on the last day, preparatory to leaving Hungary, and the organiser of our party, an expatriate Hungarian who farmed in England, went to pay the bill at Mavad, the Hungarian government sporting agency. They advised him that I had a charge of £120 to pay for a red deer stag shot. He explained the incident, but they were adamant. Eventually he pointed out that I wrote in the British sporting press from time to time and that I could create very bad publicity for them. At this they said that they would check with the head keeper at the estate where we had been staying and confirm the situation. Having done so, they reluctantly finally agreed to waive the charge. Twenty years ago £120 was a good deal more significant a price to pay for a deer than it would be today, but it would still have been possible to face a bill for £1,000 had the animal been one of the monster stags that are there. Thank goodness that such an invidious dilemma never faced me. I do not know which alternative I should have taken if faced with the nauseating choice of putting a clearly badly suffering animal out of pain and certain slow death and risking a bill that I could not possibly afford, or turning a blind eye and letting the animal go. There is no doubt that such a situation occurring in this country would be settled more easily by private owners than by a bureaucratic government agency, but nonetheless a period of indecision over the choice could lead to a lost opportunity. It is likely that the system and attitudes in Eastern European countries will change over the next few years, but the problems arising from this sort of situation will always be there when charges are dictated by the rules of an organisation.

Thus, pricing bucks according to the size of antlers, or number of CIC points, introduces the rather distasteful 'shopping' element whereby the stalker goes out looking for a £100 buck or a £200 buck, or maybe two £100 bucks rather than one £200 buck, and so on. A second aspect of this system is that the wealthier stalkers generally look for prestige trophies, which usually means that the hunt is on for the best bucks, so that the culling of the poor, weakly, sick beasts is not paramount in the plan. While food quality and lack of disease and disturbance are clearly the factors that affect the development of roe antlers and bodyweights more than heredity, the actual importance of the latter in roe is not fully known. With red deer, fallow and sika, the antlers of the male develop in sequence over the years, but there is no evidence of this in roe.

Stalkers often refer to bucks' heads going back from the previous year, or developing, but they can never be sure that it is the same animal. In Denmark, where the Game Biology Station at Kalo has carried out probably the most extensive research on roe in the world, including the monitoring for many years of marked animals where identification is positive, a known yearling buck has produced a gold medal head. We were able to watch roe kids from our house in Surrey and knew some fairly well, though of course we could never be absolutely certain of identification. Any yearling bucks that did not produce quite nice six point heads were regarded as poor.

It is inevitable that the continual quest for trophies amongst stalking clients puts great pressure on the better bucks. It also puts pressure on the professional stalkers taking out paying clients. The result of this system of charging has been seen in other parts of the world where it is increasingly difficult to find good quality beasts. Perhaps consideration should be given, in this country where deer are yet abundant, to devising a fairer system of charging that takes greater account of the long-term management of the deer. In fishing or bird shooting charges are made on a time scale rather than on the result. That is to say that one pays for a day's fishing without any guarantee of catching anything, let alone the size of fish. In bird shooting one pays for the day or season, and though some idea of the bag total may be estimated, especially on the manipulated commercial shoots, the quality of the sport is not guaranteed. There would seem to be much merit in charging woodland stalking on the basis of an outing for a period of hours, and while there might be some benefit in financially penalising the best bucks, it would not only save anguish, but add excitement to the prospects, and assist long term management if the professional in charge was given complete authority, within the agreed plan for the area, of what deer should be shot. On the basis of his judgement, the client would be required to shoot whatever beast the professional instructed, for a flat rate for the stalking opportunity, irrespective of the quality of the beast or the ability of the client to pay. For longer stalking lets a number of deer of different types could be agreed.

Yet another result of the current system of charging is its effect on the composition of the deer population. Clearly the more male deer present, the greater opportunity for renting out stalking, and the determining factor for deer numbers is the quantity of females. Herd deer – fallow, sika and red – require only a small proportion of males to females for successful procreation. Roe deer are generally regarded as largely monogamous, but in some areas, such as the part of Aberdeenshire where I now live, they are definitely not so: there is a noticeable preponderance of does over bucks, without a noticeably large proportion of yeld does. Thus the more does or hinds, the more young and the more deer there are. The shooting seasons for the female deer occur in autumn and winter at the same time as those for gamebirds and wildfowl. Consequently many keepers and stalkers divert their attention and efforts at that time of the year to bird shooting and pay little attention to culling does and hinds, which in any case are less easy to find during short winter days, when their habitats become more crepuscular and nocturnal. This is unfortunate, since the stalking of does and hinds can still offer fine sport, even if there are no trophies involved, and if sensibly priced, there is undoubtedly a market for it that would give sport to keen stalkers and an income and extra venison revenue to the estate, as well as achieving the necessary cull of the female deer population.

That the ideas on management and control of woodland deer have been ineffective in this country thus far can be demonstrated both by the remarkable expansion in the areas colonised by roe that has taken place in the past twenty years, and by the lowering of quality in some areas. Both fallow and sika have expanded their range, too, though to a more limited degree.

If deer management is to be contemplated with a view to minimising damage to crops and gardens and ensuring a healthy population of high quality animals, then the emphasis on commercial cropping will have to change to one where long-term management is paramount, and the quality of the sport is important. This need not necessarily impinge adversely on the financial return if buck stalking remains sought after, but scarcer, and doe culling also becomes a recognised part of the commercial scene.

In much of the country roe, unlike fallow deer, do little damage to agricultural crops, although in the north, especially in severe weather, they can do considerable harm to root crops, particularly turnips and swedes. They can also create havoc in a garden by browsing on young plants, flower buds, and shrubs. However, the most common and obvious damage is to forestry, fraying newly planted young trees. The killing of odd trees may only be irritating, but when significant patches are destroyed, or a buck goes down a whole row in a narrow shelter belt wrecking trees that have been growing well for a year, or even for two or three years, then understandably owners can become angry at the loss of time and expensive investment. Fraying saplings is a sign of territory marking, not merely the cleaning of antlers from velvet, and the proximity of a number of bucks in an area can lead to increased tree damage. A farmer who sees six or eight roe deer out in his turnip field in winter is also likely to be unhappy at what seems to be a high roe population.

As well as obvious damage caused by a high deer population, this usually leads to a noticeable deterioration in quality, both in terms of body weights and antler growth, the latter often being indicative of the condition of the animal. This is not merely due to the actual amount of food in the immediate environment, though obviously this has much bearing on their well being, and a habitat of plenty of thick cover and abundant food throughout the year can carry a far higher resident population. Equally important are disturbance and disease. The latter may be more relevant to animals living in herds or large parties, and the former especially important to the more solitary roe, which establish clearly defined summer territories. Disturbance by the presence of other deer can be especially unsettling for them, and when one studies roe it is not long before one appreciates that does can be equally as vigorous as bucks in the defence of their territories. Examination of lists of roe trophies containing details of the areas where these were shot frequently reveals that many of the best heads came from areas either recently colonised by roe, or outlying areas with good habitat for them but comparatively low numbers of deer. It is not customary to record body weights of roe deer as it is for red deer, unfortunately, but if it were so then such records would almost certainly show a similar trend.

Therefore there is clear evidence that the optimum roe deer population is not the maximum, but the level just below which animals cease to achieve their best apparent condition for their environment and where the level of damage that they cause is acceptable. Such a level should still provide not only adequate opportunity for commercial cropping, but increased demand for the better quality bucks available. Breeding success is a measure of the health of a population in most animals. Inadequate food, and excessive disturbance and competition inevitably lead to lower breeding levels. The extreme is reached when the population is at crisis level and what young are born are weak and sickly: few of these survive. Nature has its own safety valves that come into action in an endeavour to avert disaster. A noticeable number of barren does, or where single kids are normal and twins unusual, suggests that a roe population is high, perhaps too high. The presence of occasional runts, or weak small beasts is also an indication that all is not well with the population. This situation might be caused by some endemic disease, but mostly strong healthy beasts can overcome such problems, while animals in poorer condition cannot do so.

In order to formulate some idea of a management plan, or estimate the numbers of deer that should be culled from an area, first of all one has to form an impression of or estimate the population of the area, as well as the proportion of sexes present and the sort of age distribution. The establishment of population figures for roe is exceptionally difficult. This has been highlighted by the famous experience of the Danish Game Biology Research Station at Kalo, where it was decided to remove the entire roe population on the estate and start again with fresh blood. The roe population at Kalo was reckoned to be quite well-known and recorded and the researchers had a good estimate of the population. It was arranged to organise a large deer drive, moving the deer from the woods to waiting rifles. The operation was completed quite successfully. When the tally was added at the end of the day it was found that the woods had contained over twice the supposed number of deer. It would seem likely that any population estimate will be on the low side of reality rather than too high.

I am always reluctant to be pedantic about animals, especially wild deer. When I read or hear comments about how someone knew or knows a particular roebuck, especially when they claim to have done so for more than a season, doubt always enters my mind. I recall reading a book by Richard Prior, who has considerable experience of roe and probably knows as much about them as anyone in the world, in which he related how he knew well a particular buck that inhabited a part of a wood. Eventually he shot that buck. Going back to that part of the wood a short time later he was astonished to see the same buck!

On two occasions that spring immediately to my mind I have shot atypical, freak bucks in a woodland clearing that I would have considered to be easily recognisable, and then subsequently shot almost identical beasts in the same place. On the first of these instances I was sitting up a high seat that I had made in a large beech tree overlooking an area of about five or six acres of trees newly planted that spring. There had been some damage to these and I wanted to take a buck from the place to appease the forester. It was early August, in the middle of the rut, and I hoped to call a buck from the large area of woodland that lay behind this new plantation. My wife, Diana, was sitting up the seat with me. We had not been there very long, peeping on the call at intervals, when a yearling came out of the wood well down the clearing and started making its way towards us. We both felt that it was a buck, but until he got fairly close we were unable to see underneath him for confirmation, and he appeared to have no antlers. We confirmed his sex first by the tush on his belly, and it was not until he was about sixty yards away that we could discern tiny spikes on his head. I shot the beast, and he ran about ten yards and fell dead.

As it was so early in the evening we decided to wait a while in case a more mature animal appeared. Very often a single shot causes little disturbance, and we remained quietly up the tree. I did not mind leaving the yearling ungralloched for a short while under the circumstances, and we could see him clearly, obviously quite dead. I continued calling for half an hour or so, when another young deer appeared from roughly the same direction and wandered towards us, though rather less obviously responding to the call than the first. We identified him by his tush, too, and when he offered a clear shot I took it. When we examined the two deer our immediate reaction was that they must be siblings since they were so similar, both with a pair of tiny spikes only a couple of inches long. This was in Surrey, where all reasonable yearling bucks had, at that time, six point antlers, and those with only four points were regarded as rather poor. I am quite sure that not only myself, but all my stalking friends too, would, on seeing one of those bucks, have remembered the beast and on seeing him again have said that they had seen him before – but which? Moreover, were there others similar? And if so, why? Answers to such questions can only be in the realms of hypothesis at present.

A similar experience occurred to me years later in Aberdeenshire. I had made a high seat up an ash tree overlooking a small clearing in a wood on my march, adjoining a substantial area of forestry conifer woodland. This area has always showed a lot of deer sign and I have always considered that there is a lot of roe movement there rather than fixed territories. Over the years I have seen a lot of bucks there that I have not seen again. That does not mean that they are not there, of course! The seat is still there and effective, constructed from a board about eighteen inches long with holes drilled at either end for fixing strong cords. This board is wedged in a fork of the ash tree and tied firmly at either end to stop it slipping. Access is by a narrow forestry ladder given to me over twenty years ago, which I use in two halves for different seats. As there are no convenient branches for foot rests, I have driven in two six-inch nails that serve this purpose sufficiently, though I do not normally care for the practise of knocking nails into trees.

I had sat up this tree without success for several evenings and it had become almost a matter of principle to me to continue to do so until I obtained a buck from there. One evening as I sat I noticed a young roe in a lush area of tall vegetation to my left. I had to twist round hard on the seat to get a good view of the animal, and almost as soon as I started to study it the roe lay down. As it did so it appeared to look up and see me, fifty yards away. Roe rarely look up. I have had roe literally immediately below my feet on countless occasions, but do not recall another occasion when I was seen by a roe while I was up a tree or high seat. Usually any alarm is caused by scent, especially from where one has approached the tree or seat. Red deer and fallow both look up, and closed high seats are advisable, or at least well-camouflaged ones. I was sitting up a seat that I had made in a birch tree on my hill one evening, hoping to ambush a roebuck as it came out of a forestry plantation, when I heard noises in the plantation close by and in due course spotted two red deer hinds feeding on broom pods about thirty yards away. Eventually they jumped the fence to my side and started grazing grass, one coming straight for my tree. I could hear her eating so clearly that I felt sure that she would hear me breathing, if not my heart beating! Fortunately the beast that came towards me was the younger hind, a yearling. She stood right under the tree and then looked up at me from perhaps seven feet away. I was fascinated by her great, big, enquiring eyes. She stared hard at me for a few moments and I froze, scarcely breathing; then she resumed feeding, having either decided that I was part of the tree or an inanimate object without danger, and it was not until about five minutes later when she went round the other side of the tree and crossed my line of approach that I heard a deep 'Woof!' and they were away.

Another season a friend was sitting up a different birch seat, hoping for a roebuck, and he told me later that he had a hind come right under his tree only a couple of feet from his own feet, and he was amazed that she did not scent him, perhaps because of a fair breeze. This hind did not look up and passed by without being aware of his presence, which was unusual.

To revert to the roe, I believe that this beast just happened to glance up as it lay down facing me and caught sight of the large object up the tree. I suppose that it did not know what to make of what it saw, but was clearly suspicious and remained staring at me. I moved as slowly as I could to observe the rest of the clearing, and then back to look at the lying roe. It lay at such an angle to my left that I could not turn properly, especially trying to avoid obvious movement, and had to balance my binoculars on the fingertips of one hand to study the beast. For some reason I felt convinced that it was a young buck, but I could not see its genitals, of course, and I could see nothing on its head save for a strange bump that appeared to be a single lump or tiny piece of horn on its forehead. I dared not shoot it, relying without proof on my intuitive conviction that it was actually a buck, and what I saw on its head mystified rather than convinced me.

After a while, throughout which the roe seemed to lie staring fixedly at me, I became aware of another buck moving along the edge of the clearing to my right, going rather purposefully. He would pass in front of me at about sixty yards just on the edge of the open area if he continued, so I cautiously took the rifle off the branch where it hung beside me and made ready. A glimpse at the lying roe showed no change, and it crossed my mind that maybe I could solve the question of its sex if it stood up at the shot. The other buck, a mature but rather unimpressive beast, moved slowly into view and paused to nibble a raspberry plant, which was his undoing. He ran about twenty yards and fell dead. When he did so I turned to look for the lying roe, but it had vanished. I subsequently recounted to Diana about my 'unicorn' roe.

A couple of weeks later I again went up that seat for an evening's vigil. After an hour and a half of seeing nothing but rabbits, hopping about and sitting motionless in quantity, I saw a deer over to my right proceeding along the route, a deer path, taken by the buck I had shot earlier. I could see nothing on his head, but his tush underneath was clearly visible, and I was excited at the prospect that here was my 'unicorn' buck and the chance to solve the mystery. At almost the same spot as the previous beast he paused and looked across the clearing and I fired. He too ran less than twenty yards and fell. It transpired that this roe had two tiny spikes as antlers, only a couple of inches long, and both were bent inwards, coming quite close together, hence my illusion of a single bump on his head.

During the season I had seen several other bucks in that area and I decided to try for a third from that wood that year. However, I did not return to that seat until towards the end of the season. I saw nothing for a couple of nights, but on the third evening, after some wait, a beast approached towards the clearing along a damp track to my extreme left. I had to manoeuvre right round in the seat. It appeared to be a yearling buck, since I had a good view of underneath him, but I could see only stumps on his head. I managed to get the rifle swivelled round for a reasonably comfortable shot and took him. This was again a beast with two very tiny spikes, not quite so close together as the first, perhaps, but had I shot him first I would certainly have taken him to be the beast that I had watched lying staring at me earlier in the season. Why there should be two bucks with such poor heads and whether they were related I shall not know. It is not as if the area is poor, for not only have I seen several good bucks there, including the best I have seen on my ground, but recently a friend shot from that seat the best head from this ground so far, and I believe it was not the animal that I mentioned as having seen myself, of which I had a good view since it ran to within fifteen yards of me chasing a doe in the rut.

This perplexing question of certain identification can really only be resolved by the sort of procedure undertaken at Kalo, where they capture roe and place numbered collars on them. The roe are captured in traps baited with food, and the opportunity taken to make certain measurements and so on at the same time.

We used to watch a buck on our back clearing in Surrey one summer that had as long antlers as I have seen on a roe in this country. Length estimation on a live animal is slightly confusing since one's assessment is inevitably based on comparison with ear length. I recall one day that several stalking friends were assembled in my kitchen, and one was relating how he had noticed that some roe had hairier ears than others. We were discussing characteristics such as roe tusks, occasional abnormally long tails (which at even double normal length are still small and probably unnoticed by the majority of stalkers), and so on. It so happened that I had five roebucks hanging in my larder at the time, so we went out to look at their ears and to measure these, for we had also been discussing this question of assessing antler length. We discovered that three of the roe had ears six inches long and two had five inch ears. Actually I now forget which way round it was, but I have measured ear length since, and they do vary. Clearly, then, judging antlers to be twice ear length could mean ten inch or twelve inch antlers.

With this proviso, Diana and I had decided that this buck had antlers at least twice its ear length and perhaps more. We saw him frequently that summer, presuming him to be the same beast, of course, and were able to watch him both from our bedroom window and from Diana's studio on the edge of the clearing. He had strong six-point antlers, but rather straight and narrow, as antlers in that part of Surrey tended to be, with quite heavy pearling. I tried photographing him, but my equipment was not good and my ability to use it worse. Looking at the poor prints that resulted we found it difficult to believe that the antlers were so large. Nevertheless when he next appeared we could confirm this in reality.

We saw that buck consistently through that summer but never saw him again after that to our knowledge. The next spring I shot a buck at least half a mile away from the house. I knew that the roe had long narrow antlers when I fired, but when I first got up to him the thought crossed my mind, with a certain degree of horror, that I had shot our 'house buck', to which I should never have dreamed of raising my rifle. His antlers were much narrower than those of the 'house buck' that we had watched so often, and at eleven inches we felt that they were not as long as his had been; our impression at looking at the dead animal was the same. It seemed to us that it was not the same head. However, particularly since we never saw the big buck again, we always had the doubt in our mind as to whether this beast was him, with a much poorer head, or a totally different animal, in which case did our 'house buck' die, or move on, or have quite different antlers the following year? We shall not know the answers.

Assessing a woodland population of deer, and roe in particular, is made difficult by problems of identification, as illustrated, and underestimates are likely in a fully populated area. Equally problematical is the question of sex ratio and age groups. One is able to form a general opinion as to sex ratios after a period of observation of the ground, but probably the best time is during the second half of July and the early part of August, or even as late as the end of August in northern parts, when the roe rut is likely to be in progress. Intensive observation over this period should give one an idea of the proportion of bucks and does seen. In Surrey at rut time one rather took the view that if one saw a doe one then looked for the buck that one expected to be in the vicinity. In this part of Aberdeenshire one frequently sees quite a few does at this time of year with no sign of a buck, or sometimes a buck with two does in proximity. I refer continually to these areas of which I have most experience, since generalising can be very dangerous, inaccurate and misleading. What happens in one area does not necessarily apply elsewhere, and the two areas where I have had most experience of roe show differences not only in the appearance of the deer, but also in their behaviour, noticeable even if slight.

The subject of the ageing of deer on the hoof or on the hook is as contentious as the subject of ballistics and suitable rifles and ammunition for differing purposes, where most stalkers are concerned. Roe are perhaps more difficult to age than most, insofar that their antlers are not especially helpful in assessment, having no progressive trend as is the case with other deer. By this I mean that roe antlers do not grow and develop through recognised stages as those of, say, red deer or fallow deer do. One can make a fairly intelligent guesstimate by the look of roe antlers as to whether they belong to a young, mature or very old beast, but little more. Analogising between deer and other animals, let alone with humans, is mostly unwise, if not absurdly incorrect. However, perhaps one can point out that things like tooth wear, hair colour, eyesight and hearing, and so on, all vary considerably with people and one would not dream of ageing someone on the basis of one of these alone. Even impressions of behaviour and carriage can be quite erroneous, and the golden rule with anything to do with animals is never to be dogmatic. Someone who insists that a certain deer is, say, a five-year-old rather than a four-year-old or a six-year-old is likely to appear foolish to wiser people who have learned better than to be pedants.

An example of how easy it is to be fooled occurred to us quite recently. One of our sheepdogs, who happens to be six years old (we know his birthday!), suddenly, apparently became very lame. None of us, including the vet, was able to identify the problem, but came to the conclusion that it must be something like arthritis or a slipped disc. Instead of always leading the race of our four dogs across a field, he whimpered and would not leave my side. In the matter of a day or two the dog's coat lost its lustre and his whole appearance changed to that of an old dog. Indeed, a visitor who was unfamiliar with our dogs referred to him as the old dog and presumably 'retired', and was astonished when we said that he was only six years old. His indisposition lasted several weeks, but then gradually he improved, and soon he was back to running, if not so fast, with the others, barking at vehicles and the ponies, snapping neurotically but not seriously at the younger dogs, and his coat shine returned. He no longer looks an old dog, and works the sheep as normal again.

This example may be an unusual occurrence, but if one spends one's life working with animals one appreciates that such things are not all that uncommon. In recent years we have had a ewe give birth to a lamb while she had a three-week-old lamb at foot, a cow produced a calf a week after producing a previous calf that she then rejected, and we have had a calf that was newly-born survive on the hill for thirteen days without its mother (she now has a calf of her own!), so we no longer expect all matters concerning deer to be completely stereotyped and normal!

So how does one age roebucks and does on the hoof, walking around alive and undisturbed, or later by post-mortem? The answer to the former really is that one does it the same way as one does for any animal, including humans – by experience. Seeing a roe walking about, or even lying down, with a little experience one can form an impression by its appearance and behaviour as to whether it is young, mature or old. Few people, even the pedantic experts who claim to be able to age bucks to their nearest year, bother to be more accurate with age estimates of does, and it may well not be necessary to do so anyway. Describing the different appearances of these age classes is better done by illustration than by words. Young roe are slimmer and perhaps daintier in appearance, often carrying their head higher. Old beasts, like humans, may rather plod along with head and neck lower, as if it's a bit of a strain to hold them up. This overall impression of age gained from watching the live animal is, in my opinion, by far the most important and valid ageing assessment. It can be confirmed, or otherwise, by examination of skulls and jaws and eyeballs, and whatever else the scientifically minded feel may assist them, but the person who has seen the beast alive has a great advantage over the person faced with the task of ageing only from remains.

Young male   Old male

With most young animals it is possible to be accurate with age determination by examination of teeth early in its life, and deer are no exception. Until the milk teeth are replaced at just over a year old the animal can be shown to be a yearling. After this age examination of a leg bone can establish the next stage. The small joint below the cannon is separate in a yearling, but by about the age of two and a half years this becomes completely fused. Another guide may be the suture in the centre top of the skull and running down the forehead, which gradually fuses in older beasts. Old bucks usually have much thicker pedicles than young animals, and sometimes the angle of the coronets may suggest age, when the coronets tend to slope downwards from the horizontal. Old does quite often have bony projections on the skull where pedicles might be, and loss of teeth may be a guide, as in other herbivores such as sheep. However, I have shot a buck that I have no doubt was a youngish mature roe from his appearance and behaviour and from the look of his face and antlers, but which had a whole lot of teeth missing at the front, for which I was unable to establish an explanation.

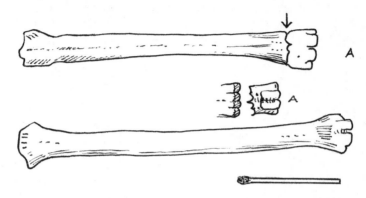

Some scientists claim to be able to assess age by sectioning teeth, and even by sectioning eyeballs I believe, but this is outwith the realm of the normal stalker. In earlier days I kept all jaws of deer shot with the skulls, and I went through the stage of believing that I could put an accurate age on the beast from examination of tooth wear. However, I gradually came to the conclusion that much depended on diet, and deer from one area could have quite different wear from those in a different environment with different food. Moreover, I then began to feel that the teeth of different animals in the same area could vary according to the idiosyncrasies of the animal and its individual diet preferences. Nowadays I prefer not to regard the appearance of deer teeth as other than one of several guides to age assessment, of which the impression given by the live beast is by far the most indicative; I would also be reluctant to be dogmatic about specific ages, but prefer merely to classify an animal as young, mature or old.

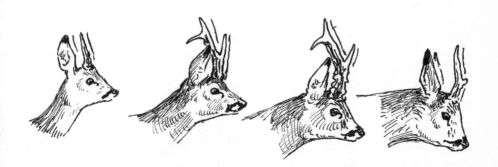

In order to form a plan for managing a deer population and deciding what should be shot one first of all needs to consider all these aforementioned factors in connection with the population level, or the actual number of deer in the area, and what is perceived to be an optimum number for the habitat concerned. As with any animal community a balanced population is desirable, so one does not want to shoot all young or all old deer regardless of other factors, and the temptation to shoot only mature bucks, let alone as many of these as possible, should be avoided, unless there is a particular reason for doing so, such as an excessive population where reduction of roe numbers is paramount. In most parts of the country it is accepted that a normal ratio of bucks to does in roe is between one to one and one to two. The normal based on twin kids being produced by most does on a fifty-fifty sex ratio would be one to one, of course, and perhaps this should be the objective for a management plan in good habitat. In areas such as this part of Aberdeenshire there is a very noticeable preponderance of does and the ratio could be as low as one buck to five does. It is likely that factors causing this disproportion are that the large estates of which the area is composed, and where the deer are mainly shot by keepers or fee paying clients taken out by them, concentrate on the shooting of bucks: these are not only more financially rewarding, but easier to shoot in summer than does are in winter, at which time of year the keepers are more involved in matters other than roe. It is also possible that male kids are weaker initially than females and succumb more easily in hard weather, but this would be unlikely to account for such significant imbalance. Where such a situation occurs, and the overall number of bucks available seems reasonable, the solution is clearly a determined effort to reduce the doe population over a large area.

In an expanding population of newly colonised ground, where deer are to be encouraged, clearly light shooting is essential, sufficient to alleviate any damage that might be caused, but assuming that the roe numbers are high those in charge have to decide whether they feel numbers are about right or too high: the amount of damage being caused is one criterion, the quality of the roe another, and the apparent birth rate another. If the quality of the roe does not appear to be good, and occasionally very poor specimens or late kids or runts are seen, and if a lot of yeld does are seen and very few twins, then the chances are that there are too many roe for the area for optimum quality. It does not require a great mathematical brain to appreciate that if most does bear young and the normal family is twins, as in much of the better land in this country, then a pair of roe can double the population of its territory. Even allowing for some young does not bearing offspring, and some mishaps, the compound population growth rate over the district without culling would be very high, which explains the impressive expansion of roe through England into areas previously without them. Even if single kids are the norm, and many young does do not conceive, the population of an area could still be expanding at a compound rate of twenty-five or thirty per cent without some form of control.

It is important to remember that it is the doe population that governs the growth rate primarily, for whereas one buck can serve several does, only does can produce young. Consequently does must be shot to keep a population at a constant level. In an area of a disproportionate number of does, an estate owner or keeper is not carrying out the job properly if he takes say sixty bucks in a season unless he also takes out at least sixty, and probably 120 does. If the number of bucks seems less each season they may be taking too many, but if the buck numbers seem as high as ever then clearly not enough does are being culled. In order to achieve successful culling it is important to plan forestry blocks and woodland areas with that in mind. Roads and rides strategically laid out can be good culling areas, and it may be possible to leave small open areas in places where trees are unlikely to grow well anyway, such as boggy or rocky ground.

A 250-acre block on my march is an excellent example of bad planning with regard to deer control, and although this was pointed out at the time to the manager of the commercial company in charge of the planting, the advice was ignored. A single ride runs through this block, with a short branch off it. In fact the area is not a ride, merely a strip left unplanted, but with a vigorous growth of long heather. A small boggy area, the site of the emergence of a spring that feeds the burn watering my fields below, was ploughed and drained, and only my protest saved the spring itself from being traversed by the forestry plough. An acre left there unplanted would have made an ideal area for shooting deer. This block is not deer fenced, so now has a high resident population of both red deer and roe. The forestry company was anxious for the deer to be controlled, and with the approval of the estate owning the land I undertook to shoot deer there for them. No attempt was made at liaison or co-operation by the company or the forester, and a number of times I went out to spy for deer only to find piece workers beating up, planting new trees or spreading fertiliser late in the evening, rendering stalking impossible. The plantation is now at the dense thicket stage, where seeing deer is impossible, let alone shooting them, but I abandoned stalking there some years ago, when the young trees already made it difficult to shoot a red deer stag, let alone a roe, after the forestry company called in a couple of professional stalkers, I believe from the Red Deer Commission. They came on a day of thick snow, herded some families of roe into an area and, according to reports, shot a heap of twenty or more, irrespective of sex or age.

The Red Deer Commission has estimated that the roe population in Scotland is between 150,000 and 200,000. How this estimate is produced I am not sure, but it is almost certain to be an underestimate, especially with the significantly increasing areas of new plantations providing new habitat. Estimates of cull figures are more difficult to obtain than for red deer, since a significantly larger number of shot roe than the larger deer will be home consumed and never pass through dealers' hands. Figures of roe population guesstimates for England are not available, but it is very clear that the present cull rate is nowhere near sufficient to maintain a steady population, and a strong imbalance of sex ratios in the total cull figures is very likely.

Having said all this and theorised about the formulation of a plan for the management of roe in woodland, what can be done? No owner is going to be keen to try to improve the quality of his deer without the co-operation of his neighbours. The plethora of stalking agents that has appeared in recent years complicates the issue. Sporting agencies who take a percentage in return for producing clients will be keen for large numbers of preferably high-quality bucks to be shot, irrespective of long term problems caused, since they will want both to please their clients by their obtaining the best trophies, and to maximise their financial return. The same will apply to the numerous one-man professional stalkers, though many of these have the long-term effect on the roe population in mind and would like to see their areas carry a high average quality of deer. Few sporting agencies are interested in the idea of roe doe stalking, for this is appreciably less predictable in short winter days and bad weather, and clients prepared to pay well for such

sport are not abundant. As yet no strong body exists in this country to influence field sports, let alone stalking, though growing pressure may force a merger between the various organisations now existing to avoid duplication of effort and endeavour to exert maximum influence. Such a future body might be strong enough to influence

stalking policies by indicating a standard for stalking charges felt desirable under various circumstances, and publishing these along with suggested cull figures in various areas and the subsequent degree of success in the achievement of these in those areas commercialising their stalking.

Chapter 8
Equipment, Calls and High Seats

When I started stalking deer in the 1960s very little equipment was available in this country for woodland stalking. Not that one needs much equipment, but as in all pastimes enthusiasts are attracted to gadgets and paraphernalia. I took the opportunity on a trip to Australia to divert from a stopover in Germany on the journey home to visit a large hunting store offering all kinds of equipment and ideas that were quite unobtainable then in Britain. One of these was a clamp device for guiding a small saw for cutting roe skulls to various desired shapes.

Another was a roe-carrying sling bag which has proved extremely useful and of which I have not seen another amongst stalkers of my acquaintance. I also purchased a Buttolo rubber roe call, which I have found to be by far the best of the several types of call that I possess, and a loden cape. None of these is especially necessary, but they do make woodland stalking measurably more comfortable.

Good gralloching knives are readily available at most gun shops, and the only important requirements other than the ability to be kept sharp are that the blade should be strong and the handle comfortable. For this reason I always prefer a small, fixed-

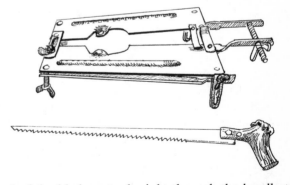

bladed knife where the metal of the blade extends right through the handle to ensure strength and enable one to use the full power to open up the rib cage of a roe or even a large fallow buck. Pocket knives with locking blades are handy, and I have a German one with gadgets such as a blunt nosed blade for gralloching and a saw blade for cutting bone. However, these are not really necessary, and I would never trust a folding blade in situations were I wish to exert strength in a cut, such as opening up the rib cage of a roe. These days one has to be careful walking around in public with a sheath knife on one's belt, since this would be regarded as illegal.

A small case for ammunition is also obtainable quite easily, and is preferable to carrying spare rounds in the box in which they came, which is generally not rattle-free and can get squashed in a pocket. Spare ammunition should never be carried loose for any type of stalking, for the clink of two cartridges together is sufficient to spook any species of deer within earshot.

Most stalkers will be familiar with loden cloth, favoured not only by German and Austrian hunters, but also by a large proportion of the population of continental Europe for winter overcoats. Loden cloth varies greatly in quality according to the wool content, the pure wool being most expensive. A substantially cheaper alternative in pure wool, obtainable in the familiar green colour, but not in the same styling, is found in Swanndri garments imported from New Zealand. Wool has a number of valuable attributes which man has as yet been unable to simulate satisfactorily with artificial fibres in such combination. Wool cloth is porous but offers excellent insulation, so that it can help keep a person warm without being soaked in perspiration, and it offers excellent water-resistant qualities. Hill stalkers know all about this, and most Highland stalkers wear tweed plus fours not for reasons of fashion, but because plus fours are easier to walk in on the hill, and tweeds remain comparatively waterproof yet readily blow dry in a breeze, at the same time keeping the wearer warm. Wool has the added advantage, of considerable importance in woodland conditions, of being quiet, unlike man-made materials or the ubiquitous waxed cotton garments.

Although unsuitable for hill stalking because it would be hopeless for crawling, a wool cape is unsurpassed in the woods in wet or cold weather. Not only is one able to keep much of oneself dry, but one can also keep rifle and binoculars dry too. My loden cape has kept me and these quite dry throughout four hours of heavy rain, though it is so light that holding it up to the sky one can almost see through it.

The roe-carrying bag is made of strong waterproof material and can easily be washed clean. It is not a rucksack. I have a German one of those, purchased at the same time, complete with waterproof lining and a similar hooked shoulder-strap arrangement, but I used it for carrying a roe on only a couple of occasions and then abandoned it as being considerably less comfortable than the roe sling or bag described below. Recently I rediscovered the rucksack and find it useful for carrying rabbits, when I shoot more than I can carry in a conventional game bag. The shoulder straps of the roe-carrying bag or sling are wide enough to be comfortable on the shoulder, and are adjustable, of course. The left shoulder strap is joined by a buckle, but the right by a hook into a ring, enabling one to put the left arm through the strap loop, swing the pack on to the right shoulder with the aid of the loose strap and hook this on to the bottom of the bag. It fits well up into the middle of the back to make for easier carrying. The bag itself is basically a single piece of material that when doubled is almost triangular in shape with the straps going from the apex to the bottom corners. Two small straps and buckles on each side hold the doubled-over material together to form the bag. For use one simply undoes these and opens out the bag into a single sheet, upon which one places the roe. The flap is then doubled over to form the sling, in which the deer now lies, and the top and sides are buckled fast to hold the dead beast inside securely. Simple, yet robust, it is the easiest and cleanest method of carrying roe that I have seen. On two occasions I have actually shot another buck while carrying one in the sack on my back, and at least twice I have managed to squeeze two bucks into it for carrying home, though under such circumstances the comfort deteriorates considerably!

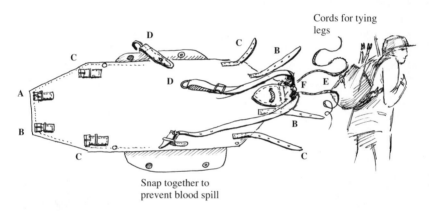

Cords for tying legs

Snap together to prevent blood spill

Topside of Roe Sack

A, B & **C** join to each other.

D. Shoulder straps

E. Cords around legs

Roe placed on underside and folded – legs to **F** and tied with cords **E.** Buckles done up.

G. Strap put over left shoulder and sack heaved onto back.

D. Hook put through D ring.

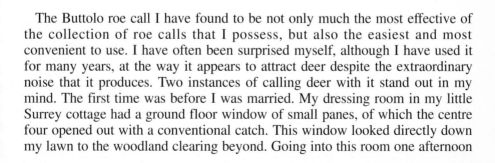

The Buttolo roe call I have found to be not only much the most effective of the collection of roe calls that I possess, but also the easiest and most convenient to use. I have often been surprised myself, although I have used it for many years, at the way it appears to attract deer despite the extraordinary noise that it produces. Two instances of calling deer with it stand out in my mind. The first time was before I was married. My dressing room in my little Surrey cottage had a ground floor window of small panes, of which the centre four opened out with a conventional catch. This window looked directly down my lawn to the woodland clearing beyond. Going into this room one afternoon at the end of July, when I knew that the rut was in full swing, I spotted a roebuck just at the far end of the lawn. I was intrigued to know how he might react to hearing a doe call from the house, so I went and got my Buttolo call. This is a hollow rubber thing about the size of a tangerine, with a call in the form of a small tube with a reed in it, covered with rubber, at one end. Squeezing the hollow rubber ball-like call expels air through the reed, which produces the squeaking noise. I put my hand containing the call out of this small window and proceeded to squeak three or four times. I was not particularly surprised that the buck immediately showed interest and started across the lawn towards the source of the noise, but I became increasingly surprised as he drew near to the house. At one stage I thought that he was going to come and lick, or attack, my hand! I do not suppose that he actually came nearer than perhaps twenty yards or a little less from the window, but at the time it seemed remarkably close. At this range he became extremely nervous and kept turning to move away from the house, but each time that he did so I squeaked again and he turned back to face me. Finally the tension was too much for him and he made off barking. I do not know how long I held him on the lawn thus. It seemed a long time, but I suppose that it was only perhaps a couple of minutes. However it was certainly one of my most fascinating roe-calling experiences.

The second occasion, also in the middle of the roe rut, was one of the first times that I had taken Diana out with me stalking, and the first time that she ever saw me call a buck. The Buttolo call makes two sounds. The first, by gentle squeezes, is the usual 'fiep' noise representing the call made by the doe when being run by a buck. The second call, made by squeezing the rubber violently, is the 'geschrei' noise, that seemingly represents the cry of a doe desperate for the attention of a buck, a sort of loud shriek. I have never heard a deer make this sound and always feel that it is most unrealistic, but nevertheless it can have startlingly effective results.

We walked along a narrow footpath with woodland and thick bushes on either side, my two labradors at heel, until we came to the edge of a large clearing with an area of recently planted young conifers. Standing looking at us about a hundred yards away was a roebuck. I hissed at the dogs to sit, but the buck turned and ran into the adjoining wood, from which he barked at us. I got out my Buttolo call, though one can operate it quite well, but more quietly, from within one's pocket by merely squeezing the outside, and pressed it sharply to give a couple of loud 'geschrei' yells. Diana, not having heard the sound before, was astonished, and incredulous that I should make such a row or expect the deer to respond to it. I felt that with the buck so disturbed he was unlikely to respond to a 'fiep' call, and I was not optimistic that the 'geschrei' would attract him either. I was surprised, therefore, and Diana even more astonished, when the buck suddenly leaped back out of the wood, into the clearing and then ran towards us. He stopped about sixty yards away, staring at us, and I shot him. A more impressive demonstration of calling a roebuck would be difficult to imagine, though it was rather similar to my first experience of ever seeing a roebuck called, when a buck leaped out of a wood after only a few moments of calling on the part of my Polish companion, and pranced up a wide grass ride towards our high seat before stopping seventy yards away, presenting me with an easy chest shot from the comfort of the high seat.

Other items of stalking equipment that have been invaluable and have afforded me many hours of pleasure as well as successful deer-hunting forays, acquired over twenty years ago and still giving good service, are three portable high seats. Two of these were made for me by a friend who copied them from a design in a German hunting magazine. These take apart into three pieces and are quite portable, and there is just room enough to squeeze two people into the seat. They rest against a tree and are chained or tied to this at the top and halfway down to give rigidity and security. These two have spent most of the time since I acquired them standing out in position in the woods, and only recently have they started to show signs of deterioration, requiring slight repairs. Clearly it is extremely important to ensure that such seats are quite safe before ascending them at all, let alone doing so with a rifle.

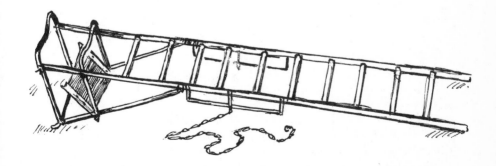

The third seat, which I use only occasionally, is one that I bought in the late 1960s. It is made out of a standard aluminium ladder of the type that takes down into four separate pieces, which slot together and are secured by wing nuts when erected. These ladders are very light, and I carry mine inside a sack with straps attached to it to enable me to sling it on my back like a rucksack. On two occasions I have shot a buck while carrying this seat on my back. The seat arrangement is a little difficult to describe and requires some experience to sit in confidently since the footrest and armrest are balanced by the tautness of the same rope. However, once one is used to it the equipment is very satisfactory. Were I requiring another seat I might well use one of these very light aluminium ladders that take apart into five separate sections, but I should probably not use a seat attached to the top of the ladder as in this case; I would rather simply use the ladder to enable me to climb to a plank seat or suitable branch up a tree.

Some stalkers appear to regard high seats with disdain. I suspect that these are either people who cannot be bothered to make a high seat or carry one around, or people of little patience who dislike the idea of sitting still all evening. I regard a high seat as a vital part of stalking and I believe not only that all woodland stalking areas would benefit from having high seats placed at strategic places, but that they should have these in order that the area is stalked efficiently. In my early days of stalking, before I had portable high seats, I was fortunate in that both my own ground and the commercial forestry ground next door on which I controlled the deer, had a number of ancient large yew trees dotted around. Many of these overlooked clearings and newly planted areas, or were situated on the edge of rides. These made very satisfactory high seats, since they were well supplied with branches, commencing low down near the ground, that made for easy climbing; at the top one had an adequate choice of branches for seat and footrest, and only limited pruning was necessary to give a good view.

High seats have the obvious merit of offering a relatively comfortable shot, and also a safer shot because this tends to be angled downwards. However, in my opinion the greatest advantage of a high seat, if the field of view is a good one, is the opportunity that it gives to see what deer, and other creatures, might be in the area. The dictum that one should stalk on one's feet in the mornings and sit in a high seat in the evenings, which I believe is of German origin or tradition, is founded upon a lot of sense. In the evenings the deer tend to be more alert, having laid up in cover during the day and now being eager to come out to feed. In the mornings when they have been up and about feeding for some time they are perhaps a little less cautious. I have a watercolour painting by the late Hubert Pepper of a roebuck feeding in a clearing with a woodcock roding overhead. I remember him describing it to me as the buck eagerly taking the first few mouthfuls, lifting his head suspiciously and alert as he chewed these, and then feeding again. As the appearance of the first star in the evening often heralds the time when the first ducks start to flight, so the appearance of the woodcock roding often signals the time when deer start to appear. I have noticed so often that as one hears the approach of the familiar croaking of a roding woodcock, so, as if by magic, deer appear feeding where a moment or two earlier there was nothing.

A high seat, whether it be up a tree or even on a high ground vantage point, gives the stalker the opportunity to study deer more closely and in an unhurried way, and is particularly useful when one is calling deer, whether bucks or does. Quite apart from this chance to study deer, rather than simply walking round a corner and finding oneself confronted with an animal, one also has the opportunity to see and study other animals and birds. that may occupy the same territory. There can be no stalker worth his salt who does not have an interest in other wildlife, and one has to remember that these are all part of the environment in which the deer live. As such they may be significant in some way so far as the deer are concerned. I believe that one can only begin to achieve a proper knowledge of the population of the deer of an area by both walking and stalking around the area extensively, and spending hours patiently sitting watching and waiting.

A portable high seat has much advantage over a permanent one because of its mobility, but has the disadvantage that it is necessarily small. unsheltered and not especially comfortable in poor weather. If the seat is likely to be required to be used by more than one person at a time, obviously a larger and more substantial permanent high seat will be required; but before this is erected clearly one needs to be quite sure that it is sited in the most favourable position. Moreover, to justify the work and expense of the materials it probably has to be erected in a position where it is likely to be of use for at least several years, without growing foliage obscuring the view.

During those frustrating early days when I started stalking on my own and was trying to see deer before they saw me, I learned that two of the important factors are movement and shape. This can be demonstrated easily to someone new to stalking by placing them inside a wood and getting a companion to stalk carefully along the outside of that wood and then turning into the cover and proceeding slowly towards the stationary person. If the latter has his eyes at deer level he will quickly see how easy it is to detect movement and to discern suspicious shapes against the lighter background of the outside of the wood. One has always to remember that under such circumstances the deer has this advantage, even though it may be concentrating on feeding rather than continuously on the lookout for danger. That noise is also a vital factor goes without saying. Deer have acute hearing as well as an acute sense of smell, and just as one can oneself be made aware of the presence of another body by the cracking of twigs or shuffling feet, so the deer is substantially more aware. On many occasions, when sitting up a high seat, I have been astonished by the noise made by a roe deer walking along. Even a hedgehog can make a seemingly obvious rustling on a still evening. How much more obvious must be the large and stumbling feet of a human!

The deer themselves seem to be fully aware that by remaining motionlesss they may well escape detection. Frequently driving around my own land I have seen roe that are used to seeing me pass and are cautious rather than alarmed; they step behind a bush or indeed even remain in the open if caught in such a predicament, and stand there watching me pass with no more than the very slightest head movement as their eyes follow me, thinking themselves unseen. Occasionally under similar circumstances one disturbs a deer out in the open and sometimes if one gives no hint of having seen the animal and merely passes on without hesitating the beast will just stand there, placing faith in the hope that it remains undetected. One frequently sees this in red deer on the hill, which will stand or lie observing walkers below so long as they remain in sight and continue walking, but the moment that the people stop, or, worse, disappear, the deer start to become agitated. How often out stalking one sees or hears a deer crash away from some place or other that does not seem to be thick cover and wonders how one can possibly have missed seeing the animal! Thus, patiently waiting up a high seat, one has this great advantage over other animals that are on the ground and moving about, and one may have one's attention attracted by their movement and thus spot their presence.

Trying to control the deer on the area managed by the commercial forestry company, I liked to take one buck at least from every newly established plantation that was suffering deer damage. I have always been a little sceptical of the dogma put about, and seemingly almost universally accepted, that if one leaves a master buck to guard a territory, taking out smaller bucks, one's problems of deer damage to the young trees are over. It may be true in some cases, but I certainly would not accept it as a panacea for tree damage.

It seems to me that while the presence of smaller bucks may activate the territory markings of a master buck to some extent, such a buck is liable to do far more ferocious fraying than a smaller buck, and is likely to mark his territory anyway whether younger bucks are about or not. Undoubtedly much

depends on the deer population, and in the case of my Surrey stalking I believed that the roe population was very high and that the first consideration was to reduce the number of deer. I suspect that good feeding and lack of disturbance has as much influence on the growth of their antlers and of their body weights as heredity, and probably more so. Moreover, there is no evidence that roe antlers show a progression of growth from season to season as is the case with other deer. Certainly it is likely that the finest antlers, of medal quality, are found on mature beasts, but it has been known, in Denmark where a great deal of research has been done on roe deer, that a yearling roebuck has produced a gold medal head. The animal in question was marked and was well known. Accordingly I took the view that if there was bad fraying damage in a new plantation it was better to reduce the source of this damage as effectively as possible rather than to indulge in theory or dogma, or speculate that either the buck in question, in the rifle sight, was in fact the master buck of the area, or that he would stay there, in the same territory, for the remainder of the season, let alone in ensuing years.

This is not a retrospective way of justifying the shooting of deer with particularly fine antlers, since I have always believed that these look better carried around on a live animal than hung on a wall. Despite ample opportunity to have antlers measured and assessed, with the official judge staying in my house quite often, I have never yet had any deer antlers assessed for measurement on the CIC scale. I have always placed more emphasis on beauty than on weight and size, although these clearly have much of interest too. I have never found reason to question my own attempts to reduce deer damage to woodland based upon these views.

In my attempt to take at least one buck from each newly planted area suffering damage, or in the case of very large areas to take a buck from each part of the plantation, I found high seats of considerable assistance. Frequent stalking on foot to these clearings often yielded no sight of a deer. Sometimes hours of sitting up a high seat produced a similar lack of result, but I found that if there was an area suffering deer damage and I was able to make a seat overlooking that area, if I resolved to sit up that seat on consecutive available evenings until such time as I got a, or the, buck, then even if it took a good many evenings of patience I generally succeeded in the end.

Parts of the woodland consisted of large areas of plantations of perhaps eighteen to twenty-five years old, affording thick cover and some difficulty in finding deer. Even in some of these plantations there were patches of bramble and so on and it was not always necessary for the deer to come out to feed. On morning stalks one would occasionally see deer in the rides but it was often a question of luck as to who saw whom first when a deer walked out on to a ride in front. Rather than shoot a lot of bucks and does throughout the year on the small cleared areas and new plantations, I felt that one should spread one's effort to include these more difficult woodlands. In these situations a high seat placed overlooking a ride, or preferably at a junction where it overlooked several rides, gave one the opportunity to take out the deer that one might otherwise not have been able to shoot. This was particularly so in winter or in bad weather when the open areas were perhaps less attractive to does than the sheltered rides. These high seats also presented opportunities for thinning out the ubiquitous foxes.

Chapter 9
Calling Roe

Soon after I became interested in stalking roe I was invited to accompany a stalking friend on a weekend trip up to Thetford Chase in Norfolk and found it most interesting. The stalking was quite different from our own area, and the palatial high seats scattered throughout the forest offered splendid viewpoints from which to study deer and their activities. I was never particularly attracted by the prospect of shooting roe in this forest since the animals were of remarkably poor quality, for the most part, both in antlers and body weights. This may have been due to overpopulation, or to heavy parasitic infestation, and it was my first experience of roe that were heavily infested with ticks. On all the large number of roe that I handled in Surrey over the years I only ever found one tick. The animals in Thetford Chase were literally covered in them. However, I found Thetford in the middle of the summer, during the roe rut, a fascinating place, both because it offered opportunities that I have never seen elsewhere of watching, and specifically hearing, bucks chasing does, and also because it gave splendid opportunities for calling deer. It was on one of the visits to Thetford Chase, after I became a member of that stalking club for a short time, that I was initiated into this practise.

My friend and I had gone up there to spend a few days during the roe rut. Staying at the rather primitive cottage used by the club at the same time was a fellow club member of Eastern European origin. I rather think that he was Polish, but had lived in this country since war time. Apparently he was the acknowledged club expert at roe calling, and he very kindly offered to take me out and show me how it was done.

I have always paid more attention to a practical demonstration that obviously works than theoretical written advice, and so I found it most interesting to see and hear this man calling very much more vigorously than I had ever seen described in literature. He told me that he had learned from a keeper when he was a young man, and that this keeper had told him that at the right time of the rut a buck would come to the call, and the only doubt was whether one would actually see the buck first, or whether he would approach in thick cover or downwind and become aware of the human first. Though I cannot claim to have had a buck come to me every time that I have tried to call one by any means, it has given me encouragement to remember his telling me that if a buck is within earshot it must come. He carried with him a pocket full of different roe calls, although these were all of the plastic or wooden blowing type and he did not have the rubber Buttolo call which I described in the previous chapter. I have found this latter call by far the easiest to use, as well as the most effective, though I do use the others for variety for my own amusement.

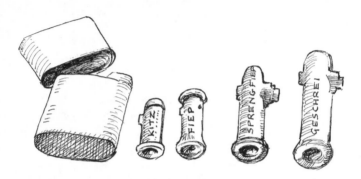

He started off by using the 'fiep' call, which is the noise that I was able to hear at Thetford and actually watch does making it as they were pursued by bucks. He told me that the doe makes this squeak every second step when being pursued by a buck, and certainly my own observation would support this. If one watches a buck running a doe, and one is able to hear the doe making the call, one realises that it is a continuous noise, even though the doe is running around the wood and one cannot necessarily hear it all the time if the doe is further away or facing in the wrong direction, for instance. It is not simply a matter of her squeaking five or six times and then stopping. Nevertheless, this was the procedure that he adopted. Having sat in the high seat for a few minutes to let things quieten down he proceeded to call five or six times with the 'fiep' and then wait five minutes or so, or perhaps less, and call again. It seemed to me that he was rather impatient, and after a certain time, if he had no success, he changed the call to another representing a doe in more urgent need of a buck's attention. Finally, if that was still unsuccessful, he would resort to the 'geschrei' call, which represents a 'come quick' shriek to the buck. I have never consciously heard either of these more urgent calls being made by a deer, but there can be no doubt that the latter certainly works when other calls fail. On numerous occasions I have used it when I have failed to attract the attention of a buck with other calls and his reaction to it can sometimes be quite dramatic, charging headlong to the source of the sound.

I visited three different high seats with my calling mentor in two days. On the first occasion we had not sat up the high seat very long before, quite clearly in response to his calling, a buck sprang out of the wood and advanced purposefully down a ride towards the high seat. When he was at about sixty yards I shot him through the base of his throat. This demonstration of calling was extremely impressive so far as I was concerned and I was anxious to learn more about calling bucks. On that outing I did not see all the other calls that he used, since the buck had responded to the first 'fiep' call. However, the next day I went out again with him and we visited two different high seats. In fact he was unsuccessful in calling another buck. Nevertheless, it gave me the opportunity to see him in action with a range of calls with the benefit of the previous day's demonstration still impressing me, and in the knowledge that this man had managed to call some extraordinary figure – I forget the exact number, but I believe that it was in double figures – of bucks in a single day in different areas of Thetford Chase.

Since that time, a good many years ago now, I have tried to emulate him, and have been rewarded with what I regard as a satisfactory rate of success. I find calling roebucks extremely exciting, whether one has the intention of shooting the animal or not, and it is also particularly effective if one wishes to take a buck from thick cover where stalking and patiently sitting up a high seat have proved unsuccessful. On more than one occasion this has been very useful. One small area of newly planted trees on the edge of the commercial forestry block on which I controlled the deer I found especially irritating. There was obvious deer fraying damage there, and countless morning walks and evening waits were completely unsuccessful with regard even to seeing a buck on that clearing. When rutting time came and I knew that it was in full swing, as a result of seeing bucks chasing does elsewhere around the area, I put up a portable high seat against a large tree that had been left right in the middle of this new planting, and having waited half an hour or so to let things quieten down after my arrival I commenced calling. I do not suppose that I had been calling for more than perhaps quarter of an hour, which meant that maybe I had given four or five series of calls at most, when a large buck sprang out of the wood and headed directly towards the high seat. The clearing was only a small one and he was within about thirty yards of my tree before he stopped, pausing somewhat suspiciously. It was an easy shot, but I was very satisfied finally to kill a buck in this little plantation after so much unsuccessful effort previously. He weighed 55 lb cleaned from throat to anus, which was the normal weight for mature roebucks then on my ground, and had a fine six point head that would probably have scored bronze medal points, according to judgement by fellow stalkers.

Using the smallest and highest pitched call, simulating the noise made by a roe kid, can be very useful for calling does at the start of their season when they are beginning to become crepuscular, if not rather nocturnal, and difficult to find during daylight. Calling does is even easier in summer if for some reason the doe does not have her kid or kids with her. Sometimes she will simply go off to find them where she left them, but at other times she will come rapidly to the call. Once during rutting time I saw a buck with a doe and kid at the far side of a newly planted area of conifers. His attention was entirely on the doe, and he took no notice whatever of my attempts to call him. Finally I took out the kid call, a little black plastic one on which one can vary the reed tone, seemingly the only roe call available in this country thirty years ago, and proceeded to squeak. To my surprise the doe did actually respond, despite having the kid with her, and came towards me with the kid behind her and the buck following on. After a few squeaks they came right across the clearing and I was able to take a successful shot at the buck.

I have managed to call bucks from considerable distances, not only in Surrey but in various parts of the country. One instance that I remember specifically was the second buck shot by the well known wildlife and sporting artist Rodger McPhail. We were sitting up a comfortable yew tree seat overlooking a very large clearing, and after a while I spotted in the distance through my binoculars, at the far corner of the clearing, a buck emerge from the wood. Doubtful that he would actually hear the call, let alone respond at that range, which must have been four or five hundred yards, I gave a few squeaks, and to my surprise he put up his head immediately and looked interested. A few more squeaks and he proceeded to run in our direction. He ran the whole way across the clearing, with a couple of pauses on the way across to listen again, when I encouraged him with further 'fieps', and came right to within forty yards of our tree, moving broadside in front of us. At this stage he was walking slowly, and I said to Rodger, 'Wait until he stops', but before I had finished uttering these words the buck was dead.

Rodger's first buck, the previous day – he shot six that week- stands out vividly in my memory. I had found a perfect figure of eight roe ring round a tree stump and a small tree on the side of a little valley immediately opposite, and quite close to, a seat I had in the top of an old yew tree at the edge of the wood facing it. It so happened that Diana had been asked by Frank Holmes to

produce an illustration of a roe ring for his book *Following the Roe*. She had gone to this seat and had watched the buck chasing the doe, accompanied by twin kids, round this figure of eight, and her drawing of this subsequently appeared in his book. Since Rodger McPhail, then aged twenty, was coming to stay with us the following week, it seemed to me an ideal seat to which to take him because of the strong probability of seeing the buck. We did not have long to wait. After we had been watching him for a while (as Rodger was anxious to watch the buck and not simply kill it) he presented an easy broadside shot and Rodger put a bullet through his heart. The buck ran about thirty yards and collapsed dead. We got out of the seat, and walked over to where he lay. I shall never forget how Rodger stood looking down at him, and then rearranged the way that the animal lay several times, standing and absorbing the detail after each alteration. I was greatly moved and appreciative that someone was so respectful of, and interested in, this lovely animal, to my mind the most beautiful of all deer and antelopes.

For those unfamiliar with roe rings perhaps I should explain the meaning. In some circumstances, but by no means all, since I have seen bucks chasing does often without any sign of pattern, roebucks chase does – or perhaps the does lead the bucks – round and round a bush or tree stump, sometimes in a circle and sometimes in a double circle, figure-of-eight pattern. The undergrowth gets trampled into an obvious path when they do this repeatedly. Sometimes this happens in open ground round a solitary bush or other object, but more often the pattern is formed in thick cover, where presumably it is less easy for the doe to run any distance.

On several occasions I have been sitting up a high seat overlooking a small clearing with thick cover all around, and especially behind me, when I have heard, in response to the calling, the rather aggressive snorting sound that a buck sometimes makes when approaching a doe in season. It can be quite exciting hearing this without yet seeing the buck, or when one can see bracken or undergrowth moving from an obviously approaching buck without knowing what sort of beast may emerge.

Of course there is no necessity to shoot every buck that one calls, and indeed on a number of occasions I have been content simply to watch the beast and sometimes tease him by holding him in the area for a while by calling, until he became suspicious at the absence of a doe and retired.

Although I consider the Buttolo call to be much the best, and the easiest to use, both the 'fiep' that results from a gentle squeeze and the 'geschrei' that is produced by a strong squeeze, generally I carry at least one other type of call simply to give variety if nothing seems to be happening. I suspect that changing from one type of 'fiep' call to another makes no difference to success, but it does have some psychological benefit to the frustrated caller.

On my return from that visit to Thetford when I had the first experience of seeing and hearing a buck called, I decided to try for myself. I had discovered a roe rutting ring in the plantation only a few hundred yards behind my house. This was in a small section planted rather later than adjoining woodland and consisting of a mixture of beech and conifer about four feet high but rather sparse. A ride divided this section from the adjoining stand of thick Scots pine, and a subsidiary short ride thirty yards long ran from this at a right angle quite close to the rutting ring. A convenient birch tree had been left by the forestry people at the edge of this short ride, and I was able to place a light ladder against this and tie a short plank as a seat to two branches on the tree, from which I could just see the ring. A short plank, perhaps eighteen inches long with holes drilled at either end and ropes or strong cord running through these, by which to tie the plank securely to branches or to the fork of a tree, makes a very convenient temporary seat, and not too uncomfortable provided that one has adequate footrest on top of a ladder or on a tree branch.

Having positioned the seat the previous day, I went to it in the evening after I got home from work and had fed the dogs and so on. I did not know whether the ring was still used, but inspired by the calling demonstration that I had seen I was intrigued to have a go. I had not been sitting up my seat for more than twenty

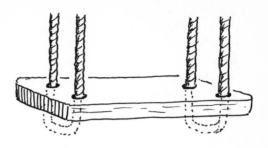

minutes, during which I had only called about three times, when I heard a snorting sound and a thundering of hooves and was aware of a buck galloping down the main ride. Fortunately I had not approached the seat down the ride but had circled round the edge of the plantation and crossed the fence on the march and walked through the trees to reach it, so my scent was not on the ride, nor on that side of the seat at all. The buck paused at the junction of the rides, looking down the short ride in the direction of the rutting ring, and more or less directly at where I sat. Warned of his approach by the noise that he had made, I had my rifle ready and the shot was an easy one despite my excitement. I felt quite triumphant at having actually called a buck for myself, and having such a spectacular result.

One of the lessons learned over the years, which applies to all forms of deer stalking, is that when one has spotted an animal it is as well to keep that animal under as continuous observation as possible should it be a beast in which one has interest and proposes to stalk. As deer can appear as if by magic, so they can disappear equally mysteriously. A roe has only to walk behind a bush or into some tall grass to disappear. At rutting time in particular, when bucks and does tend to be in close proximity, this is even more important and a mistake of identity can easily be made. This may seem unlikely to less experienced stalkers, but it can happen all too easily. I have made such a mistake myself, so I have that experience. There is no acceptable excuse for it, of course, and with the benefit of hindsight it seems extraordinary that one could be so stupid, but are there many among us who can honestly deny perpetrating stupid mistakes at some time or another?

On this occasion I was walking across a large clearing when I saw a buck in a mature beech wood at the edge of the open area. He had not seen me and was browsing contentedly perhaps a hundred yards away. So I sat down and had a look at him through my binoculars. The beech trees were quite big, and certainly large enough to hide a roe completely. As I was looking at him he disappeared behind one of these, and so I got my rifle ready with a view to taking him when he emerged at the other side. After a slight pause, a beast appeared and when I was able to see sufficient of its shoulder I fired. I had only concentrated on watching its shoulder for the shot. The beast ran a few yards and fell dead, but to my consternation as it did so I saw another deer run off in the opposite direction from behind the same tree. I had not seen another deer there and had been totally unaware of its presence. Worse, I got the impression that the beast that had run off was a buck. I hurried forward to see what had happened, and to my horror I found a doe lying dead. Since this lesson I have tried to be as careful as possible always to check on the beast immediately before firing to ensure that it is the one that I intend killing.

Chapter 10
Dogs

My dogs were my constant companions when stalking. They gradually learned a routine that they would carry out almost without my telling them. I developed a procedure with them too, which involved referring to them constantly in the knowledge that they were able to scent things, and deer in particular, when I was not able to do so. Frequently I was warned of the presence of deer ahead or to the side by the dogs, which indicated clearly that they had scented something by becoming alert, sometimes stopping and sniffing obviously. They used to follow at heel as I stalked, however slowly I moved, and if I paused they would stop, or sit. The gentlest of hisses would make them sit if they did not do so voluntarily. They got used to my calling deer, too. I never managed to train them to bark over a dead deer but I was always able to hear by their movements what was going on – usually, being labradors, a gentle attempt to retrieve the beast – and I came to rely on them completely to find shot deer that had run into thick cover, such as rhododendron thickets or bramble tangles, where blood trailing would have been difficult if not impossible. Indeed, I found myself becoming so reliant on their finding the deer, and so confident in their ability to do so, that I realised that I was becoming casual in looking for pins (hair) and paint (blood) at the site of a shot, and not bothering to follow blood trails. So from time to time I would deliberately keep the dogs back and make the effort to find the deer myself.

I never ceased to be amazed that none of the other stalkers in the local Deer Control Society, and indeed few stalkers in all the Deer Control Societies of which I had knowledge, had dogs. While it is possible to trail deer efficiently and find the beast in most cases, and a dog may seem superfluous much of the time, there are always instances when this is not so. I already had my labradors when I started stalking, and indeed had had gundogs long before that, so the idea of not having a dog available to help never occurred to me. Many of the other woodland stalkers that I knew lived in urban situations, a number of them were also bachelors, and I am sure that they would have pleaded that the circumstances made it extremely difficult for them to keep a dog. In most cases I would have rejected such an excuse. It is quite possible to keep a small dog like a Jack Russell terrier or a wire-haired dachshund, or similar, in urban surroundings, and possible for these dogs to become excellent deer trackers.

Nowadays, with the number of woodland stalkers having increased manyfold, the number of stalking dogs has also increased, but, I fear, not in proportion. I resent those who go out shooting or stalking without a dog being available to assist in the retrieving of dead or wounded animals or birds. At worst a stalker should insure that he knows of someone nearby with a dog who would be prepared to come out and help him to find a beast if necessary.

It is surprising how often it can be extremely difficult to find a dead deer, particularly a roe, which, lying flat on the ground, is small and easily hidden. I recall an instance a good many years ago, before we moved to live there, when I was in Aberdeenshire stalking roe for a few days and had not taken my dogs with me. There were two keepers on the estate where I was stalking and I knew well that I could call upon them and the assistance of their dogs if I encountered any difficulties. On this occasion I had climbed a small rowan tree overlooking a little marshy valley, into which I hoped a buck would come. Eventually he did so and I shot him. I marked carefully where he fell dead where he stood. However, by the time I got down out of the tree and walked to the spot I realised that there were some quite large tussocks of rushes, and I totally failed to find any sign of the buck whatever. The light was beginning to go after I had made a lengthy search, so I walked the three or four hundred yards to the house of one of the keepers and he kindly came back with me with his dog to look for the deer. The dog quickly found the beast: it had fallen between several tussocks of rushes and was very difficult to see even when one was standing over it knowing where it lay.

On another occasion, also in Aberdeenshire as it happens, indeed in the same area, but seventeen years later, after we had moved to live there, I had taken a friend out to try for a roebuck on my own ground before lunch one day. In this undisturbed area one can often find deer feeding at any time of day in the spring when the new foliage is tempting food. We saw nothing stalkable until on our way home we spotted a buck feeding inside the edge of a birch wood. My companion was again Rodger McPhail; he had shot a number of roe with me in the past, and I signalled him to move a little closer so that he could take a shot. He managed to get up to a willow tree, which enabled him to take a very steady shot. He fired, and the deer ran off into the wood and disappeared. We hurried forward to the spot where the buck had been standing and found only a small amount of hair, but no blood. Rodger had been quite confident about the shot, and sure that no twig or foliage was in the way of the bullet. We checked back to the firing point to make certain that we had marked exactly the right spot, but failed to find any further sign. Having known Rodger for a good many years I had complete confidence in his shooting and his knowledge of deer and their likely reaction to shot, and we were both convinced that the shot had been a successful one. We searched the comparatively open birch woodland for perhaps half an hour, and became increasingly concerned at the prospect that somehow or other the deer might have run off wounded.

I did not have a dog with me, but the house was within a quarter of a mile and we knew that we could fetch him easily if required. We had just reached the point where we had decided that I should go and fetch the dog when we both almost stumbled over the buck lying completely dead in quite short grass in an apparently perfectly obvious situation in the open birch wood. It seemed incredible that we had failed to find the beast earlier, but, as I said before, a dead roe lying flat is not easily seen. The shot had been a perfect heart shot and the animal had run about forty or fifty yards before falling dead. I cannot help but feel that under the circumstances somewhat less diligent stalkers would have given up the search and put the incident down to a miss or a wounded deer run off.

One day I was out stalking in the early morning with my Hungarian vizsla at heel when a small roebuck stepped out on to the ride about 120 yards ahead of me and stood broadside looking at me. I took a careful shot at him but just as I pulled the trigger he moved forward and I realised that my bullet had hit him too far back. The buck ran off into the wood on the other side of the ride and I encouraged the young dog to pursue him, knowing that the beast was hit. I had no idea whether the dog would tackle the buck or what he would do, since the circumstances had not arisen previously. By the time I reached the spot where the deer had been standing I realised that the dog had not actually chased the deer but was trailing it, and I could just see him fifty yards off in the wood. As I started to follow I saw the dog stop and point, and I hurried forward to find that he was pointing at the wounded buck which was lying under a holly bush. I promptly shot the roe and found that the first bullet had indeed hit too far back. I believe that without the help of the dog I should never have found that beast.

I can recall many instances over the years when the help of a dog in stalking has been invaluable, if not vital. Twenty years ago I took Rodger McPhail out to shoot a buck, and we sat up a high seat overlooking a wide ride with conifers on one side and a dense rhododendron thicket on the other. When the opportunity came, Rodger shot the buck through the heart and the beast ran off into the thick rhododendrons. We had much difficulty in entering the thicket ourselves, let alone looking for a blood trail, and I went to fetch my dog from my Land-Rover, which was parked not far away out of sight. He followed without

problem where the roebuck had run and showed us the dead beast. I think it unlikely that we would have ever found it without him since the direction was not quite what we had anticipated. The painting Rodger McPhail, made of that buck emerging on to the ride was his first of a roebuck. I still have it.

In the early stalking days a number of the first woodland roe stalkers favoured the .22 Hornet rifle for roe deer. This was before the days of the substantially more powerful .222, which I have always regarded personally as the perfect roe rifle. However I have never cared for the idea of the Hornet as a rifle for roe, for although it can kill them well, as indeed can a .22 rimfire in good hands, it has neither the shocking knockdown power nor the ability to spill blood of a more high-powered weapon. Once I took out a fellow to try a .22 Hornet on a roebuck, rather against my better judgement, but having given in to his earnest request to try out his newly acquired weapon. We located a buck across a little valley in a rather bare patch of small conifers. He shot the beast and it ran off into a thicker part of the plantation that was heavily overgrown with brambles. I had two dogs with me, and since we both thought that the beast was well shot we foresaw no difficulty in locating it. This proved to be the case, but I pointed out to the fellow that the beast had left absolutely no blood trail that we could find, and we were not able to locate exactly where it had run without following the dogs tracking the animal's scent. I am convinced that we would never have found that buck without the dogs. Indeed, as a result of this particular incident I made up my mind that I would not permit the use of a .22 Hornet on my ground again, even if the situation were to arise. The owner of that weapon had no dog at that time, but subsequently acquired one. The .22 Hornet is no longer legal for deer, of course. In England even the centre fire .222 is now illegal for use on deer, but it is still allowed for use on roe deer only in Scotland.

When I was gralloching roe and the dogs were with me I invariably gave them some titbits, usually the heart, and I have no doubt that this encouraged them to know what was required of them. However, some dogs follow deer trails by instinct, and indeed I have often heard it said that roe scent in particular seems to have an irresistible attraction both for foxhounds and for pet dogs being taken for walks in the woods.

I think that the most memorable occasion for me concerning a dog and a roebuck, which did not turn out entirely well, due to my own stupidity, was with the first roe on which I used my then newly acquired vizsla puppy, Wizzy. Diana and I had gone on a sunny evening to sit up a high seat that I had made in a large yew tree overlooking a very big clearing that had been replanted a couple of years earlier, and over which there was still very good visibility. There was a considerable amount of roe damage to the young trees in this clearing and I wanted to take out several bucks to appease the forestry company that managed the woodland. Wizzy had never been out after deer before, but we took him in the Land-Rover and left him in this, parked out of sight about 250 yards away on the track by which we approached the clearing. We had not been up the yew tree very long when a small buck appeared, perhaps a hundred yards away, having come up a bank behind us through an open piece of woodland of tall beech trees. The buck paused broadside in the open at the edge of the clearing and I shot him.

It was a comparatively easy shot and I had no doubts about it. I turned to Diana and said, 'That's fine! We can go back and I have time to mow the lawn this evening as there is plenty of light left. ' We got down out of the tree and walked over to the spot where the buck had stood and then followed the little deer path up which he had come and back down which he had fled at the shot. To my surprise there was no sign of the deer at all. I had expected to find him lying there under the beech trees. Still believing that the beast was lying dead somewhere fairly obvious, despite our failure to find it, I went back to the Land-Rover, got Wizzy and took him to the spot where the deer had stood when I fired. He showed clear signs of interest and ran quickly down the deer path, but to my annoyance he continued down the slope through the open beech wood for perhaps a hundred yards and started to cross the track at the bottom of the little valley and continue up the other side. I called him back because there was no possibility that the deer could have run that far. Diana and I, with Wizzy's help, searched that wood until dark. We went home very dejected and I did not sleep well, worrying about what could have happened to the buck. At dawn next day we both rose, and with Wizzy we drove back to the site. A further lengthy search still revealed absolutely nothing.

Finally, in desperation, the thought occurred to me that maybe Wizzy had been following the deer initially the previous evening, and maybe it really had run such an unusually long distance, crossed the valley bottom and gone up the other side. So I took him down to where he had crossed the track the previous evening and set him on a deer path going up the other side. He quickly followed this and I went after him. About twenty or thirty yards up the other bank from the track, in some cover, we found the remains of the roebuck. He had been heart shot, and I do not know why he had run so far, but I can only speculate that perhaps because he had run down a steep slope in his death rush this gave him greater momentum to go further. I said that we found the remains of the buck. Unfortunately a vixen and her cubs had clearly dined off him during the night. A haunch and other parts of the carcase were missing, but I was able to salvage the remaining haunch and the front shoulders. If only I had had faith in the puppy initially, as I came to have subsequently, the waste of venison would have been avoided, as well as that of time.

It is my strong view that all woodland stalkers should have access to a dog when necessary, preferably their own dog, but if there is some good reason why they are unable to keep a dog, then they should have a specific arrangement with someone that has a dog capable of locating a dead or wounded deer. Indeed, I believe that to go woodland stalking without a dog, or without the knowledge that a dog can be readily obtained to help search for a beast, is irresponsible.

My personal experience of dogs for roe extends only to my first labrador retrievers, who were excellent, and then to a succession of Hungarian vizslas and one Irish water spaniel. Apart from one puppy, with whom I dragged a roe carcase short distances for him to trail, the other dogs all picked up their training as we went along. I admit to never having been good at training dogs, never having had the patience, I suppose, nor the ambition to have a dog that did fancy tricks like dropping to whistle at a distance and so on. Even my succession of sheepdogs have had limited specific training. However, all my dogs have fulfilled their roles to my complete satisfaction, and I believe that this has been due partly to the instinct bred into them, and partly due to our frequent companionship, whereby they have learned what is expected of them merely by being with me, particularly accompanied by an older dog that knew the expected behaviour already. My dogs are my companions, not solely my servants, and though the sheepdogs live outside, largely because with thick coats they seem to prefer this, the vizslas always live in the house, and are invariably allowed up on the bed while I drink my early morning cup of tea. When I have taken my dogs on shoots, including stalking, their behaviour has always satisfied me, and their performance has often been better than that of so-called professionally trained dogs; whenever they have been required to find a deer for me they have never failed to do so when it was possible. The confidence this gives me is not only reassuring, but a completely necessary part of responsible stalking or shooting.

Chapter 11
Abnormalities and Noises

May and June are exciting months in roe stalking. In the south it is already early summer, but in the north it is spring, and the countryside is bursting into life, a new, clean, exhilarating life, with fresh plants emerging and the pleasure of finding the first violets, the first primroses, cuckoo flowers in the wet areas, and even the cuckoo itself, though this all-pervading call we sometimes hear first at the end of April. At the end of May and in early June the roe are moving about, seeking their summer territories, coming out into more open ground from the winter protection of the thick woods to where the food is lusher. Wood anemones, or windflowers as Diana calls them, begin to carpet the ground, and this is usually a sign for seeing roe about, for they like these to eat, as pheasants like the roots or tubers. The Highland roe are looking scruffy at the end of May, and in early June one can see them in all stages of change from winter to summer coat, a long way behind the deer in the south that have been bright red for weeks before that. Bucks in particular are moving about then; we probably see more at this time than at any other period of the year, as they have split up from winter family groups and are seeking out summering ground of their own, some out into fields and small blocks of shelter, others out on to the hill.

Everything in the countryside seems clean and fresh in late spring and early summer, and the pressure on the farm eases in mid May when feeding of stock ceases as grass grows sufficiently to appease the eager cattle and sheep. Birds are nesting, and some already have young. The tadpoles have hatched in the ponds by their thousands, and on the hill the air is filled with the noise of curlews and lapwings. It is a time to be out in the woods and fields appreciating the wonderful beauty of the rich part of the world in which we are fortunate to live.

July and August are the months of the roe rut, and this time of year carries for me the connotations of chanterelles, flying ants and toads. It is the time of year when sometimes one sees the bucks that one never sees at other times, and when there is the chance of calling out roebucks from thick cover, just as mayfly time often brings the opportunity to tempt out and catch those monster trout that are never seen at other times, mostly lurking unseen in deep holes and pools. In July I ensure that my pocket always contains a plastic bag, for

July is the start of the chanterelle season, which continues into September when the yellow birch leaves on the ground make finding the last of these delectable fungi more tedious. Those who have never had the pleasure of returning from a morning stalk on a warm autumn day with a bag of freshly picked mushrooms for breakfast have missed out on the aura of stalking, for it is not just about shooting deer – that attitude is for deer killers and those who degradingly think of deer only as live targets or trophies to measure and hang on the wall, or as income from the meat merchant or paying client. The true stalker has some of the atavistic opportunism of the hunter-gatherer, as some of our evolutionary forebears are described. The fruits of the woods and fields and hill are all part of the way of things.

Personally, much as I love mushrooms, as a variety I always preferred chanterelles. Not only can I eat chanterelles frequently without tiring of them, and indeed a plate of chanterelles fried in butter, with a little garlic, served with home-cured bacon, is a dish that I can eat, and have eaten, daily over a period in late summer without wearying of them as I would mushrooms, but they have the great advantage that they do not get fly-blown and maggoty. Occasionally they are attacked by slugs, and are sometimes favoured by harvestmen, but these are easily removed. Excess chanterelles can be dried or frozen for use in venison stews in winter.

Chanterelles and the roe rut go together as far as I am concerned, though the first of these yellow fungi appear in early July before the rut has started. Wandering round the woods with the combined objectives of gathering chanterelles and looking for deer sign, and perhaps hunting for roe-rutting rings, can be doubly advantageous. These rings are not easy to find, and in open country may be used less than in cover. Whether rutting rings are only formed by some bucks, or pairs, I do not know, but I rather suspect this to be the case. On more open ground the roe may chase round a bush or tree a while, but do not seem to do so with the consistency involved in clearly well-worn rings and figures-of-eight that can be found in thicker undergrowth. This may be due to the question of visibility, with the doe going round in circles in cover where at roe level this is poor, but not doing so in open ground where she is easily seen by the buck, but this is certainly not always so. The weather appears to have an effect on the roe rut, cold, wet weather often apparently dousing the ardour of the deer, while warm, close, thundery weather seems to promote much activity. These conditions are those that promote the instincts of ants, too, and at this time of year on a warm, close day the winged males and females emerge to fly and mate, providing a feast for a host of birds, and an abundant meal for toads after darkness has fallen. I recall one such evening in particular, returning from a stalk with a companion along our farm track discovering this to have toads hopping about every few yards where earlier in the evening flying ants had swarmed.

Deer come into season like sheep, not like cattle. That is to say that both bucks and does come into season together. What actually stimulates this is not certain, but probably the light factor and the length of days. It would seem that frost can bring stags into season more quickly than mild weather, but the reverse is true for roe. Although hinds and does come into cycle at the same time as their mates, as with sheep there can be exceptions. Whether this is less frequent or that out of normal season progeny are less likely to survive is not known. Undoubtedly most late-born calves, fawns and kids do not thrive, and those born too early would suffer from adverse weather, nature having devised a breeding season for the various species that suits their environment and gives the young the optimum time for growth, under normal circumstances, before the onset of adverse conditions of weather and food scarcity.

Abnormalities in deer are always of interest, though mostly these are against the welfare of the deer, as one might expect. Malformed antlers are generally due to mechanical damage to them in velvet, or the growing stage, but can be the result of disease or parasitic disorder. Often collision with a fence, or even a vehicle, results in damage to the antlers or to the pedicle, which may itself lead to unusual growth. Testicular damage or interference with hormone supply may result in strange antler growth, or the rare peruke heads, where the antlers do not stop growing and velvet is not shed. In extreme cases this has resulted in a revolting mass of growth on the head that has flowed down obscuring the unfortunate brute's vision, or becoming maggot-infested to the desperate distraction of the animal. Mostly deer that are exceptionally late in cleaning velvet off their antlers have some defect. Hummels, male deer without any antlers, are caused by internal and hormonal defects. In red deer these often grow into large, strong animals, probably through not having to waste energy growing their antlers, and if they are large bodied they are able to dominate smaller horned beasts. Whether the condition is hereditary I do not know, but I doubt it, though the opportunity for experiment is seldom offered, since most stalkers regard hummels as a prime target for removal from the herd. Hummels in roe are much rarer, even allowing for their being less easily identified, but they do occur. A young roe without antlers was shot recently in eastern England, having been seen, presumably the same beast, during two seasons. Diana has watched and sketched a young roebuck without antlers in this vicinity, identification confirmed by the obvious tush or pubic hairs on his belly and by watching him urinate.

Many old does develop bony growths on their heads, though generally these are no more than small lumps below the skin, but antlered does have been shot. Mostly the post-mortem examinations of these have not been thorough enough to determine the extent of hermaphroditism present. Vestigial upper canine teeth, called tusks but actually only as large as small teeth, occur in red deer, wapiti and other species. In Germany these are called 'grandeln', and are prized as trophies for jewellery. Most professional stalkers regard these as perquisites, which they can sell to their advantage. Although these 'tusks' do not normally occur in other deer in this country (not to be confused with the proper tusks in Chinese water deer and muntjac – or with the word 'tush' that is the name given to the pubic hairs of a roe, both male and female!), they are found occasionally. I have had reports of them being found very rarely in fallow, and have found a grandl in roe on rare occasions myself. I have five of these now, and certainly have not found more than six personally. I believe that one of these came from a doe. It is difficult to judge frequency of occurrence and a small sample is valueless in this respect, but for what it is worth it would appear to me that roe tusks occur in no more than one per cent, and perhaps less, of the population. I have never seen a pair in one roe. The lack of data on the subject is exacerbated by the undoubted fact that the overwhelming number of stalkers do not automatically examine the mouth of all deer handled. This unfortunate omission and apparent lack of interest should be rectified, and responsible deerstalkers of all species of deer should make a practise of looking at carcases not only for tusks but for any other abnormalities.

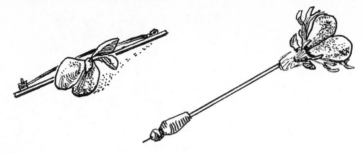

Roe tail length is another factor where abnormalities have occurred. This is more easily seen, but not necessarily noted, when cleaning the rectal passage and pelvic arch during gralloching. I have come across two roe, both bucks, which had tails that, though still small, were two or three times normal length. Roe tails are not very obvious and many people may think that they have none, but they become more obvious when deer are observed defaecating.

Apart from the obvious barking of roe, other noises or vocal sounds produced by the deer are somewhat of a mystery, made more so by the strange artificial calls used to entice them at rutting time. The clicking often heard from rapidly departing roe has been suggested by some to be a warning signal, and certainly it emanates from animals disappearing hurriedly, but it can be heard from cattle, too, when running, particularly young beasts careering about a field, and Père David deer make the clicking noise when walking about. So it seems likely that while this sound may act as a signal, it probably does so coincidentally, being caused by the cleaves clicking together from any running cloven-hoofed animal.

The barking of roe is usually first heard in spring, the deer being largely silent in winter. Why this should be so, and whether it relates to cover and visibility, or to some other factor, is uncertain. Through the summer roe are frequently heard barking, and in autumn they become silent again. This noise would seem to be related to uncertainty and aggression. It is sometimes possible to call up a buck by barking back at him, and I recall a demonstration of this being given to me by the late Louis Petyt in the Ardennes some years ago, my own powers of impersonation being quite hopeless. I have heard it said that it is possible to distinguish not only a buck from a doe by the tone of the bark, but also an old buck from a younger one. Personally I doubt this, based on my own experience of watching barking deer, but perhaps my auricular faculties are lacking. I have watched more than one roe barking simultaneously in close proximity and been unable to associate differing tones with any particular sex or age groups.

Most experience of roe barking is from human disturbance, of course, and usually this is so when the animal is uncertain as to the origin of its anxiety: it may hear something downwind, say, or see a suspicious body, but be unable to identify it by scent or otherwise. The bark usually denotes caution rather than alarm. Surprisingly, what would appear to be a loud signal to other deer often seems to be ignored, and I have frequently seen several roe in a large area apparently oblivious of their fellow deer barking some distance away, but well within earshot. Often one hears roe barking in a wood where human disturbance is unlikely and one wonders as to the cause. Sometimes it may be a fox that is responsible for the disquiet, but I suspect that at other times it is other deer causing the disturbance, whether unseen by the barker or identified but unwelcome in the vicinity. Sometimes if a roe is not badly disturbed it will bark only two or three times and then settle down again, occasionally resuming feeding but giving low barks with its mouth full.

Red deer are far less vociferous than roe. Their bark is definitely an alarm signal and warning to others in the vicinity. I have been barked at by hinds on the hill, of course, but mostly it has been in woodland, and usually when the hind has spotted me before I have been aware of her, or is downwind and has just caught my scent. The deep, hollow-sounding bark of a red deer hind when close and unexpected can be quite startling. I have read that stags make no noise other than their roar at rutting time, but this is nonsense and I have frequently heard parties of stags making grunting communication to each other when down on the river flats for their evening grazing. Hinds and calves chat to each other, too.

Roe clearly communicate vocally, and kids make a peeping noise, which can be demonstrated by the efficacy of a 'kitz' call in either bringing a doe running to the call or causing her to go off to look for her own kid. Roe also have a terror scream reminiscent of the cry made by a frightened hare only considerably deeper. I have heard it on several occasions, and it is indeed a most unpleasant noise. Once a roebuck wounded by a companion fell in a ditch and proceeded to scream several times before my companion was able to dispatch it. One time on a pheasant shoot we had gathered for lunch at the 'big house', when our host came and said that a roebuck had been in his garden, had jumped out over the substantial iron gates and seemingly had hurt itself and was unable to move. I always carry a knife, so I immediately went with him to see what had happened, also bringing the shotgun in case it was necessary. The buck was clearly unable to move for some reason that I was unable to ascertain, but screamed in a disquieting manner when we approached, so I seized the terrified creature by its antlers and cut its throat to dispatch it rapidly. I was not able to examine the carcase subsequently – was attended to by the keeper – so I never learned the reason for the initial injury.

On the possibly incorrect assumption that the powers of reasoning of a Jack Russell terrier that we once had did not allow him to realise that snow would cover tracks, it appears that the onset of a snowstorm creates good scenting conditions. This tiresome terrier, given the slightest opportunity, chose such a moment to vanish on a rabbit hunt, usually persuading one of the other dogs to go along for the fun. Try as we might, short of keeping the brute permanently encaged, he contrived to grab the moment when one's head was turned momentarily, and to signal his accomplice to vanish. On one such occasion Diana and I immediately donned suitable clothing and went in forlorn pursuit, and by chance found their tracks in the wood. We followed these, but they did not go in any particular direction and clearly the dogs were chasing rabbits. In the middle of the wood we were appalled to hear a roe scream and concluded that the dogs had caught one. We ran in the direction of the sound yelling for the dogs, and our anger was tempered by relief when they suddenly appeared. Immediate examination revealed no evidence of contact with deer, so I back-tracked them until I came across roe marks. I concluded that in fact they had not even chased the deer, but had come face to face with it, or very close to it, and the animal had screamed and run off.

More recently I was shooting rabbits in thick bracken with my two vizslas. Under such circumstances they behave in most un-field-trial-like manner as they pursue the rabbits unseen, hopefully flushing them into the open. Despite the bells with which I normally fit their collars, so that I can locate them or, more correctly, establish when they are pointing and not moving, it would be useless for me were they to point the rabbits in the midst of thick bracken, so I encourage them to give chase. During the course of this usually successful and quite entertaining form of rabbbit control one day I heard a roe scream quite close, and yelled at the dogs, thinking that they had a deer. I rushed in the direction of the scream, and met a well-grown roe kid running down a path in the bracken towards me. When it saw me it turned tail and disappeared in the opposite direction, subsequent to which both dogs appeared and quite clearly took no notice of it or its scent. Obviously they had disturbed the kid at close quarters and it had screamed in fright without being touched.

From the success, on occasion, of roe calls at rutting time, with bucks responding to what often seem outrageously strange noises, including those made by blowing on a blade of grass held between the hands, I assume that roe must make such noises; otherwise they would not respond to them, but personally I have not consciously heard them made by the deer themselves. I have heard strange noises in the woods on occasion and been uncertain of their origin. Perhaps noises I thought were caused by young kestrels and other such possibilities were actually made by roe? Who knows? The only rutting call of which I am certain, and which I have witnessed quite often as a doe was chased by a buck, is the continuous 'fiep' or peeping sound, which could easily be mistaken for a bird by a listener unaware of the deer. I do not believe anyone that I know has heard the more violent noises represented by the 'sprengfiep' or 'geschrei' actually uttered by deer, though the latter might be regarded as not totally dissimilar to a scream of anguish.

Chapter 12
The Woods and the Hill

Imprinted on my mind is the caption of a photograph in a book entitled *Wildfowling* by the late Christopher Dalgety. The photograph is of two dead swans and a dog sitting beside them. The caption reads, 'A dead Whooper is not beautiful'. I hasten to point out that the book was published in 1937 when, of course, wild swans were legitimate quarry. I have so often thought of this when looking at dead birds and animals. A dead deer is not beautiful either. The majesty of a fine stag guarding his harem, and the grace of a little roebuck, are both vanished from the corpse lying on the grass. Some of us can feel a little sad at the anti-climax at the end of a successful stalk. Many never have such feelings. Their hearts are full of pride and their heads sated with success, thinking only of fine antlers to display on their walls. But there should be room for a little sadness at the lifeless form, as well, perhaps, as relief that the wretched beast doing all the damage has now been removed, or that the big switch or hummel is no more, if such are the circumstances. The true hunter has a feeling for his quarry that is difficult to reconcile with his atavistic instinct to pursue it. Many of the greatest conservationists, who have done most to preserve species, started life as hunters of those beasts, coming to love them in that strange relationship that cannot be understood by many, and gradually undergoing a change of emphasis as that admiration for the animal swelled yet further.

I have spoken with a good number of stalkers of various types over the years, and I have been increasingly saddened and embarrassed by the realisation of how many of these see stalking deer as a thing of statistics and ballistics, and perhaps a bit of venison. Their talk is only of numbers killed, medal heads and rifles. For them a stalk is a deer hunt, no more and no less. I feel sad for these people, for they miss so much of the fascination of a stalking outing. When a young man comes back from a stalking evening and reports that he saw only a couple of does 'but it was a fine walk, and the smell of the gorse was magnificent', and goes on to tell of the owl that landed on the fencepost ten yards away from him, of the strange bug that he saw on a fence, which he is off to look up in the book, and asks if we saw the spectacular sunset, then my heart lifts a little in pleasure to know that here is someone that I regard as a true stalker and not merely a shooter of deer.

There is so much to see in the woods and on the hill, and for the fortunate ones the stalking is in part a *raison d'être* for being there. If we shot deer every time we went out, and going out was always with the certainty of success, some of the fascination would evaporate, and fewer people would wander the woods, or sit watching, or climb the hill, merely to enjoy  the environment as some can. The rifle on one's shoulder gives a sense of purpose, and the stealth and secretiveness that the stalker tries to achieve give the opportunity of observing not only undisturbed deer but many other creatures, too. The woodland stalker has a great advantage over the person whose interest is confined to hunting the red deer on the hill, not just in variety of environment, but in length of opportunity. The stalker of roe in particular can be out with hunting purpose almost the whole year through, while red deer and sika are in season only from July to February between stags and hinds. The fallow deer stalker has a respite in early summer from May to July, which is a glorious time to be in the woods, so may lack the incentive to enjoy this period of new life for plants and creatures.

The fortunate, or perhaps resourceful, stalker will seek to pick the best of these opportunities to give a variety of incentive to be out following the deer. By the end of August the roe rut is over and roebucks tend to be elusive and not in evidence to a great degree, which gives the roe stalker the opportunity to savour the glory of autumn in the Highlands. Late September and early October, the time of the red deer rut, often bring some of the best weather in the north, and I should hate the prospect of being unable to relish the fabulous autumn colours of northern landscapes, which I have contrived to enjoy every one of the past twenty-five seasons without break.

Increasingly I find myself employing the word 'hunting' as it is used in most other countries, rather than the possibly more definitive stalking and shooting. This is because I find it more descriptive of the sort of atavistic pursuit that I enjoy. In recent years I have found less and less pleasure in driven bird shooting, which is often little more than live bird target shooting and does not give the satisfaction of seeking out an elusive quarry for the pot. In the same way I feel that hunting is more descriptive of many situations on the open hill where it is a question of seeking out and finding the deer before even considering stalking them.

I never return from a stalk unrewarded, though I am sometimes empty-handed. There is always something of interest to tell those at home, and perhaps a feather to bring back, or a little bunch of bluebells or bog asphodel or cotton grass. Frequently the highlight of my stalk in woods has not been deer at all, but watching a badger out late or early snuffling about, or observing a pair of amorous and rather noisy hedgehogs oblivious to my standing ten yards away, or sitting fascinated as a stoat executes a remarkable dance or game seemingly out of pure *joie de vivre* and friskiness. Often the stalk has turned into a cautious gathering of chanterelles, or picking of brambles, trying to be alert for deer at the same time. The vigil in the high seat is always enhanced by the appearance of a woodcock, with the male bird patrolling his territory with that peculiar croaking flight, often signalling the time when deer will emerge from the woods to feed in the open; and later, in some areas in the south, the churring call of a nightjar, reminiscent of somebody trying to tune an ancient wireless set, signalling the failing of the light and little time left for a shot even were a buck to appear.

Sometimes, when there is no requirement for a deer to be shot, I take an air rifle out into the woods instead, to stalk rabbits. In many ways this can be as exciting and rewarding, especially if we need a rabbit for the dogs' supper. Perversely the creatures often change their roles when I do this. The rabbits that seemed to be everywhere sitting upright and alert but unmoving at close range when I carried the heavy rifle, apparently aware that they were not the quarry, now silently disappear into cover as one approaches within shot, and occasionally I come face to face with a roebuck that I have been trying to outwit. An air rifle is quiet, and fully effective on rabbits at thirty to forty yards, with little damage to the carcase, and a rabbit stalk is excellent training for the would-be deer stalker, teaching him to move silently through the woods, to observe and notice and then to place a steady, effective shot. All young potential stalkers should serve their apprenticeship stalking rabbits with an air rifle for a season or two first, before progressing to a higher powered weapon and larger animal.

Chapter 13
Aberdeenshire, Fallow Bucks and Rifles

In the early 1970s we began to find the pressures of living in the south of England too onerous and circumstances that would involve a different story altogether resulted in our moving from Surrey to a farm in Aberdeenshire. There can be no doubt that one of the factors that determined our attraction to this farm was the evident roe population. At the time that we moved we did not know that there was also a significant red deer population in the area and that a few of these spent time in the summer on the wooded hill part of the farm. They were an undoubted bonus. Since neighbouring estates shoot both species of deer on a commercial basis, I decided that the farm should become available as a partial sanctuary for some of the red deer. Consequently I rarely shoot red deer on the farm unless crop damage to neighbours necessitates action. We derive far more pleasure from seeing the hinds and calves grazing peacefully in the summer and having a stag rut within sound of the house each autumn.

One year when we grew oats behind the house two hinds, a calf and a yearling staggie used to come regularly each evening in late summer to feed in the field. They were easy to see from the back window of the house, but we often used to go up the steps to the corn loft at the back of the steading, where we could look down upon them only fifty yards away at times. We were sure that they were aware of our presence but did not seem disturbed. They used to come out of the wood in the evening, some time before the light started to fade, cross over the farm road into a field of rape and then over the dyke into the oat field. They always made for one spot in this field initially and I was interested to mark this carefully and on several occasions examine it to try to discover the attraction. I came to the conclusion that this was a damp part of the field with an old drain running through it below ground, and the crop there was a little thinner and had more weeds growing at ground level. So far as I could tell it was these that the red deer were eating. They were not eating the oats to any great extent, and indeed the only damage they were doing was making a track through the crop. We watched them on a number of evenings, and even took friends up the loft steps to see them. Their routine seemed to be much the same and they worked their way over to this damper patch in the field to spend a few minutes there before wandering off further into the field. The yearling staggie was a rather poor specimen with deformed antlers that were small in any case. Eventually I decided that no harm would come by taking him and with the deer having fed in my field for a week or two I felt that I might take some venison in return. I suggested this to Diana, who, to my surprise, agreed and felt that this staggie might well be shot since his antlers were so poor.

We had a young Canadian boy staying with us at the time and I thought that he might be interested to accompany me in trying to shoot this staggie, as he was quite keen on shooting, if unfamiliar with deer. Early in the summer when I had sowed the field of rape I had placed an old diesel tank, with a side and part of one end cut out of it, in the field as a permanent hide from which to shoot pigeons that raided the crop. With an old sack closing the doorway made by the cut out end, it formed a comfortable hide into which two could squeeze. Since the deer had crossed past this tank every evening and were thoroughly used to it, I felt that it would make an ideal ambush. I did not wish to shoot the animal in the rape because of the damage that would be caused in removing him. So I hoped to shoot across the farm road on to the wooded slope beyond, which would be a range of perhaps 120 yards.

We went out to the tank about half an hour before the usual time that the deer appeared, and settled down to wait. Sure enough, at the usual time I saw the older hind coming down through the birch trees on to the road. She spent a little time walking up and down the fence, as deer are wont to do, despite their ability to jump it perfectly well. I saw a movement in the trees in the background and I knew that the other deer were there, but obviously waiting for the leading hind to establish that all was clear. She finally jumped into the field, but seemed to be suspicious. I cannot think that she could have smelled our presence because of the wind direction, and we had approached the hide across the middle of the field so that the deer would not cross our path. I think that she must have sensed our presence somehow, though, because she walked up to within about ten yards of the diesel tank where we were crouched scarcely daring to breathe. We could hear her snorting about outside; then she gave a deep bark that almost caused us to have involuntary evacuation of the bowels, ran back to the fence and jumped out of the field again. We remained quite still, and though obviously disturbed and unsettled, it seemed that she could not make out the reason for this, for she continued to move up and down on the other side of the farm road in the edge of the trees, clearly wanting to come across into the fields, as had become her habit.

At that stage the younger hind, calf and yearling appeared a short distance behind her and, having located the staggie, I prepared for action. He stepped out of the trees on the bank and stood looking down on the field, presenting an easy shot. I duly put a bullet through his chest. At the shot he ran straight down the bank and very conveniently fell dead precisely in the middle of the road. This meant no dragging and easy collection with the tractor. I felt a slight sense of guilt or regret at having shot him. I knew that not only would it mean an end to seeing him each evening, it would also scare off the rest of the group.

Another stag that I shot with reluctance, but I felt that if I did not do so the neighbouring keeper probably would, was one of a small party that had done much damage trampling a neighbour's oats with nightly visits across my fields. Their presence was all too obvious since they stayed in his oat field until well after daylight and he was doing much roaring. As the rut was almost over by then, and I knew that there was at least one other stag in the area to take charge of the hinds if required, I decided to waylay him on his return across the fields. I had been ferreting in my grass field, across the burn from the neighbour's oats, on the previous day, and had gone down to the edge of the burn to see where they crossed. I was horrified by the obvious trampled deer path. Later I checked on the opposite side of the field and found a well-worn path through some boggy scrub leading back on to the hill.

I chose to ambush him as he came out of this scrub on his way home. I had to do a long detour because the wind was in a difficult direction, but reached my chosen ambush site in time to hear a roar that I estimated indicated his entering the scrub on the opposite side, perhaps 250 yards away. I was only just in time to catch him returning from his nightly outing. I got into position behind a small knoll covering their exit path from the scrub area on to the hill and had barely done so when I heard a movement and a staggie emerged on to the path forty yards away. I could have taken him, but I felt that to take the stag might be more effective both as a deterrent and diplomatically. Another roar sounded nearer and the staggie moved up on to the hill out of sight amongst the birches. Yet another roar and I glimpsed a hind crossing the rough ground in front of me with the stag close behind. He was quite a large animal with longish antlers, although no magnificent trophy. Having seen how briskly the staggie had moved off up the hill once out of the thicker cover, I was a little concerned in case the stag took off too quickly for a shot. Suddenly a hind came out, trotted a few yards and paused, looking behind her. She was only about fifty yards away, level with me or even slightly behind me, and I was frightened that she might look round in my direction and see me, since from that position I would have been perfectly obvious to her had she done so.

After a moment's pause the stag also appeared and the hind moved off with the stag behind her. I realised that he was not going to stop, but as he was walking slowly I decided to take him, it being a comparatively easy shot at that range. Knowing that the range would be close I had taken with me my open-sighted .256 Mannlicher, which, with its shallow back sight, is very much easier for taking moving shots than a telescopic sight. The bullet was perhaps a little high, but it was a high heart shot and the stag fell where he stood. I went over and checked that he was dead and then gralloched him. There was no need to 'stick' him to bleed him, for I gralloched him fully as I do woodland deer with no dragging involved. On the hill, where one has to drag a beast, it is desirable to have a small opening into the body cavity for gut removal, to minimise dirt and so forth entering, and one is unlikely to wish to carry heart and lungs, liver and kidneys separately, so these are left in the carcase; in which case it is necessary to remove blood as soon as possible. This is done by sticking a knife into the base of the beast's throat into the heart or large blood vessels and allowing the blood to flow out. Rapid removal of blood and cooling of the carcase is essential for best eating quality subsequently. Where a deer does not have to be dragged and transport is no problem it is easier, and indeed best for achieving these objectives, if all viscera are removed immediately from gullet to anus, retaining those organs required separately in a plastic bag or whatever.

Some may consider that I have been fortunate to have owned roe deer and red deer stalking for a good many years, and while I would not disagree, I would counter that I have devoted considerable effort to organising my life to enable us to indulge in our interests of stalking wild deer. Others aim for fine houses, expensive cars, video sets and holidays abroad. We have eschewed all these things in favour of leading the life that we have chosen. Those who enjoy vast deer forests and fine lodges, stalkers and ghillies and expensive all-terrain machinery will doubtless smile condescendingly at the idea of our little patch of deer ground and the strenuous efforts involved in getting the deer home. An expensive restaurant with fine surroundings and a bevy of waiters in attendance is impressive, but it is the food that is important to me and it is the quality of the meal that makes the place memorable. I have been fortunate enough to stalk on deer forests where I have been taken out by professionals, had my rifle carried for me and have not been involved in getting the carcase home, but have merely been required to walk and pull the trigger when the rifle has been presented to me. I have had most enjoyable days under these conditions, and consider myself lucky to have had such opportunities. Nevertheless, there has always seemed to me to be some ingredient missing. It is, I suspect, that my atavistic hunting instinct has not been satisfied.

With a shotgun I have enjoyed a good many memorable days at driven grouse and pheasants, although in most cases the memorable part has not been associated particularly with the shooting itself but with other aspects of the day, and I have experienced miserable days of driven shoots likened to live bird target shooting, in which I have vowed not to participate again. Without doubt the most satisfying days with a shotgun have been rough shooting days where one has had to work for the bag in the company of pleasant and enthusiastic friends. So with stalking red deer on the hill my most memorable experiences have been where we have been the stalkers, both on my own ground and on that of friends, and we have done the hard work of getting the beasts home and felt the more satisfied for it, with a sense of achievement and not simply satisfaction at a successful shot.

Be that as it may, I believe that having been able to participate in my own red deer and roe deer stalking as I wished, I am in a position to make an unbiased personal judgement as to which type of stalking I prefer. There is no doubt that red deer stalking on the open hill, as opposed to seeking them out in woodland, with the exercise involved, the clean hill air and often breathtaking scenery and remoteness, is appealing, especially to those who lead a sedentary life in urban surroundings. Certainly when we lived in the south, the far north of Scotland was in contrast utopian, and spending so much time seeking roe deer it was pleasant to have red deer in different habitat as a change of quarry. However, there is no doubt in my mind, and I do not believe that there ever was any doubt, that I prefer roe stalking in woodland. I have always preferred trout fishing to salmon fishing, and I have always regarded chalk stream dry fly fishing as the cream of all. Perhaps my personal taste was influenced by my initiation into this at a school with its own stretch of chalk stream, on the banks of which I spent as much spare time as I could. Some people prefer salmon fishing, with the larger fish. Perhaps they have more patience than I do. Others prefer an expedition in search of sharks, or are prepared to sit for days on end in an open boat off Portugal in the hope of a battle with a swordfish, but to me stalking a rising trout in a chalk stream with delicate tackle and the necessity of great skill to achieve success is my first choice. So I believe that the pursuit of the dainty roe deer in the woods has a magic about it, and requires greater skill than shooting a stag on the hill.

We take a number of roe here each year, but I find that there must be a motive involved above simply the urge to stalk and shoot a deer. Mostly that motive is venison, for we eat a lot of this excellent meat, as we have done now for a great many years. We have high seats scattered round the farm, some of which are used only occasionally, from which we can observe roe, and occasionally red deer, as well as other wildlife. I enjoy sitting up these seats even without the intention of shooting a roe, and Diana also finds them useful for observing and drawing deer. I particularly enjoy sitting up a tree at the time of the rut, calling bucks.

Our interest is in wild deer, but we have an ideal piece of ground for running a deer farm and with judicious deer leaps could acquire some wild stock. Although we have never seriously entertained this idea, we became early members of the Deer Farmers Association in order to learn more of that side of things. However, disregarding the economics, which are doubtless extremely attractive to those estates capturing and selling off wild live hinds in large numbers rather than shooting them, but which are rather more doubtful where stock has to be bought at great expense, we have never been encouraged by the sight of fenced deer. For some reason tame or fenced in deer, even if captured in the wild only a short time before, seem to have a totally different look about them from truly wild deer and I do not find them particularly attractive. It is remarkable how one can detect deer that are domesticated rather than truly wild even in photographs and paintings. They seem to have a completely different expression. In rather the same way I found that after visits to Africa I have seen in zoos in this country animals that I saw there in the wild, and however good the zoos and however hard attempts have been made to give the animals good surroundings, they invariably look totally different, to the extent that I actually find myself rather disgusted by seeing these normally wild and free animals in captivity in spite of accepting the good reasons for their being there. I value too highly the excitement of looking up from breakfast to see a couple of wild hinds browsing 150 yards from the window, or the pleasure of being able to lie in bed watching hinds and calves grazing within a rifle shot of the house, or lying in the bath listening to a truly wild stag roaring outside at the bottom of the hill, knowing that he could be gone tomorrow.

My experience of other species of deer is limited. It may be because of this that I have never found them as attractive from the point of view of either stalking or watching as red deer or roe. I have only ever seen one wild muntjac, which I shot because I wished to examine him close up and from a culinary viewpoint. The company that managed the forestry adjacent to my ground in Surrey had asked me to visit another area that they managed, north of the River Thames, where they were complaining of a lot of deer damage. I visited this area with a stalking friend and we found that the deer doing the damage were fallow, but because the area was small they were mostly passing through rather than resident, so far as we could tell; much of the damage looked as though it might have been caused during the previous rut. The area also held a high population of muntjac and the dainty, almost fairy-like, slots seemed to be everywhere. The muntjac had then just started their massive spread from the Hertfordshire area.

I was walking through an open wood of mature beech trees at the edge of which grew thick clumps of rhododendrons. Nature suddenly called me urgently into one of these clumps, and when I emerged again I saw a muntjac buck standing browsing. I watched him for a few moments and then shot him, anxious not to miss the opportunity.

Muntjac fawn

In retrospect I wish that I had watched him rather longer, but I hoped for further opportunities which did not occur. I cannot say that I have any wish to shoot any more muntjac since they seem such inoffensive creatures. Years ago Diana and I visited a friend of hers in the New Forest, and they had a minute muntjac fawn that they were hand rearing. It was an amazing little creature and they had trained it to urinate standing over an ash tray!

Various friends with ground holding fallow deer have asked me out stalking on a number of occasions. Spotted fallow deer are undoubtedly attractive animals, especially if one is fortunate enough to see them in dappled sunlight in the woods, but somehow I never find that these animals endear themselves to me as other species do. Certainly stalking rutting fallow deer is exciting and testing; often the vigorous grunting belching noise that seems so near suddenly ceases and the deer vanish as a result of a mistake on the part of the stalker, a twig cracking or an eddy in the wind, or his being detected by an outlying young buck or doe. The first fallow buck that I shot was undoubtedly the best fallow deer that I shall ever take, and my second best was shot within an hour of the first, though compared to antlers that Diana and I saw on a herd in Denmark the heads are indifferent.

I remember the incident well for a number of reasons. It was my first outing after fallow, and a friend whom I had invited for a week's stalking red deer in the north of Scotland offered me a chance at a fallow buck in reciprocation, coupled with the hope that his partner in this stalking might be offered the opportunity of stalking red deer with me in the following year. The rutting ground was in a large yew wood on top of the Downs, which seemed to me to be full of fallow deer. The visibility under the yews was quite good because the browse line of the deer had cleared lower branches of the yew trees. It seems that fallow deer and roe deer brought up in an environment containing yew can browse it without ill effect. I often saw roe browsing yew outside our Surrey house, and Diana has frequently seen fallow deer browsing it too. It may be that only dead or dying foliage is poisonous, or that yew affects only animals unused to its ingestion. We could hear grunting in the wood, and guided by this we carefully made our way forward until we were able to have a clear view of a beautiful spotted fallow buck with a good head rutting amongst a number of does and grunting away with an almost snake-like expression on his face. It took some minutes of waiting until I could get a clear shot when he was standing away from the does, but eventually the chance came. I fired, he went down and the does melted rapidly away through the wood. One of my companions went forward and 'stuck' him.

As it was still early in the day we went in search of another buck, in the same quite large yew wood, and in due course came across another beast on his rutting stand. He was almost of the same size, but was of the dark variety. After watching the deer for a while, the buck running amongst his does grunting furiously, the opportunity for a clear shot presented itself and he too went down where he stood. Although he did not rise again, he was clearly not dead and I gave him another bullet to be sure. When we got up to him he still seemed to have some life and one of my companions cut his throat.

Although both bucks went down satisfactorily and there were no real problems, I felt then that the .243 that I was using was not heavy enough for a rutting fallow buck in woodland. These animals clearly have a great deal of adrenalin flowing through their veins and can be difficult to kill, and I felt that had the shot not been in the right place the .243 might not have given sufficient blood trail for following up a wounded animal. I resolved then to acquire a heavier rifle in case of further such opportunities. I was not sure what calibre to choose, but for some reason that I find difficult to quantify I have never favoured a 30.06 or .308. Had other occasions not arisen I might have ended up with one of these, but it so happened that two opportunities presented themselves more or less simultaneously and I took advantage of both.

The first of these was when I happened to mention my interest to a friend of mine, the late Christopher Dalgety, and he told me that he had an 8 mm combined 16-bore drilling that he was about to sell. I knew that he already had a lovely drilling that I had admired on visits to his house over a number of years, and it seems that he had acquired the second one in a sale and had quickfit mounts made for a Zeiss telescopic sight to fit it, as well as a tool for sizing rifled slugs to a precise fit for improved accuracy. However, he eventually decided to keep his original weapon and resell the second one. I coveted the weapon as soon as I saw it and bought it from him. It remains my favourite gun and I have often used it at pheasant shoots as well as for stalking. I have shot roe, red deer and sika with it, but I cannot recall if I have taken fallow deer with it as well. I have certainly shot all manner of birds with it at different times, and one day I shot several ptarmigan, a grouse and a red deer hind with the same weapon.

About the same time a client of mine who knew that I was interested in stalking told me that he had a pair of .256 Mannlichers that unscrewed in half and fitted into a leather case, both fitted with peep sights as well as open sights. He was retiring and felt that it was extremely unlikely that he would ever stalk again, and that there was no point in passing the weapons on to his son since ammunition was no longer made for them. He had acquired these rifles second-hand many years before when, as a young subaltern, he had been part of the guard detail at Balmoral Castle, where the officers usually had a chance to go stalking. The opportunity to buy this pair of rifles, with the smoothest actions that I have ever handled, plus eighty rounds of ammunition for twenty-five pounds was one that I could not resist. I took the precaution of obtaining permission to acquire and hold a substantial amount of ammunition on my Firearms Certificate on the grounds of acquiring obsolete stock before it became unavailable. A diligent search of London gunsmiths and a gun shop in the north enabled me to acquire a total of 2,000 rounds, sufficient for me to use the rifles for target practise without inhibition and last me a lifetime of stalking with the weapons used only sporadically for particular purposes.

That first outing after fallow was memorable for two other reasons, the first amusing and the second embarrassing and detracting from the experience. After we had gralloched these two bucks one of my companions said, 'We had better bury these grallochs because there is a woman comes round here watching deer, called Diana Brown, and she might find them.' In less than two years Diana Brown was to become Diana Alcock! The second, and rather sad reason for recalling this day in particular was that I discovered some time later that actually both of these bucks had been poached! I remembered that we had to drag them out of the yew wood and over a fence into deciduous woodland, where we later collected them with a vehicle. I remember, too, that one of my companions covered up the drag trail. What I did not know at the time was that the yew wood adjoined the stalking where my companions controlled deer and, although they knew the owner, the area was normally regarded as a sort of sanctuary for the fallow herd. The owner did not know that the bucks were shot and the carcases were sold for the benefit of my companions. The subsequent discovery of the true situation, quite a long time later, naturally soured my memory of the outing and my relationship with those who had taken me to shoot these bucks. Perhaps this and the fact that on two occasions I was offered the opportunity to shoot impressive fallow bucks in deer parks, both of which invitations I rapidly but politely refused, of course, have contributed to my lesser enthusiasm for fallow deer stalking. I have both stalked and sat up high seats for fallow, and taken part in moving operations to cull does in various parts of the country, but for some reason I have never found fallow stalking as exciting or fascinating as the pursuit of other deer.

My experience of sika deer is limited to a couple of outings in Dorset and a number of forays in Argyllshire. I sat up a high seat in the former area, where there are good sika, and was successful in shooting quite a large stag, though without exceptional antlers. I had watched him for a while, with a good lot of hinds in a field a long way from the seat, and despairing of anything nearer had descended from the seat, usually an unwise move, and stalked him. It so happens that I had shot a roebuck at home the day before, and I rendezvoused with a friend on the way home from the sika expedition for an early morning fallow stalk on the following day, during which I shot a fairly large buck. Three species of deer on three consecutive days! That fallow buck was taken with one of my .256 Mannlichers, a two-hundred-yard running shot across a valley, which I took with confidence but which nowadays I should be unlikely to contemplate at all, let alone with open sights.

The sika in Argyll, on the beautiful estate of a friend, are significantly smaller animals than the Dorset ones, but very numerous, and we killed quite a few over a number of visits in an effort to reduce the population somewhat. This estate has a number of roe on the ground, which the owner preserves since they do him little harm, and quite a high number of red deer that we pursued with the sika. We had several stalking days taking both species, which caused quite a lot of damage to both agricultural crops and forestry. My best red deer head, in my opinion, came from there. It is only an eleven-pointer, but heavily pearled and nicely shaped and appeals to me more than any of the others.

Chapter 14
Sutherland and Red Stags

When I first became interested in roe stalking, after realising that I had a lot of roe on my ground and that there were plenty of other opportunities locally, my interest not surprisingly extended to encompass other types of stalking and I developed the ambition to try red deer stalking on the open hill in Scotland. I arranged a week's stalking at a lodge on a famous forest in Sutherland and duly set out. I had never stalked red deer before, but I knew roughly what was expected from much reading about the subject. This particular forest and lodge had recently been leased by a retired businessman from England, who was running it as a small hotel with stalking and fishing for the guests. It appeared that this was his first season. There were only two beats on the forest attached to the lodge and so there was only one other guest staying during the same week as myself. Unfortunately we were misted off the hill for three days, but at least I managed to shoot a stag on each of the other three days.

On the first day I was taken out by a local crofter, who had been hired for the season as second stalker. I explained to him that I was not as fit as he was, and that since I was to take any shot that presented itself it would be pointless for me to arrive puffing and heaving and unable to shoot straight, so he had best not go too fast up the hill.

We came across a party of hinds, two or three of which were on a bank, with the others invisible in a little gully by a burn. The stag was clearly in this gully because we could hear his roaring. We got as close as we could and then found that we could proceed no further to enable us to look into the gully to see the stag because of the hinds on the opposite bank, which in any case were perhaps only a hundred yards away. We presumed that the stag was lying down roaring, but could see nothing of him. The stalker decided that the best thing to do was simply to lie there and wait until he eventually showed himself, and this we proceeded to do. We lay for a long time, eating our lunch 'piece' as best we could lying flat on the ground and almost in view of the forward hind. I do not know precisely how long we lay there – it must have been at least an hour, though it seemed longer at the time. Finally there appeared to be a movement among the hinds, and the stag at last appeared at the far side of the gully. The stalker told me to take him and I fired. I remember seeing a spray of blood as the bullet hit him and the stalker crying, 'Oh! The blood! The blood!'. At the strike of the bullet the stag leaped up a peat bank at the far side out of the gully and fell dead. He turned out to be a twelve-pointer, a royal. It is coincidental that my first roebuck with a rifle had the best head that I have ever shot, and so also did the first fallow buck that I killed.

We then had a rather exhausting drag, having to move the dead stag, once gralloched, three or four hundred yards up a rise in order to reach a down slope of the hill, from which the beast could more easily be dragged to a point accessible to a tractor fitted with rubber tracks, which was the machine used for bringing in the deer.

The second shot on that holiday is also pictured firmly in my mind, for the stag was standing broadside on a rock roaring in a classical pose, like Landseer's *Monarch of the Glen* when I fired. He was a ten pointer.

My third stag was only a spiker that we came across after a long and tedious stalk in mist was wrecked at the last moment by a sheep. At the end of what I regarded as a pleasant and satisfactory week I went to settle the bill with mine host before departing south. I was rather surprised when he told me that the cheque for the venison would be sent on to me. At that time I had no idea of the normal procedure, so I did not appreciate that this was unusual. A few weeks later I received a cheque for the venison and found that this exceeded the cost of the stalking holiday, such that the week had actually yielded me a profit! I understand that in subsequent years this procedure was altered and guests did not receive payment for the venison they shot!

This stalking holiday gave me great food for thought during ensuing weeks. My enthusiasm for woodland deer stalking most certainly extended to red deer stalking on the open hill as well, and I intended to go again. Although that first week stalking on the hill had actually resulted in a profit rather than a cost, I felt that this was highly unlikely to occur again and I reasoned with myself that it might be cheaper in the long run, as well as being prospectively much more fun, if I was able to acquire an area of rough hill for myself where there might be an opportunity of shooting a stag, even if it only involved the odd wandering beast. I certainly could not afford to buy a deer forest as such! I got together a list of estate agents in Scotland and wrote to all of these, hoping that somewhere or somehow I might be able to find a piece of rather useless rough hill of little value that might have an odd stag wandering over it from time to time. I confess that I had little hope of achieving this, but there seemed to be no harm in trying.

To my surprise I received a letter from one of the estate agents not long afterwards advising me that a corner of an estate in the far north of Sutherland might be available for sale. It was part of a large sheep farm on which the owner had decided to give up one sheep hirsel with the reduction of one shepherd. There was no house available, and though there were thought to be deer on the ground there were no records. I studied the map carefully and it looked to me to be promising ground. A friend of mine, with whom I had been at the university and who now lived in Edinburgh, had also shown interest in this idea; we had agreed to try to buy some ground jointly. Accordingly I contacted him and told him about it. He mentioned that a mutual friend, who had also been at Cambridge with us, had a cottage not all that far away from the ground that might be for sale and that he might know something about it. I wrote to him, and subsequently spoke to him on the telephone, and he told me that there were plenty of red deer on that particular ground and that he had actually stalked on it himself. The problem then was to decide how much to offer for the land. After much thought I formulated a figure and spoke to my prospective partner, but he got rather cold feet and we decided that I would go ahead with the project alone; if I was successful he would be a welcome guest anyway.

This sheep farm, or estate, was owned by trustees, one of whom was the tenant who farmed it. I discovered subsequently that he actually lived only seven miles away from me in Surrey, though we never met until after the deal was concluded. The agent fixed a date by which I had to make up my mind and put in an offer. A week before the deadline the telephone rang late on Sunday night after I had retired to bed. Somewhat disgruntled at the late call, and half asleep, I answered the telephone, to find that it was one of the trustees of the estate. He was a farmer, with a big farm in the Borders, and said that he was free the following day, Monday, and that he felt that I should see the land before making an offer for it. He suggested that I came up the following morning; he would meet me in Edinburgh and drive me up to the north of Sutherland to see it. The trip would take two days because we would spend the night in the north, visit the property early the following morning and drive back to Edinburgh that day; I would then get a sleeper south overnight. Half asleep, and barely able to think straight and absorb the ridiculous idea of playing truant from the office and heading north, I agreed. I told him that I would ring for an aircraft booking and telephone him back. I discovered that for some reason there was a strike on flights to Edinburgh and that I should have to fly to Glasgow, and then get a train to Edinburgh. I arranged this and rang him back; we agreed that he would meet me at the ticket barrier on Edinburgh station, from where he would drive me directly north.

Early next morning I got to London Airport and caught the plane to Glasgow, from where I telephoned my office to say that I should not be in that day or the next. Fortunately there were no urgent appointments and this caused no inconvenience. I met Tom at the railway station as arranged and we had a pleasant drive north to Bonar Bridge, where we stayed the night in the hotel. A good deal of whisky flowed that night, but with no ill effect so far as I was concerned, as I was completely determined that I would remain sober. The following day we went to see the property, which involved a ferry journey over a river in a rowing boat to save an extra hour's drive round by the north coast, and I met the shepherd and his wife who lived close by and herded the adjacent hirsel. We never actually went on the land in question since it lay a mile from the shepherd's house up a rough track, but we had driven along one side of it on the road and I liked what I had seen and had even spotted a single stag on it. The shepherd told me that there were a good number of deer on the ground, but of course I was aware that he was an employee of the sellers. Actually what he told me turned out to be quite correct.

I had a good journey home and enjoyed meeting and spending time with Tom, who seemed quite interested that I should buy the place, without in any way encouraging me to do so. He told me that when my offer was in there would be no 'horse trading' and that it would either be accepted or otherwise. Accordingly I formulated a figure in my own mind of what would now appear a derisory sum – the capital value accorded to perhaps only a single stag or little more – and wrote off to the agents with my offer. I then sat back with crossed fingers until the end of the week and the appointed day. On that day I telephoned the agents but was told that I should probably not have a response until the following Monday. I telephoned again then and was overjoyed to learn that my offer had been accepted. I was also astounded to learn that I had not been bidding alone. Apparently the property had also been offered to a neighbouring estate. Had I known this beforehand I should probably not even have bothered to put in an offer, since this was a huge estate belonging to one of the richest families in the world! I learned later that the other adjoining estate, which had tried to buy the land in the past, had never been told that it was for sale now! Subsequently I learned that the two bids had been the same, but that the trustees had decided that they preferred to sell to me. My hasty trip north had clearly paid dividends.

Unfortunately the ground carried no house, but after the deal was completed, Tom's brother, the tenant of the estate as well as one of the trustees – the one who ran the farm but lived close by me in Surrey – contacted me and we met. He advised me that there was a small bothy close to the house of the shepherd that we had visited up there, which had been the home of the bachelor shepherd who had tended the hirsel, but which was now vacant and for which he had no plans. He told me that I could rent this if I wished, but he would not sell it. This cottage was a mile from what was now my ground, but there was a track from it to my hill and it was really quite convenient. It was subsequently agreed that I would rent this cottage for five shillings a year, now twenty-five pence, for a fifty-year lease. So began my love affair with Sutherland, and the source of many happy and memorable holidays in years to come. I did not then realise that the site of the cottage was already immortalised as a beauty spot in a well known Scottish popular song, and that a lesser known Gaelic song spoke of the beauty of the glen at the far end of the ground.

A couple of years later I was able to borrow the game records of the estate from which I had bought the ground. These shooting and fishing records went back to well before the turn of the century. From them I discovered that some stags had been shot every stalking season for almost the past hundred years, and the majority of these had been killed on what was now my hill. Therefore the estate had originally been a sporting estate prior to the war, when it was purchased by a sheep farmer who had no interest at all in the sporting. My hill had actually been a small deer forest for almost a hundred years. I was never quite sure of the acreage, since this was never mentioned at the time of the sale, but I tried to work it out from a map. On the flat it appeared to be about 6000 acres of triangular shape, but with much of it rather vertical I always reckoned it to be nearer 8000 acres. The actual acreage was really quite irrelevant since the ground provided daily stalking for our three weeks' holiday, and the extent of the ground was too great for us ever to go to the southern end when stalking. I only once visited the loch at the extreme southern corner, and that was when Diana and I approached this from the southern end where the road came nearest to the ground, and we walked across country to it over a corner of my neighbour's land. That was a good few years after buying the ground. I never really minded that there was a large area of land that we could never stalk because we had no hope of dragging a stag out from it – I felt it was a good idea leaving this ground undisturbed as a sanctuary.

At one stage I did consider the prospect of building a road from the edge of the ground, which we were able to reach by Land-Rover from the house, up the northern end to the high ground, where it was hard enough to drive a vehicle with ease. Given quick access to the high ground we could easily have taken a cross-country type of vehicle the full length of the hill. However, as it transpired I decided that the operation was too expensive to be worthwhile and I did not fancy the idea of creating a scar on the landscape with a new road.

The cottage that I rented was a traditional shepherd's bothy consisting of one large room inside stone walls with a corrugated-iron roof. The living area had been divided off from the kitchen area by a wooden partition and had been panelled all round in wood with a similar ceiling. Above the living room was a loft that I converted into a dormitory that could sleep six. At the far end of the kitchen area, cubicled off with a large glass window looking into the kitchen, was a loo. Water was piped to the house from a settling tank fed by the burn about a mile away, the water being taken out of the burn just above the sheep fank there to avoid pollution by the latter. This water supply also fed the shepherd's house that lay about three hundred yards away across a small green field. The bothy was heated by an old cooking range that also heated the water supplied by a hot tank in the loft. This range burned coal or peat. The former inhabitant had obviously used the latter, judging by the axe marks on the concrete floor where he had cut the peats, but the stove operated far more efficiently on coal and gave out a remarkable heat both for drying clothes and for the water.

The house was situated about a hundred yards from the river and the site of an old ford, having originally been a ford-keeper's house, and according to a reference in an old almanac that I found was once also an inn of sorts. At that time the main road had crossed the ford and passed the house, but twenty years before I moved in a new motor road had been built on the other side of the river and the old one abandoned. When we first went there the ford was quite passable at low water in a Land-Rover, but as the years went by the neglect compounded and it deteriorated from spates to washing away completely. The house stood at fifty feet above sea level and looked straight out on to a mountain that rose impressively above it to 3050 feet at the summit.

Although I spent my first holiday there during the spring with the bothy in its original state, my purpose in travelling north to be there then was to plan some improvements and to organise a builder to carry these out. The two houses were approached by a five-mile stone track, originally the old main road but severely deteriorated, which when we first went there was just negotiable with great care by an ordinary motor car, but which soon became impassable except by Land-Rover or cross-country vehicle. The alternative approach, which saved an hour's journey round the long loch at the end of which the house was situated, was by a track off the main road about half a mile long and then crossing the river by the ford at low water – for those who were able to find it and had a suitable vehicle! – or by boat if the river was at normal height or higher.

I managed to get the work on the house carried out that summer so that when I went up at the start of the stalking season the alterations had been completed. The corrugated-iron roof had been stripped off and replaced by an insulated asbestos one. The walls had all been repointed; a proper bathroom had been made at the far end of the large kitchen, with the necessary intervening corridor, and the kitchen area had been re-done, wooden shutters made for the windows to keep out bad weather in long periods of disuse, and the whole place decorated. Outside a smart new deer larder had been built, large enough also to house a boat and subsequently the three-wheeled Gnat that we used initially for taking deer off the hill. For the first year or two before I was married this simple accommodation suited us well since our stalking parties were men only and there was adequate room for four or five of us, and six on occasion.

During the first visit staying there I went with a couple of friends and we walked part of the hill to see what the deer situation might be. From what I had learned, I had thought that perhaps we might manage to achieve five or six stags in a stalking season. On our walk we were astonished at the numbers of deer that we saw. Quite clearly the removal of the 900 ewes that used to run on that hirsel had made room for a significant number of deer. Although our highest ground only extended to 1500 feet above sea level, which seems low by standards further south, the ground rose from almost sea level to this height, and the vegetation on top of the hill at that latitude was the equivalent of what I have seen at 3000 feet further south. Indeed, there were a few ptarmigan living on the very top of the highest hill. Parts of the ground had good grazing, particularly an area in the middle that we named 'the green valley', that showed signs of drainage attempts in the distant past. Much of the lower ground was wet and peaty and this made for hard walking going up the hill.

Before we started stalking I was faced with the problem of how we could take beasts off the hill with the least discomfort and effort. We were never able to overcome the problem entirely, though I have no doubt that had we lived up there permanently we could have arrived at a more satisfactory solution. Staying for only three weeks in autumn and two in spring we could not keep a pony there, of course, and though I believe that a suitable route for taking a pony up the hill could have been evolved, there would have been problems with much of the lower ground wet and peaty.

It so happened that the brother of one of my friends lived on the west coast and had acquired the agency for that area for a new three-wheeled low ground pressure vehicle called a Gnat. He brought one up to demonstrate it and I bought it. Although subsequently we decided that really this machine was unsatisfactory for our hill, the struggle of getting it up the first steep part on to the main ground being scarcely worth the effort in dragging that it saved later, I had it for over twenty years. I finally sold it to a neighbour in Aberdeenshire for half its original cost, and his keeper still uses it, in modified and much repaired form after a number of years' service there too, for taking stags off their ground.

We had a great deal of use and fun from this machine, but it had a number of snags for use on our particular ground. However, all other vehicles shared the same snags or were even less suitable. Despite having a very low centre of gravity, its two seats being very close to ground level, the machine was still rather unstable on a steep slope, especially if loaded with deer. Consequently it was always necessary under such conditions to have someone walking on the uphill side with a rope tied to the top of the anti-roll bar above the driver's head to apply sufficient leverage to stop the machine overturning. Though it would go over surprisingly wet ground with its fat low-pressure tyres without getting into trouble, ubiquitous burns, peat hags and other such obstacles invariably meant that a considerable amount of time on each outing was spent digging, pulling and heaving the machine out of difficulty, it was rare that we went out without being bogged down at some time or another, and spades were permanently strapped to the machine.

One day during our first stalking season we shot three small stags and we decided that we would leave these overnight and come back next day with the Gnat to collect them, rather than the three of us dragging one stag apiece off the hill. At that stage we were inexperienced with regard to one of the dangers of leaving a dead beast on the hill unprotected. When we returned next day, four eagles lifted off the carcases when we were quite close to them. It was my first close up view of golden eagles in the wild, and although I have since had closer views, including one bird getting up literally at my feet out of a peat hag on a very stormy day and almost causing me to have an involuntary evacuation of the bowel from fright at its enormous size as well as its unexpected appearance, I have not seen so many eagles so close together again. We found that they had caused considerable damage to the carcases, both tearing large areas round the bullet holes and damaging other parts of the animals.

This was the first of many journeys up the hill with the Gnat, but I doubt that we would have achieved this without there always being three of us to help manhandle it through problems. Subsequent journeys were marginally easier because in the course of time we got to know routes that we could negotiate with minimum difficulty, but on this first occasion it was a whole day's exercise to get the stags down the hill back to the larder. In later years I decided that it would really have been far easier for each of us to drag a stag down from that particular place. However, the exercise was all part of the adventure, and we finally got the three stags loaded on to the Gnat and faced downhill and home once more. At one stage I was going down a steep slope on this little machine with the three stags roped to the back when a ditch or narrow burn appeared directly in front. Because of the steepness of the slope, it would have been quite impossible to turn the Gnat to go in another direction, so there was no option but to go on directly downhill. Having stopped the vehicle the three of us went down and had a look at the situation and decided that the best course of action was just to charge the narrow, but quite deep, ditch and hope that I could get across it without the front wheel getting stuck in it at least, for this would certainly mean the whole machine overturning. The Gnat was steered by a tiller that guided the front wheel and provided I could keep this straight there was some chance of getting over the ditch. Fortunately the manoeuvre was successful, and only one back wheel stuck momentarily before pushing from my two companions enabled the whole machine to get out on to smoother ground again.

We used the Gnat on occasions for two or three years for bringing back stags from the hill, but there were so many incidents involving the machine getting stuck, and even overturning, that, after one particularly tiresome incident when it took us an hour and a half of digging to extricate it from a burn, I decided that really it was much easier to drag the stags down manually. Thereafter we used the machine for collecting beasts from the foot of the hill and driving them back along the track to the house, and for other chores such as ferrying supplies up to the house that had been brought across the river by boat. It never ceased to amaze me that this machine could stand in a shed for months on end unused and yet one could rely on its Briggs & Stratton engine starting on the third pull of the cord almost every time.

Chapter 15
Red Deer Stalking

Having acquired a little deer forest with no recent records and no detailed information of the ground, I had to decide what I thought one could and should shoot in a season. Clearly, as I learned from that first walk with friends, there were a large number of deer on parts of the ground. I knew that there were also a few deer on that part of the estate that lay behind our house and that the stalking there was let to a local person who regularly took a few stags from it. Before the first stalking season I happened to go to some lectures on deer at which one of the speakers was an elderly colonel whose family owned a large area of ground adjoining that which I had purchased. Indeed, it was they who had once tried to buy this land and were unhappy that they were never given the opportunity to bid for it when I did so. At the end of the lectures I went up and introduced myself to the colonel as the person who had bought the small area adjoining his. I was highly amused that his reaction was, 'There are no deer on the ground! A bit of fishing, but no deer!' He really said nothing else at all to me, and I had no opportunity to speak further since he indicated that he had to catch a train and had no time to talk. I do not know whether his reaction was outrage at the upstart from the south who had bought the ground from under their noses, or whether he really had no idea of the deer population there on his neighbour's estate, or whether indeed there were fewer deer at the time when the hill carried a stock of sheep. Some of his reaction no doubt stemmed from the fact that, as I learned subsequently, we had differing views on the numbers and types of deer that should be taken from deer ground to maintain the quality of the animals or to try to improve this.

I have always held the view that, rather in keeping with the old saying that a sheep's worst enemy is another sheep, so numbers of deer that are too high are bad for the deer population and the quality of the animals. I believe that many of the traditional deer forests that have apparently maintained their target numbers of stags and hinds based on history and tradition rather than on current numbers and general habitat and circumstances, have created problems by not shooting sufficient deer. The result of this has been that the red deer population has increased from perhaps 150,000 around the time when I acquired my hill to double that figure now. This massive increase has taken place at a time when the ground available to deer has been reduced drastically due to forestry and reclamation, and the effect has been exaggerated by the ground being taken often being the best grazing ground and the best shelter for the deer.

My initial impression of my own hill was that it carried too many very indifferent young stags, and I felt that these numbers should be reduced. During ensuing years I never had any reason to consider that my initial decision was incorrect, and indeed I have always been critical of the policy still followed by a number of estates of shooting only stags above a certain level of larder weight and below a certain level of antler quality, which policy is generally designed to show good estate records rather than to endeavour to manage the deer herd on a long-term basis. I am convinced that with fewer deer on the ground altogether the overall body weights and quality of antlers would improve and that on most forests there are far too many stags in proportion to the numbers of hinds.

Having said that, of course, I acknowledge that it is the hinds that breed and control population growth and that the level of these should be reduced in number drastically, thus resulting in even fewer stags being required. I see no conflict in this view with those estates, these days the majority, that rely on commercial stalking and selling stags to be shot, for the clear result would be fewer stags of higher quality sold for a higher price, and more attention paid to the commercialisation of hind stalking.

That first season I decided that the best thing to do was to take out a number of these indifferent young stags and see how we got on, and after three weeks going on the hill every day I might be better able to judge future policy, and the numbers that might be taken. Most of the friends that I invited to come and stalk with me already had quite a bit of stalking experience, and some of them were nearly as fanatically interested in deer as I was. Therefore their opinion would guide me on future plans for the hill and its deer population.

We seemed to see plenty of beasts about as we stalked, and by the last day had shot eighteen stags. I decided that I should like to make the total twenty for our three weeks if possible, and so while my two companions went to stalk on one side on that last day. I went off on my own, approaching the east side from the river. Halfway up the hill I spied a stag with a few hinds which looked to be approachable by going up a little burn. The first part of the approach was quite easy because the burn ran down a steep little gully and I simply had to walk, or partly climb, up this burn. I wore cheap, felt-type boots, which I found satisfactory for stalking because they got wet and let in water very easily and therefore one had no inhibitions about trying to keep one's feet dry. They also let the water out quite easily, too! Other stalking companions who came up with leather and rubber footwear used to go to great pains to keep their feet dry, and some of the time they were successful, but not often. With waterproof boots, once water got into them it could not get out again and their feet remained sloshing about in water. Getting wet was not as bad as it sounds, for provided that one kept moving and warm the water seemed to act as a sort of insulation and one did not get particularly cold or uncomfortable. However, it did mean that adequate drying facilities were imperative, which the old cooker at the house provided, and a good supply of dry clothing for wearing on the following day if necessary was essential. One of our approaches to our hill was from the road on the east side, which meant a short walk across my neighbour's land down to the river, and then wading across the river. In fact at one place the river came right in close to the road and so it was possible to wade straight across the river on to my ground and then walk along on the other side underneath the hill. This approach meant that often, when there was a west wind encouraging beasts to come on to the sheltered side of the hill, one started the day getting thoroughly drenched to one's knees or to the middle of one's thighs. As a result of this we became so used to getting wet around the feet and legs that we thought little of it.

As I ascended the burn it changed from a rocky bed to a deeper channel through peaty, flatter ground, but although the sort of ditch through which the water flowed was two or three feet deep the water itself was less than a foot deep. The channel was quite narrow but just wide enough to enable me to move up it. By then there was a certain amount of dead ground and by walking stooping up this channel I remained hidden from the deer until I began to get quite close and almost within range of the nearer hinds. Proceeding with much caution and continual spying with binoculars to make sure that no heads were visible, I had managed to get a little nearer still and within shot of the nearest hind, when suddenly the channel in which the burn ran ended abruptly in a sort of hole where the water was deeper as a result of the burn trickling over a peat bank into the hole in a little waterfall. I was able to stand in this hole with water up to just above my knees and by crouching a little I was out of view from the deer, almost in a little sort of butt or dugout, and able to peer through the grass at them. It was impossible to proceed further since had I tried to crawl out of the hole I should have been in full view of the deer. I could see three or four hinds lying down below a little knoll and another one feeding, but no stag. I could hear occasional roars and knew that the stag, and probably more hinds, were behind the knoll just out of my sight. I could do nothing but wait and hope that the stag would eventually come round to the front of the knoll, or over the top, and collect these other hinds or check up on them, rather than that they might wander back out of sight to him. At least if they were to do this I would have an opportunity of clambering out of the hole and advancing nearer. I simply had to be patient and wait for the deer to move. I laid the rifle case on top of the bank in front of me and took out the rifle, which happened to be my .222 (now illegal in Scotland for red deer, of course). I am not sure now why I had taken this smaller calibre rifle, but perhaps I had wanted to try it out on a stag, knowing that many stalkers considered it an excellent weapon for hind shooting. I was quite confident about it, of course, though I had no personal experience of its knockdown power on red deer.

The nearest hinds were perhaps a hundred yards, or a little more, away from me and seemed quite settled and content. I had to wait almost an hour before anything happened to change the situation. By that time my legs and feet were extremely cold, although the protection of my position did allow me to move them a little, sloshing up and down in the water to keep the circulation going. My feelings were a mixture of some discomfort and boredom, coupled with the realisation that sooner or later there must be some movement amongst the deer that would enable me either to get a shot, or to move forward, or at worst to lose them altogether.

At this point there was a rather louder roar from the direction where I presumed the stag to be, and I saw his antlers appear over the top of the knoll. A quick check with the binoculars revealed that he was a rather indifferent seven-pointer. He quickly moved round the side of the knoll and amongst the hinds that I had been standing watching for so long, and stood and roared again. It was the opportunity for which I had been waiting for rather a long time. As soon as I had checked his antlers I had got the rifle ready, and so by the time that he came fully into view I was prepared. As he stood he offered me quite an easy shot, almost broadside, slightly uphill, at what I estimated to be about 140 yards, and my position was comparatively comfortable for the shot. At the shot, which clearly hit him, he ran about twenty yards and stood. As he was the first stag that I had ever shot with the .222 and I was not quite certain of the reaction, I was not prepared to take chances, so when he did not drop immediately after running a short way I gave him another bullet, at which he dropped. In fact this second shot was probably quite unnecessary, since both were heart shots, but it is my firm belief, and always has been, that if in any doubt at all when shooting a beast one should try to make as certain as possible that it is killed quickly, irrespective of disturbance to the area or meat damage or whatever. I believe that a prompt kill of a wounded beast is of paramount importance.

The hinds dallied for a little, alarmed but slightly puzzled, and I let them get well away and out of sight before I emerged from the hole to go and deal with the stag, which was quite dead. Fortunately this was on the side of the hill and there was mostly a downwards slope with very few flat patches, if I picked my route well, and by careful navigation I was able to avoid any up gradients. This factor was already one whose importance we had started to appreciate as a major reason for learning the terrain of the hill well. One had to be able to judge, before shooting a beast, the relative ease or difficulty with which one could drag it off the hill and the route that one would have to take to do so. Even with the Gnat in the background to assist the operation one had to be able to plan precisely how to enable it to arrive on site, or as near as possible. Starting off in a wrong direction could mean a tiresome and extremely hard uphill drag if one was not careful. On the east side of the hill there was no access for the Gnat anyway, since it rose steeply from the river. Only in the centre part of the ground could we get the machine right out on to the hill.

I had arranged a rendezvous with my companions at the point where the river bent right close to the road. If I arrived there before them I was simply to wait until they came, since their stalking involved their going back to the house, where they could then cross the river by boat to the vehicle on the other side and drive to meet me. I had the option of dragging the stag down the hill and then across a long flat to the point where the river was furthest from the hill, or alternatively making for where the river came right in to the foot of the hill and then trying to float, or drag, depending on the depth of the water, the stag down the river to the road. I chose the latter as being the easier, especially since I was already drenched from the thighs down from my long stand in the burn. The drag down to the river was comparatively straightforward, except that the last part was fairly steep, but taking the beast down the river was not simple: although in places where the current was strong and there was sufficient water the carcase was washed down comparatively easily, tethered by my drag rope, there were long stretches where it was shallow shingle with rocks and not enough water to float the carcase properly. In these stretches I had mostly to walk down the middle of the river dragging the carcase, with perhaps less friction than on dry ground but certainly with less satisfactory foothold for myself. The drag off the hill had taken me around an hour. Taking the stag down the river took half an hour, though this was proportionately longer for the shorter distance, since by then I had tired. I was in no great hurry, except that I had decided to get the stag up on to the road by myself, if at all possible, and be ready waiting for my friends to arrive.

The worst part of the whole operation was dragging the sodden stag up the final twenty yards of steep slope from the river to the road when in a state of exhaustion. I was able to shift him only inches at a time up the little pathway, but with frequent rests, and fortified by the contents of my hip flask, I managed to complete this and had him lying on the road several minutes before I saw the vehicle coming to collect me. I felt satisfaction at having achieved success with the first stag that I had stalked and brought off the hill entirely single-handed. Moreover, as I soon learned, my friends had also been successful, which meant that this was number twenty for the season and our target achieved. Only a little later did I discover, when thawed out a little, that I had partially sprained both ankles in my stumbling down the river bed.

It seemed to me, from what I had seen during these first three weeks, and my view was endorsed by my companions, that from the number of deer that we had seen, particularly indifferent young stags, an annual target of eighteen to twenty was reasonable, at least for the following year, when the situation could be reassessed. This meant one daily for the three weeks' stalking holiday, perhaps two if circumstances permitted. When I had the opportunity to examine, and copy out for my own records, the Game Records for the estate that related to that part of it which I had bought, going back into the 1880s, I found that the previous sporting tenants – for the estate seemed to have been taken by such over a long period until the war – seemed to have taken about eight stags from my ground in most years. Taking into account both the considerable increase in the deer population that had taken place, and was still taking place, coupled with the fact that forestry planting on an adjoining estate had shifted a number of deer from traditional sheltering areas, and the doubtless fact that a good deal more deer had moved on to the ground subsequent to the removal of the large sheep flock on to what the sale catalogue for these described as one of the finest hirsels in Sutherland, the target that I had set seemed not too far amiss.

Although our figures varied between fourteen and twenty beasts during ensuing years, I detected no change in the deer population on my ground to cause me to reassess this target. Indeed, I felt that the deer population of all the ground surrounding my own was probably too high and undershot, and that without this being remedied little improvement in the quality of the deer in the area might be seen. The problem was complicated by the fact that I did not live there permanently, nor have a resident stalker on the ground, and I was perfectly aware that as a result of this my ground was poached in my absence. From time to time we found evidence of this and it seemed to me that without knowing the numbers of beasts taken in this way it was difficult to arrive at alternative decisions anyway. My hill was primarily stag ground, with only small numbers of hinds, though in the evenings a good many hinds crossed from neighbouring land, over the end of my hill, to graze on the flats in the strath by the river.

Chapter 16
The Green Valley

The experience of getting to know one's own hill without any assistance whatever from anyone else was fascinating. Compared to being the stalker oneself, having to plan all the movements and work out the logistics, a day's stalking under more conventional circumstances as a guest elsewhere seemed tame indeed. Although seeing other ground is always interesting, as is seeing how other people operate, following in the footsteps of the professional stalker, having one's rifle carried – pleasant as it is to be relieved of the weight – and being more or less pointed at a stag, handed the rifle and asked to take the shot, and then to have no need to gralloch one's own stag, has little attraction for me now. I have had the opportunity, due to the kindness of friends, but I found that my own experiences had spoiled me for such gentlemanly stalking and I did not enjoy it when my sole contribution to the day was taking the shot, the result of which should hopefully be expected to be a foregone conclusion anyway. I do not decry conventional stalking with a professional by any means, but feel thankful that circumstances gave me the privilege to experience what one might perhaps term a wilder sport that offered more scope to atavistic hunting instincts than when under the guiding hand of others.

I found quickly that while I liked to shoot a few stags myself, I really enjoyed more taking out friends to do the shooting, particularly appreciative guests after their first stag, or going out with longstanding companions whose company I enjoyed and with whom one shared the logistics of the stalk. Many happy stalking holidays there with two good friends from Edinburgh, as bachelor parties in the early days and later with our respective wives, are forever engraved in my memory with gratitude. To go out with friends who dearly loved the hills and the wild places as I did was always a pleasure. To learn the idiosyncrasies and facets of a particular hill under many varied conditions of wind and weather takes many years, and even then it is unlikely that one can go through a stalking season without encountering situations not experienced previously.

The interest in stalking on the hill is not merely the deer themselves, but in getting to know that in differing winds the air currents seem to travel uphill in certain gullies and burns against the apparent wind direction, or that in a certain valley or corrie the wind will eddy this way or that, or that approaching

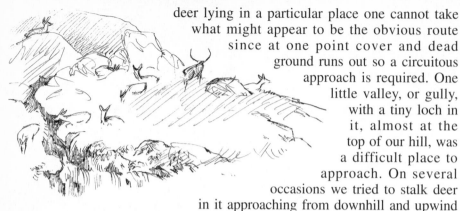

deer lying in a particular place one cannot take what might appear to be the obvious route since at one point cover and dead ground runs out so a circuitous approach is required. One little valley, or gully, with a tiny loch in it, almost at the top of our hill, was a difficult place to approach. On several occasions we tried to stalk deer in it approaching from downhill and upwind and always seemed to arrive at the firing point to see the beasts disappearing over the top of the hill. We could not risk approach from above with the wind blowing down the hill, so eventually we adopted a sideways approach. This meant being extremely cautious, but, depending on the exact angle of the wind, could be successful if all went well. There was one particular place at the north-west end of the hill which we found impossible to approach. We had a long climb up from the house, alongside a burn on a much used deer track when we stalked what we called 'The Green Valley' which lay in the middle of the ground. We could approach this by following a little burn, once we had got on to the higher ground, and going through a pass in the entrance of the valley. If beasts were on the east side and we could spot them early enough we could sometimes branch off and climb straight up the hill to try to get above and round them, but if they were on the west side we could not cross the pass into the valley without being observed.

One day four of us decided to visit this part of the hill. As the burn that we had been following flattened out below the approach to the pass to 'The Green Valley', down which one of this burn's little tributaries came, we spotted half a dozen deer high up on a crag on the west side of the valley. Spying these through a glass I saw that it was five hinds with what seemed to me to be the largest stag that I had ever seen on the ground. I do not now remember what his antlers were like, but I do not believe that they were exceptional or I should have remembered; it was his body size that seemed enormous and I was very excited and anxious to try to get nearer for a better look. At this point he was perhaps half a mile away. I believe that he may have been the largest wild stag that I have seen, but distant memory may have exaggerated.

We immediately got down into the burn and debated a plan of action. It seemed to us that the only possible course for moving at all, if we had not already been seen, was to follow the burn up, trying to use it as cover, shallow as it was; then we would round the shoulder of the hill and somehow try to approach sideways from the west. We were sufficiently far off that we hoped that even if we had been seen we would not have disturbed the deer unduly. By

wading up the stream under the shelter of the bank we would probably have
sufficient cover to transverse the open ground to the dead ground beyond.
Pausing at intervals for surreptitious peeps over the burn bank, we proceeded
apparently quite satisfactorily until almost the point of reaching dead ground.
To our dismay, a final look over the bank revealed that the deer had vanished.
We never saw them again. We had no idea whether we had disturbed them or
whether the place that they were in was a little too windy and they had just
moved on, or whatever other reason might have made them shift. I often
looked up at those crags when we passed that way and thought of that stag, but
we never saw him again.

'The Green Valley' contained deer most of the time, but unfortunately the
bulk of these were low down at the southern end and we had to consider
whether we might be able to drag one from there, also bearing in mind the time
factor because it was a long way out. One day three of us went up to that area,
and spying the valley from the pass we spotted a couple of small stags part way
down on the west side. We figured that if we retreated a little, took a circuit
round the back of the hill and came over the top we might have a chance of a
downhill shot. This manoeuvre was completed quite easily, and it was fine,
easy walking on top of that ground, being hard and comparatively level, a
pleasant change from the wet, soggy ground under foot on most other parts of
the hill. We had marked a rock on the ridge as the point at which we should
start going over to look down the other side to locate the beasts. The wind
appeared favourable, and cautiously we started to move over, stopping for
careful spies at intervals to make sure that we missed nothing.

Eventually we were able to see where the two stags had been lying, and after
a search we discovered that they had moved on further down the valley. We
located them again about half a mile away. They seemed to be approachable if
we continued downhill to the burn at the bottom of the valley and followed this
until we reached a knoll, upon climbing to the top of which we estimated that
we should be in shot. This all worked according to plan this time and one of
my companions killed one of the stags. Had we been closer to home we might

well have given the other fellow a chance at the second stag, since this beast paused well within range before departing at speed. However, we knew that we were now in for a long tedious drag uphill and resisted the temptation. The beast was gralloched and the drag ropes attached to his head and horns; we then each had a fortifying nip from the hip flask, since we were faced with at least a mile of steady gradual uphill drag before getting out of the valley and heading down again. The smooth wet grass offered minimum friction, but the drag was tiring enough and took a long time. At the pass out of the valley there were various obstacles to overcome, including rocks and some very wet boggy ground. Although the going thereafter was all downhill, provided that we estimated the contours of the route correctly, it became very much rougher ground and with several burns to negotiate.

By now the light was beginning to fade and we realised that we could never drag the beast home before darkness fell; indeed, there was no chance by then of getting back to the house in daylight, even unencumbered. Reluctantly we had to leave the stag for the night and come up next day to collect him, though it meant wasting a day's stalking to do so. We took the usual precautions of tying a plastic bag to the beast's antlers and placing pieces of lavatory paper between the cleaves of its hooves. We rarely left beasts out overnight or unattended for any length of time if we could possibly avoid it, but when we had done so in the past without such precautions we found invariably that the carcase was damaged by eagles. We never saw ravens or crows on a carcase and I was always surprised that grallochs, even in obvious places, remained untouched for days.

Leaving the stag we wended our way down the hill and by the time that we were still perhaps a mile and a half from home it was completely dark. Fortunately I was very familiar with the deer track on which we were walking and my companions were able to follow me. At one stage we were fascinated by the spooky effect of seeing phosphorescent footprints crossing the path ahead of us. A deer must have passed that way just a short time previously. I do not know how long the phosphorescence of this disturbed peat lasts, but I think not long. I was familiar with this phenomenon because there was a patch of ground down by the river where we kept the boat moored and where if one scuffed up the soil one could see the same effect after dark – a number of tiny phosphorescent particles glowing in the darkness. My companions had never seen this before. I can imagine a phosphorescent trail being quite scary if one was walking alone on the hill in the dark, not knowing what kind of creature might have caused it. Walking on rough and slippery ground in the dark is extremely dangerous and foolish because it would be so easy to fall and damage an ankle or a leg, and we were fully conscious of our stupidity in breaking the rule of making sure that we returned home in daylight.

Whilst the 'do-it-yourself' deer forest may not be to everyone's taste, and is really a young man's domain, the fact that one has to expend a great deal of energy and thought to getting a stag and then face the expenditure of even

more effort in retrieving the carcase undoubtedly adds piquancy to the whole
exercise. Anybody shooting a stag on our ground felt that they really had to
work for it to a degree that could not be experienced by most stalkers taken out
by a professional and merely contributing to the exercise by the firing of the
shot, and perhaps paying a handsome fee for doing so. One friend who came
up to stay with us and stalk several years suffered from a degree of insomnia.
He was short and stout, and surprisingly he found going downhill more
tiresome than climbing up, contrary to those of us with longer legs. He was
telling us about his insomnia at the begining of his first week north with us. On
his first day out three of us went to the hill, a mutual friend accompanying the
two of us. The stalk was successful and our stout friend got his first stag. He
also received his initiation into dragging such a beast. When we finally got
back to the house he was quite exhausted, hardly surprisingly. The following
morning he announced that the previous night he had slept soundly throughout
the night for the first time for a good many years. Moreover the experience
seemed to cure his insomnia. Not only did he sleep well on the following
nights at our little Lodge, but I gather that he continued to do so when he got
home again.

Another friend who came to visit us in the north for a week's stalking
announced that he never sweated. It was a particularly dry autumn that year,
and even quite warm on some days. On one of these, when we decided to
climb straight to the top of the hill before spying, I happened to glance round to
see sweat pouring profusely from his face.

'I thought you said you never sweated,' I said.

'I do now!' he said. He was to sweat a good deal more in the next few days,
helping to drag stags off the hill.

During that week another friend of ours, Leif Ragn Jensen, the leading
Danish sporting and wildlife artist, under whom Diana had studied many years
ago, came with his wife to visit us for a couple of days, during a tour of
Scotland. We took him out on the hill for his first stalk at Scottish red deer
stags. He was familiar with Danish red deer, and indeed deer in a number of
European countries, but had not stalked in Scotland on the open hill before.

We came across a party of young stags quite early on in the day, none of
them very impressive, and we agreed that he should take one of these, which
he achieved satisfactorily. As it was still early we decided to leave this beast
temporarily, having gralloched it, and proceed a little further. There was a
strong wind blowing and we did not think that our shot would have disturbed
very much. We had not gone far when we discovered a switch lying in the lee
of a rock slightly below us, and after a short stalk, which was really more of a
climb downhill, our friend obtained his second Scottish stag. The beast
gralloched and our hands washed in a nearby trickle of water, we ate our piece
and had a dram from the hip flask to celebrate. We then had to face the task of
getting the two stags down. Fortunately the first was comparatively easy in that
it was downhill all the way, and with a bit of careful planning of our route,

making sure of keeping to the contour of the hill, we were able to move the second stag round the shoulder of the hill to a similar position. We all three dragged the first stag to this point, quite close to the first beast, and I suggested that the two of them continued to drag this beast home while I went and fetched the first stag, which was rather smaller, and took this down on my own. Having already had a fortnight up there I was a good deal fitter than they were.

I dragged my beast for some way, making much faster time than the other two in a deliberate attempt to show off, until I came to a steep bank. With the stag perched on top of this it seemed a good opportunity to try carrying it. I had heard stories of people carrying stags off the hill and never understood how they had managed to do it. Indeed, sometimes I queried the veracity of such reports, but I know of at least one that was certainly true, and I had carried a sika stag a long distance on one occasion, and twice had carried two roebucks at once. I am sure that half the battle is arranging the beast into a comfortable package. I imagine that some of the carcases carried off the hill on a man's shoulders have head and legs cut off first to make the task easier, but not always. I managed to get this stag on to my back quite easily from this ledge and drape it round my shoulders, without the head and antlers being too tiresome and poking me in the back of the legs. All went well for two or three hundred yards until I came to another obstacle in the form of a large rock down which I had to climb. I could see no way round this, and considered it too dangerous to try to negotiate the small descent with the beast on my back, so I put it down and lowered it over the rock. Once down myself I found that I was quite unable to get the animal on my back again and had to abandon the attempt and continue dragging it home. Having deposited the stag in the larder I went back to meet my companions and assist them in the final part of their drag home.

The only other occasion when I tried to carry a stag was totally unsuccessful, as I was quite exhausted by the time that I made the attempt. A friend and I had been out and secured a beast, which involved a long drag back down to the river. We had managed to ford the river rather higher up than usual and had dragged the stag across the flats on the other side to the foot of a sharp upgrade of perhaps three hundred yards to the road where we had left our vehicle. This steep bank would still have presented some obstacle had we been fresh, but by now we were both tired. Unfortunately we were faced with a patch of long bog myrtle, and then a slope of long heather, neither of which are recommended terrain for the dragging of stags even on the flat. The prospect of trying to drag the beast up through this undergrowth was daunting indeed and I volunteered that perhaps it would be easier if I tried carrying it. With my companion's help we got the stag on to my back, but whether or not I could have carried it normally, I was by then so tired that after a couple of steps it simply fell off again and we had no option but to continue dragging. With the aid of frequent rests and liberal use of the hip flask we moved the brute up in stages until finally, with a massive sigh of relief, we got it on to the road.

That some people can carry a stag I do know, because apart from being told by the shepherd who lived nearby for the first few years that the grieve (farm manager) there for a short time, who apparently had a reputation for poaching, used to carry in deer that he had shot, though without head and legs, I was also told of another instance by a completely reliable source. On one trip north we stayed for a few days in Argyll to stalk both red deer and sika with a friend who had a beautiful estate with a high population of both species of deer. On the way north from there Diana suggested that we might call in to see another friend of hers who was in charge of a large property in Wester Ross. He kindly offered me a day's stalking, as he had a number of stags to cull, so we accepted their hospitality and stayed a couple of nights with them. That day's stalking was one of the most memorable that I have ever had, partly because of the beautiful surroundings, partly because it is the only time that I have had four stalks in a day, but mainly because our host was easily the most impressive person who has taken me out after red deer.

We began the day by walking quite some distance, well up the hill, on an excellent pony path, until we came to a splendid little shelter. Two of them had apparently carried up one of those plastic rounded shelters in which one sees roadmen and others sitting and drinking tea. They had then turfed this over to camouflage it and make it unobtrusive, and later had carried up seats, a calor-gas cooker and so on. This made a totally weatherproof warm and comfortable hut in which to enjoy a cup of tea before serious stalking began. It was situated at a point where one could start spying out the ground and possibly vary the direction in which one decided to proceed depending on wind and deer.

My friend told me that he had gone up one day to take out several stags to make up the numbers required. He had shot a stag early on in one corrie and asked his assistant, who had come up with him, to go down and fetch a pony to collect it while he went off to try for another beast that he had spotted. Having succeeded in shooting this stag he went back to the hut, where he found his assistant waiting with the pony. He asked why his colleague had not taken the first stag down on the pony instead of waiting there, to which the reply came that his assistant, an extremely fit and strong man, did not see the sense in walking all the way down to get the pony, bringing it up the hill, going down again with the stag and then coming up yet again for the second stag – so he had simply carried the first stag down to the deer larder when he went to get the pony!

Having finished our tea, I followed Dick out to look for a stag. I knew that he was extremely knowledgeable on all sorts of wildlife, and also a good photographer, but what made the day so memorable for me was that it is the only occasion when I have been out on the hill, anywhere, with somebody who was not only a very good stalker, but who seemed to know the names of all the flora of the area and could give me information on all the plants about which I asked, as well as all the birds and other fauna on the hill. I felt privileged to be taken out stalking by such an outstanding practical naturalist. It is rare to have the combination of a naturalist and competent and enthusiastic stalker combined in one person, sadly, and I constantly deplore those stalkers who show no interest in the environment in which they pursue their pastime and exhibit what might be called deer bigotry, with little concern for anything else. So many stalkers live all their lives in rich environments, out on the hill through all seasons, and when asked about deer answer fluently and authoritatively, accurately or not, but when questioned on the plant on which they have just trodden or at which one is lying staring while waiting for a stag to rise, or asked to comment on a small bird or frog, the reply so often takes the form of non-committal grunts or plain disinterest. I have little time and no respect for these people, and I always regard their observations on deer themselves with consequent caution.

We had four stalks that day, with the luxury of the beasts being readily collected for us by pony. The first was comparatively easy because a stag with hinds was spotted on a patch of green ahead of us and with the wind in our favour we had only to make a short climb to get above these and approach within shot. It was not a difficult shot, but the angle was quite steeply downhill and as I raised the rifle to my shoulder I thought to myself that I should aim a little low because at that angle the bullet might well go high. Needless to say, as I put the point of the reticule of the sight on to the stag, I forgot all about this and aimed straight for his heart. The resultant shot was high, but not too high, and the animal fell where he stood, the bullet having hit over the top of the heart in the area that I actually consider to produce the most satisfactory result, which is dropping the beast quickly. Dick gralloched the beast and I was fascinated to see the way that he cleaned the flesh off the oesophagus and tied a knot in this, then pinched the rectum clean to close this to ensure that no contents were spilled inside the beast to spoil the meat. I have not seen any other stalker take such meticulous care, yet it was done with speed and efficiency that did not prolong the job. I confess that I have not subsequently emulated this procedure myself. I do not understand why it is, but I have found that with a sheep, or a pig, of which I have butchered quite a large number, especially the former, one has to take great care about absolute cleanliness, and even a very small quantity of spilled gut content can taint the meat of a lamb, whereas deer seem to eat well even after the appalling mess of a gut shot or a bad gralloch, provided that the carcase is subsequently well washed out, of course. Nevertheless, it is imperative to gralloch all creatures as cleanly as possible for the best quality meat to result.

We left this stag where it lay, for Dick said that he would send his assistant up for it with a pony later. The ground was hard, with a good path for the pony most of the way up, so it would make good time. We moved on and had not gone far before we spied another stag with a party of hinds on another patch of green. This involved rather a long belly crawl to approach them. I was astounded at the speed with which Dick, carrying a rifle – for we both carried rifles – was able to move flat on his stomach, emulating a snake. My attempt to keep up with him resulted in several buttons being torn off my jacket. I am ashamed to say that the missing buttons remain off this jacket, now in its final stages of use, as a reminder some twenty years later! We got in fairly close to the deer and again it was an easy, but steeply downhill shot. I proceeded, once again, to reflect that the downhill angle would make the bullet go high, and then forget to allow for this when I fired. Had the shot been at long range the result could have been regrettable. This time the bullet went rather higher than the first shot, but fortunately still felled the stag where he stood. Once again I watched Dick carry out a speedy, neat and clean gralloch with expert hands, and we left the carcase to be collected later. We then moved on round the hill to bring us in a circuit to come down on the other side of the face up which we had originally come. We spied a stag with quite a large number of hinds some distance below us. We descended down the quite steep mountainside, and then with the aid of a burn for cover got into a position reasonably close to the deer. After examining the stag through binoculars for a few moments Dick decided that the nice looking ten pointer was too good to kill, particularly since we already had two stags that day, so we watched the herd for a while and then moved on down the hill homewards without disturbing them.

As we approached almost to the loch side Dick suddenly spotted, standing above us in long heather, a switch. He wanted the beast removed and told me to shoot it. This time it was a fairly steeply uphill shot, but in the excitement of the rapid action to get the rifle out of its cover and shoot before the animal, which had seen us and was staring at us, departed, I completely failed yet again to allow for the angle of the shot. Although I might offer the excuse of being unused to such steep country with such angled shots, nevertheless it was unacceptable that I should not remember before I fired that a steep angle uphill and downhill both cause a bullet to go high. This inexcusable omission cost us a bad shot and a lost stag. I sat down to take the shot and I suppose that because the beast was standing in long heather I aimed slightly higher behind his shoulder, for a high heart shot, than I might normally have done, to ensure that the bullet was clear of the heather.

Nevertheless, at the shot the beast fell instantly, and Dick said, 'That's fine! I'll go up and deal with him if you go and get the vehicle and bring it back here.' The Land-Rover was parked only about three hundred yards away in a lay-by, as we were only just above the road, so removal of this stag, despite the long heather, presented no problems. When I came back with it I was surprised to see Dick obviously searching in the heather. I quickly went up to join him and find out what the problem might be and he told me that as he had got almost up to the beast it had suddenly got to its feet and run off looking distinctly healthy. We found a few hairs but no other sign of a hit, and searched for some time in the direction that the beast had gone without finding anything else. We concluded that I must have creased the top of the beast's neck or back, as with a 'rabbit punch', and felled it unconscious temporarily, but without doing it further damage than presumably a flesh wound. Undoubtedly the angle shooting uphill would have contributed to a high shot and I should have allowed for this.

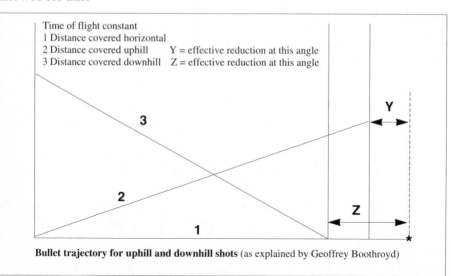

Bullet trajectory for uphill and downhill shots (as explained by Geoffrey Boothroyd)

The explanation of why a steep angle both up and down causes the trajectory to be high is based on the principles of gravity. Simple as an explanatory diagram may be, I still find it puzzling to think about and understand! Gravity causes an object to fall at an acceleration rate of 32 feet per second per second, or approximately 9.81 metres per second per second. This means that the longer a bullet is flying through the air, the more it falls. Given that a range is similar at whatever angle, plotting this range at differing angles gives the diagrammatic result that a bullet fired at an angle takes less time over the distance than one fired horizontally, so has less drop in its curved trajectory.

The experience of that day is always in my memory when angled shots present themselves. A year or two later I saw a similar occurrence when I took a friend out to look for a roebuck on my ground in Surrey. I particularly wanted to take a buck from a steep little valley that was newly planted on one side, where there was a lot of fraying damage. There was an estate road running along the bottom of the valley. Despite repeated visits I had failed to get a shot in that area and was anxious to take out at least one buck to appease the forester. We were driving along in the Land-Rover on our way elsewhere for a stalk when suddenly I spotted a buck standing towards the top of this bank above us. I asked my friend to get out of the vehicle quickly and shoot it. It was hardly a sporting stalk, but so far as I was concerned I wanted that buck because of damage and this was merely a job to be done. My friend was a very good rifle shot, and had actually competed in the British long-distance rifle-shooting team. He got out of the car and seemed to take an inordinately long time over the shot; I was concerned that the buck would not continue to stand broadside looking down at us much longer. Eventually he fired and the beast fell as if pole-axed. These days, subsequent to these experiences, if I see an animal fall like that I am suspicious, but at the time it did not occur to me that the shot might have gone wrong. As we climbed up the side of the valley to fetch the animal, to my horror, when we were about half way, the roe suddenly got up and ran off at speed. We found a little hair where it had stood, but no blood, and after a long search in the direction it had taken found absolutely nothing. We went home to fetch the dogs and again searched the area, but still found nothing. We concluded that what must have happened was that the steep angle had caused the bullet to go high, my friend not having allowed for this, and it must have creased the top of the buck's neck or shoulders and knocked it down temporarily with no more than a flesh wound.

One of the lessons to be learned from such an episode, as well as the strange ballistical quirk of a sharply angled vertical shot, up or down, causing a bullet to go high, is the necessity of advancing on an animal that has fallen to shot in a cautious manner with another round in the chamber and ready to take a second shot if necessary. This is particularly the case if the animal falls instantly on the spot. We were out on the hill one day when one of my companions shot a stag. There was no reason to suppose that anything was amiss and we advanced on the beast to deal with it. I was not carrying a rifle myself that day because both my companions had theirs. When we were about thirty yards from the stag I realised that it was not yet dead and I asked the chap who had taken the shot to give it a second bullet. I had stupidly not noticed that he had unloaded his rifle, thinking that the action was over, and he had to chamber another cartridge in order to take the shot. He did this and killed the stag. I remonstrated with him about unloading his rifle before he knew for certain that the quarry was dead, and whilst he accepted the logic and did not argue with this, I learned subsequently that he had been upset by my castigation. He had been a target shooter on rifle ranges for years, long before he took up stalking, and range drill had been drummed into him instinctively for maximum safety. Therefore he had automatically unloaded on the grounds of safety on the assumption that he would not fire again.

Some days later he was out on the hill with one of my companions – I was unable to accompany them owing to pressing chores. On their return from the hill empty handed and looking somewhat shamefaced I learned that a similar circumstance had taken place: the stag had gone down, I suppose with a shot that was too high, but when they were almost up to it the beast had got up and moved off. The same man had again unloaded his rifle and was not quick enough in reloading to get in another shot before the beast disappeared into dead ground. They were unable to find him and supposed that he had recovered and moved off that part of the hill. The lesson was learned by both these stalkers.

One has heard stories, which happily I have never experienced personally, of stalkers taking a stag by the antlers in order to bleed it and finding it to be not only alive but quite strong and active. When I approach a dead beast, if in the very slightest doubt I always touch its eye with my rifle barrel to check that it does not blink and thus ensure that it is completely dead.

Contrary to the practise on most deer forests, I always like to have at least two rifles carried out on the hill. On a conventional forest the stalker generally carries the guest's rifle and a second weapon might be awkward. Part of the reason for the stalker carrying the rifle is as a service to relieve the guest, who may be paying to go out, or a friend of his employer, of the weight and inconvenience of carrying it, but part of the reason is that he should have control of the weapon and pass it to the person who is to take the shot when he thinks fit to do so. In our case the person chosen to take the shot carried his own weapon, except in rare circumstances when I had a special guest new to the experience and perhaps not so fit, for whom I might carry it. Mostly I liked a stalking party of three and very often we all carried rifles. Initially I liked three people when we took the Gnat up the hill so that they could help counterbalance the machine with ropes on steep slopes and mostly to help drag and shove the machine when it became stuck or bogged down. Three also seemed the most suitable number to ease dragging stags and lessen the burden involved. Four is too many on one stag, and two is a perfectly workable drag team, but three lightens the strain noticeably, if only to carry impedimenta and assist in difficult places.

I like to have two rifles out partly in case a second opportunity gives the other guest a chance at a stag too, but primarily because I always like the presence of a back-up rifle in case anything goes wrong with a shot. I give strict instructions to anybody going out stalking on the hill that if a beast should inadvertently be wounded everything should be done to kill it as quickly as possible. This includes the second rifle taking the second shot and not waiting for the first rifle to finish it off if there seems to be the slightest chance of it getting away, and it also includes taking long shots or emptying a whole magazine full of bullets at a fleeing wounded beast if necessary. Fortunately the need for such a procedure has been extremely rare and of the substantial number of beasts shot on our hill over the years I can only recall two going off wounded and not being found. I like to think that in both of these instances the animal was not badly wounded and was likely to recover.

One day when I had to go to replenish stores rather than go out stalking I sent two companions up the hill to try for a stag, both of them taking their rifles. They returned triumphant in mid afternoon with a reasonable beast. One of these fellows was of Polish origin, and he was always restless, on his several visits, until he had killed the first stag of his holiday. This was his first stag on his first day out and he was cock-a-hoop. The other fellow was a generous and diplomatic person who was a frequent visitor to us in Sutherland. Not until quite a long time afterwards did I learn that what had actually taken place was that they had spotted a stag lying down across on the other side of a small gorge and had got within range of him. It being the Polish chap's turn for the shot they both got ready, but the Pole took the shot. He hit the beast, which was still lying down, in the leg, whereupon his companion, who was covering him with rifle ready, immediately fired and killed the animal, as I always requested. I do not believe that the Pole knew that I was aware of the true circumstances, and we were happy not to contradict his claim to the trophy that I subsequently saw hanging proudly in his house!

Chapter 17
Hill Equipment, Dragging and Skylines

I have always enjoyed taking friends out stalking, sharing the pleasures and excitement of the outing and hopefully giving them the opportunity of shooting a stag or roebuck, or even a doe. This has been particularly satisfying when they have obviously enjoyed and appreciated the experience, and they have made a good shot, but especially when they have clearly shown interest in the myriad wonders of nature that one discovers every time that one goes out into the wood or on to the hill. Those who show little interest in the merlin or the ring ouzel, or the vole's nest, or who are clearly bored at seeing true cranberry plants or the wonderfully coloured lichens and mosses, rarely get asked again.

As the years have gone by, I have found that I get more pleasure from my guests doing the shooting than from pulling the trigger myself. With the option always there it tends to lose a little of its thrill and it is more fun to share this with others who may not have so much opportunity.

In woodland stalking physical fitness is of less importance than it is on the open hill. When we had been up north for a couple of weeks already, and got used to the daily climb, I was always amused to take out new arrivals to the stalking party for the last week of our holiday and to see how comparatively unfit they invariably appeared to be for the first few days. I am sure that those who have taken me out on the hill have been similarly amused. When I have been taken out by a professional stalker I have always told him that there is no point in his going at a pace with which I might find it difficult to keep up: I intended going at my own pace and if I was the one expected to take the shot then it should be remembered that I could not do so with a palpitating heart, or puffing and panting, and there was no point in my arriving at the firing point in such a condition. Thus when I took out freshly arrived friends I tried to ensure that I did not exert them beyond a pace that they found tolerable. Indeed, if they were slow I too enjoyed the relief of frequent pauses.

I remember going out on the hill one day with a friend who was a shepherd cum stalker and had been so all his adult life. I was appalled that he always wore 'wellies' with the tops turned down, which I should have regarded as utterly unsuitable for the hill. I asked him about this and if he felt tired on the hill, and he told me that since he did it daily throughout the year, whether after sheep or deer, it made little difference to him whether he was walking on the flat or up the hill. It is easy for such fit people to forget that others, especially sedentary townies, are completely unused to such exercise and physically incapable of adjusting quickly to it. Furthermore there is a distinct psychological advantage in leading the party, in the same way that a winning person in a game or competition very often has this advantage over the loser. The person who sets the pace and chooses the route does so largely at his or her choice while the others follow doggedly in his footsteps. The weight of a rifle, seemingly slight at the outset of the excursion, also makes a considerable difference on a long and arduous walk, particularly to those not used to it. Mostly I carried my rifle when on the hill, but on the days when I did not do so the relief was very noticeable.

When guests who had not done so before came to stay and stalk, they rarely included a stick in their equipment. On their first morning, prior to leaving for the hill, we always offered them the use of a spare stick, several of which I kept for the purpose. Usually they looked quite surprised and said that they did not need one, thank you. Invariably on the second morning they asked if they could borrow a stick! If they came again for another holiday they always came equipped with their own hill stick, and sometimes two, in case one broke. Those familiar with hill stalking, especially on wetter ground, will be aware that a stick is of major assistance in walking over rough terrain and steep inclines. To say that a stick acts as a third leg is hardly an exaggeration at times. Apart from an additional use as an aid for steadying a telescope, or even for a rifle if one has to take a sitting shot, a stick is of much benefit when dragging a stag, either to use as a handle for a drag rope, or, if one used a harness or sling over one's shoulders to which to attach a drag rope as we did, to assist in keeping one's footing when pulling.

We developed a routine that, when the party was finally ready for the hill and assembled outside the door of the house, we checked aloud that the necessary equipment was being carried by everyone. The idea of having to share a meagre piece with the fellow who forgot to put his in his pocket, or of bullets or knife being left behind, was not one that any of us wished to contemplate.

The rifle in its cover, and a stick, were fairly obvious, and probably binoculars and telescope too. Lunch piece, knife, bullets, hip flask and drag rope were checked. The fellow who left his drag rope behind would not be popular. Under my waterproof jacket and sweater I always chose to wear a waistcoat, usually one discarded from an old suit. This I found of great use because of its pockets, which did not interfere with crawling, and which remained dry underneath the other clothing. In one waistcoat pocket I always carried a small 8 x magnification Zeiss monocular, and many times I found this invaluable when telescope and binoculars had become soaked or fogged and spying with them hopeless. Indeed, I have had two of these tiny monoculars for thirty years, both bought at sales for ten pounds each, and I have carried one of these in my pocket daily whenever I have been outside in the country, stalking or not; I use it constantly for looking at birds and animals and other items that interest me. I would not contemplate going stalking on the hill without this monocular in reserve.

In another waistcoat pocket I carried some tissues, or paper handkerchieves, or failing that some paper kitchen towels, which might have various uses, but especially for wiping dry binoculars and telescopic sights on wet days. Another pocket held a compass, in case we ever became mist bound, though this only happened very occasionally on our low hill not far from the sea. Finally, as well as the string that no countryman should be without, if I was carrying a rifle I always carried a few spare rounds in a small container in a waistcoat pocket, in case somehow my other spare bullets got lost. The readily accessible spare rounds were also in a case or in a box tightly wrapped with an elastic band so that the bullets could not rattle. These I carried in my waxed cotton jacket pocket, together with my knife, piece and hip flask. The piece was wrapped in a plastic bag that could be tied to the antlers of a dead stag if we found that for some reason we had to leave this out overnight.

It is a good idea to know that at least one other member of the party is carrying a gralloching knife, for these have been known to get lost out on the hill. The classic way to lose a knife is to leave it by the gralloch or where hands

are washed subsequently, but I have known people to lose them off a belt and out of a pocket. It may sound ridiculous to those unfamiliar with the conditions, but it is remarkably easy to lose things on the hill if one is not careful, even only temporarily, and it can be very annoying having to search for a rifle cover or binoculars or even a stick carefully left at the last stage of a stalk, when the final advance to the firing point is made with impedimenta left behind and rifle out of the case and ready for action. One imagines that it would be impossible to misplace these things, but by the time one has gone forward to a stag that has run a short way, especially if anything has gone wrong, it is only too easy on looking back to an unfamiliar view to forget precisely the spot where they were left. A good idea, if terrain permits – without disturbing the deer, of course – is to push the stick into the ground so that it stands vertically and can be seen easily, leaving other gear beside it, perhaps with the rifle cover draped over it to make it even more obvious. An alternative, if there is a third member of the party, or more, left behind at the final approach, is to put this person in charge of all items left behind with a request to bring these forward when the shot is completed.

Under some circumstances another useful item of equipment to carry in some waterproof and unsquashable place is a box of matches. The occasion might arise when it is desirable to attract the attention of somebody a long way off or down below, and a small smoky fire from a handful of heather or grass can very often be an excellent way to signal.

Clothing worn by hill stalkers might appear to be some form of traditional uniform to the lay observer, but it has evolved through practicality and suitability. The choice of top garment varies, and much depends on personal choice and terrain. On a dry hill a tweed jacket would probably be my choice, having the necessary pockets and being comfortable to wear as well as weatherproof. Our hill was mostly wet ground except in exceptionally dry weather, and if it was necessary to crawl or lie for any length of time elbows, at the least, would get very damp. Accordingly I always chose a waxed cotton jacket. I have two Maxproof jackets, which I wore on alternate days to let one air and dry thoroughly inside; I have had these for well over twenty years and still use them. They are completely waterproof despite a great deal of rough work and wear, have excellent pockets and are long enough to enable me to sit dry on wet ground. The noise factor is less important on the hill than in woods, where I should regard such jackets as completely unsuitable. The dull brown colour, especially when well used and no longer shiny, merges with most backgrounds.

There can be no doubt that plus-fours, worn by most professional and regular stalkers, are the most practical wear. Fashion, and doubtless some economy of cloth, has resulted in plus-twos, and an even more restricted version now known as 'breeks', being worn by many shooting men. These are serviceable on low ground, but the whole purpose of seemingly baggy plus-fours is to enable maximum freedom of knee movement for climbing and walking on steep ground, and I certainly find plus-fours or generously cut plus-twos more comfortable on the hill than breeches-type garments. Baggy tweed trousers of any kind not only provide better insulation than tight-fitting garments, but open weave tweed also dries out well in a breeze. None of our guests over the years, even younger ones, have been silly enough to venture out stalking on the hill in the now ubiquitous jeans. I should imagine that these were among the most unsuitable of all lower wear, quite apart from the colour: they are tight-fitting and made from material that gets wet easily and is vastly uncomfortable to wear when wet. Most people appreciate, certainly after the first time, that conventional trousers are unsatisfactory wear for walking in damp heather or grass, let alone for wading through burns and streams.

The properties of wool make it ideal for such conditions, but long tweed trousers would be unsuitable and so woollen stockings provide the best answer to the problems of comfort, warmth and being easily dried. Wet stockings remain warm insulating wear while still worn, and are much less uncomfortable than any alternative. It might be possible to remain dry with some form of protective wear, and many stalkers carry light waterproof overtrousers, which are certainly of some comfort in continuous heavy rain provided that the weather is not too warm. We noticed that friends who came to stalk without tweed plus-fours almost all either went off to the nearest place to buy a pair after a few days, or certainly possessed them on a future visit. If they did not do so initially, by the second day they wore their trousers tucked into their socks, or stockings if they had these, before progressing to plus-fours or knickerbockers.

Ideas on the best way to drag a stag vary. A hind, being without antlers, is less of a problem because one has no option but to tie a rope round its head and feet. A stag's antlers continually try to dig into the ground unless the dead beast is roped in such a way as to avoid this. Some people tie their stick across the antlers and drag lifting the beast's head off the ground. We have tried all ways over the years as different people had different ideas and preferences, and a certain amount depends on the terrain to be traversed – a long drag over wet grassy slopes, as on a lot of our hill, is quite different from the operation on hard rocky ground or steep slopes.

The pattern that we evolved and came to prefer depended on how many people were to drag. If two, then we would attach both ropes to the head. One rope would be tied to the antlers and looped round his nose with the rope coming from the top of it to keep head and antlers upright and the nose out of the ground, and the other would be round the base of the antlers. If there was another member of the party, we would attach a third rope to the front leg. I preferred not to be close to the stag's head or to have to carry the weight in my hands, involved in tying a stick across the antlers, and I found that rope halters with a webbing band, used for cattle or horses, served well if the band was untied to make a single loop to form a shoulder band. With this attached to the stag one could pull with the shoulder and have both hands free and able to use the stick to assist walking. Later on I acquired a harness that went over both shoulders, with a ring in the centre of a back to which to attach a rope, which enabled one to pull with both shoulders rather than just one. Of course, when one came to a steep slope ropes had to be untied from oneself to avoid the danger involved if the stag rolled or slid downhill too fast.

Skylines are a familiar aspect of hill country, and they are a continual experience and concern of the hill stalker. A stalking day invariably begins with climbing a hill to higher ground, and with this comes the tantalisation of those awful false summits. One climbs on looking at the skyline ahead, expecting it to be the top of the hill at last and imagining how nice it will be to sit and pause for a minute or two, resting and enjoying the view before spying the ground and starting stalking in earnest. As one nears the skyline, lo another unfolds behind it and above it and one realises that rest is not imminent. So the hill unfolds, skyline after skyline until at last there is no more and the summit is reached.

Out on the hill, especially if one is low down, one becomes conscious of deer moving over skylines, and deer standing on skylines catch one's eye. Skylines alter as one moves position and angles change. Walking or driving around on roads in hill country one sees sheep and deer on skylines, and from time to time – sadly, from the stalker's viewpoint – one sees people walking along on the top of a hill. It is then that one fully appreciates how obvious a human can be. Walkers on the hill see vast stretches of wild land and think themselves to be alone in the wilderness, but often they are mistaken in believing themselves unobserved. Humans on the hill are so easily picked out by the trained eye, and most shepherds and stalkers carry telescopes or binoculars for looking for sheep and deer. Red deer have wonderful eyesight, particularly for movement and strange shapes, and they too readily spot interlopers. Successful stalking necessitates bearing this in mind and exposure on a skyline is second only to wind as a critical factor. Often it can be the disappearance of a human, or strange shape, from view that unsettles the deer – if it is no longer able to see the danger, it becomes fearful of where it might have gone.

Observe a party of hill walkers trekking below a herd of deer and see the animals watching them intently, but relatively undisturbed. If the walkers stop to look at the deer, or if they disappear from view, then the beasts become unsettled and depart. I have seen the same situation with both foxes and wildcats walking through a field highly populated with apparently undisturbed rabbits, and I have seen antelope grazing calmly, if watchful as always, not far from lions and cheetahs that are in full view and clearly not intent on their pursuit. When these predators disappear into the undergrowth, though, it is another matter, and watchfulness changes to extreme vigilance and nervousness. The stalker has always to remember that there are skylines looking downhill, from the deer's viewpoint, as well as looking uphill towards the sky, and one may not be able to tell whether the knoll behind which one is sheltering is a skyline from where the beasts see it. If it is, then a head peering over the top of the knoll could be as obvious to the deer as a sheep on a hill top is to an observer from below. The hill is a continuous series of skylines and dead ground, and it is not always easy to judge how the ground may look to the animals being stalked.

We were given a lesson in the lack of solitude one day when three of us had set off to go up the hill. We were only a mile or so out from the house, still on comparatively low ground, when to our astonishment we suddenly spotted ahead of us and slightly below us two walkers. We had never seen walkers on our ground before and from the direction from which these appeared to have come they must have been walking cross country for a very long way, since there was no road for a good many miles. Clearly they had not seen us, since we had been in dead ground to them. They had not actually disturbed our hill, as they were too low down, but one is not happy to think of others walking about on the hill at stalking time because of both disturbance and potential danger. We kept an eye on them as they went down the hill because we were intrigued to know how they proposed crossing the river below, for they were heading for a stretch of still, deep water. They actually arrived at the one shallow part in the middle of this long, deep, pool-like stretch, but this would still involve crossing a channel that would necessitate getting rather wet or removing footwear and trousers. To our surprise, when the couple, a young man and woman, reached the river they removed all their clothing and we wondered what they had in mind! Telescopes and binoculars came into action and hidden Peeping Toms watched them cross the river and then have a short bathe followed by stretching out on the bank in the sun to dry. They were, I am sure, totally oblivious of being observed.

Chapter 18
Red Deer Management

Hill red deer management effectively applies to Scottish deer forests, where the overwhelming bulk of hill red deer exist. Whereas in woodland deer stalking the subject of management is complex and moves towards implementation of policies are applicable only to a myriad of individual owners, the situation with regard to deer forests and deer on the open hill is a very much more public matter. In Scotland, where sporting is rated, deer forests are rated according to numbers of deer shot, primarily stags, but how realistic the figures are is not known. Most recognised deer forests have had records of their ground and numbers of deer killed recorded in two well known books published many years apart (*The Deer Forests of Scotland* by A. Grimble, 1896, and *The Deer Stalking Grounds of Great Britain and Ireland* by G. K. Whitehead, 1960) and most of the red deer killed are handled by game dealers.

In Scotland there exists a body called the Red Deer Commission, which has the responsibility for the conservation and control of red and sika deer, and to a lesser extent roe and fallow deer, in Scotland. This was established in 1959 as an independent statutory agency, and has a statutory duty to prevent damage by deer to agriculture and forestry. Poaching and the implementation of close seasons for various species and sexes of deer and so on do not fall within its responsibility, these being matters for the police. Commission stalkers cannot be authorised to shoot roe or fallow deer. The Red Deer Commission has access to the records of game dealers and is thus able to formulate an idea of numbers of deer shot each year, which it can relate to population estimates made on the ground. Consequently a great deal more is known about Scottish deer as a whole than is known about English deer. This is reasonable to expect in the circumstances where a significant land area of Scotland is entirely dependent on stalking as an enterprise, and employment in these areas is affected to some degree by the stalking. Without deer and stalking many large deer forest estates would not exist, nor would the substantial outside finance required to maintain them be available, and the disappearance of these estates and their owners, visitors and employees would have obvious repercussions on other local services. Thus the red deer themselves are more significant to the environment in which they live than are the deer in areas where agriculture is predominant.

| Year | Stags killed (estate figures) | | (dealers' figures) | | Total (estate figures)(dealers' figures) | |
	In Season	Out of Season	In Season	Out of Season		
1980	13846	1664	13938	3467	15510	17405
1981	14644	1303	16725	2676	15947	19401
1982	15100	1599	16177	2920	16699	19097
1983	14526	1928	14659	2790	16454	17449
1984	13374	1626	12536	2254	15000	14790
1985	13911	1363	12799	2960	15274	15759
1986	13820	1424	13188	3155	15244	16343
1987	14327	1309	14360	2774	15636	17134
1988	15027	1646	14567	2900	16673	17467
1989	14957	1664	16687	3755	16621	20442

A further significant difference between woodland deer and those living on open hill is that whereas the habitat of the former is increasing due to governmental encouragement for small-scale forestry and wild land conservation, albeit not at a pace sufficient to keep up with the expansion of the deer population, the habitat of Highland red deer is actually decreasing for the same reason. Moreover, the forestry that is taking away land from the deer and fencing them out of it inevitably takes the more accessible, sheltered and better land for tree growing. The proportionate effect on the deer herds, therefore, is considerably greater than it might appear from mere acreage figures, for in many situations the low ground from which the deer have been excluded represented a substantial part of their food supply and areas where they could shelter from the worst of the hard weather in winter. The strath into which the deer came to feed each night from a considerable distance on what was once my own ground in the north, as well as from my neighbour's ground on the other side of the river, is now fenced off and planted with trees, the bulk of the better land there being across the river and the march. The lower ground left for the deer to feed upon is now but a fraction of what it once was, and the deer that used to cross from one hill to the other cannot now do so. This pattern has been repeated throughout the Highlands.

In the early 1960s the Red Deer Commission estimated the Scottish red deer population at around 150,000 and indicated that these levels were too high with future land use in mind. Their estimate for 1989 is a total of 300,000, or twice the level of twenty-seven years earlier. There is no doubt that when estimates for the current population are formulated the figure will be significantly higher, although with many red deer now resident in woodland any estimates are likely to err on the low side. This substantially increased red deer herd lives on a much reduced acreage of land, and that of less congenial habitat. The RDC's research shows that the annual red deer calf survival rate on the hill represents about thirty-three per cent of the population. From this it can be seen that the potential compounding increase without adequate control would mean a doubling of the deer population again in a comparatively short time. At a sex ratio of one to one these figures show an annual seventeen per cent increase in the hind population. According to Red Deer Commission figures some estates are culling annually less than three per cent of their hinds. Although in severe winters of very heavy rainfall as well as snow, substantial numbers of deer can die of starvation or poor condition, this means that, notwithstanding Nature's own culling, the overall deer herd still increases remarkably. Cull figures show that only about eighty per cent of the calves born each year are matched by the taking of stags and hinds. Thus, excluding natural deaths, encompassing deaths from starvation in this expression, the herd is increasing by twenty per cent of thirty-three per cent, or perhaps about seven per cent annually, from a figure already stated to be far too high.

Year	Hinds killed (estate figures)		(dealers' figures)		Total	
	In Season	Out of Season	In Season	Out of Season	(estate figures)	(dealers' figures)
1980	15282	373	16794	886	15655	17680
1981	15072	299	17479	908	15371	18387
1982	15658	473	18359	675	16131	19034
1983	17433	415	20817	1203	17848	22020
1984	14676	417	15077	1462	15093	16539
1985	15795	503	18473	1340	16298	19813
1986	17720	417	20380	777	18137	21157
1987	18396	368	17847	803	18764	18650
1988	20675	357	21625	692	21032	22317
1989	22770	385	25041	926	23155	25967

Among other research, the Red Deer Commission has carried out calf tagging schemes, and these have shown that most hinds die within two miles of their birthplace, and ninety per cent within five miles of where they were born, proving that hinds become hefted to an area like sheep. Stags, on the other hand, wander much more, and winter marauders are often stag parties. These figures indicate that the Scottish red deer population is mostly increasing on those large estates where there are already heavy hind concentrations, some of which are among those failing to cull sufficient numbers of hinds and therefore exacerbating the situation. Some estates are attempting to alleviate the problem by feeding the deer in winter, a few are acknowledging the restrictions placed on the herd by forestry and allowing deer back into the shelter of some mature woodland where damage is unlikely to be severe, and a few are taking advantage of the boom in farming deer domestically by feeding wild hinds into enclosed areas in winter and capturing them for sale as breeding stock for deer farms.

From what I have seen in different areas, the feeding of red deer in winter does not make a significant difference to the overall herd, though the hay or turnips or deer cobs may improve a few greedy beasts, and I am doubtful if the few fourteen point stags that may result compensate for the extra parasites picked up by the deer that hang about the feeding areas all day waiting for free hand-outs. The policy of giving deer access to shelter in mature woods seems to me to be a substantially better contribution to the welfare of the deer, and feeding them in these sheltered places has a great deal more to be said for it than flinging out a few potatoes or a bag of cobs on the open hill. Neither can compensate for the presence of a deer population that is too high for the ground, unless the degree of feeding is high enough to relieve the burden of overpopulation. So long as the commercial opportunity for the sale of live hinds is there, or the chance to build up stock on a home deer farm, the catching up of wild hinds has much to be said for it, for a live hind is worth considerably more than a dead one at present, and if the logistics are successful it is quite probable that greater numbers of live hinds are taken than might be culled extra by shooting.

The management of a herd of red deer differs little in general principle from that of managing a flock of hill sheep. One of the facets often subject to much argument is the question of the ratio of stags to hinds. Some of the ideas and convictions held on this subject are motivated by financial and other considerations not primarily concerned with what might be described as animal husbandry. That is not to say that they should necessarily be criticised. Much depends on the objective with which the deer herd is regarded. I can see no reason why one should need theoretically a higher proportion of stags to hinds than tups or rams to ewes. One good stag should easily be able to cover say twenty hinds, if unmolested. If he is going to be continually pestered by outlying stags trying to steal hinds, and thus expend much energy in chasing these off from his harem, then clearly he cannot do his job of serving the hinds as they come into season properly. The same applies to running an excessive number of tups with ewes, which will spend much time fighting over ewes that come into season and may not then be able to carry out proper service. In practise it is necessary to allow for young replacement stags and so the ratio might well be reduced, but one stag to say five hinds should surely be ample, if not excessive.

Total Annual Kill (estate figures)				
Year	stags	hinds	calves	Total
1980	15510	15655		31165
1981	15947	15371	2370	33688
1982	16699	16131	2615	35445
1983	16454	17848	3264	37566
1984	15000	15093	2516	32609
1985	15274	16298	3218	34790
1986	15244	18137	3324	36705
1987	15636	18764	3219	37619
1988	16673	21032	3479	41184
1989	16621	23155	5548	45324

On the other hand, because of the appeal of trophies and the usually more congenial weather of the early autumn, stag stalking is the main interest for owners and the primary financial earner from the herd, and undoubtedly the requirement will be for sufficient stags on the ground for a high proportion of successful stalking outings, or at least the opportunities for success. For this reason some will argue that a one-for-one ratio of stags to hinds is necessary. Given that the sex ratio of calves is equal, as one might expect, it means that even with the overall deer population on the ground at optimum level it will be necessary to take out at least a similar number of hinds.

Two factors complicate this. The first is that some areas are stag ground for much of the time and some are favoured by hinds. Whereas the stags will travel substantial distances on to other ground in search of hinds, the latter tend to stay put. Thus the theory of taking as many hinds as stags does not always apply evenly throughout the estates: some shooting significant numbers of stags may not have large numbers of resident hinds, and other ground with a high resident hind population may shoot few stags, especially if these only appear on the ground at the end of the stag season. The second factor is that the total deer numbers may already be too high, so that the requirement may well be for a target cull high enough to effect a reduction.

Given that stalkers want to shoot a large number of stags, both for commercial reasons and to gratify their sporting requirements, it may be necessary to carry an excess of shootable stags above the ratio required for breeding. Stalkers will also wish to shoot a proportion of mature stags, not merely all the surplus young ones, and this means carrying over a stock of young stags each year, and perhaps for several years with different age groups, to ensure a supply of stags purely for shooting. These excess stags will both pester breeding stags at rutting time, and increase the number of deer on the hill competing for available food, which in turn may lead to hinds being in less than optimum condition for breeding and so lower rates of conception, birth or calf survival. In this case more hinds must be sought to produce the required stag numbers, and this accentuates the problem further. At some stage the cycle has to be broken and the population stabilised for optimum rather than maximum performance.

Hind stalking, or culling, presents a number of problems that estates find difficult to surmount. The obvious one is that the hind shooting season is necessarily in winter when days in the Scottish Highlands are very short. In mid-winter it may be dark soon after four o'clock in the afternoon, and in bad weather conditions it may be almost dark a good deal earlier. Moreover, on many days, and perhaps for long periods, the weather may make it unwise, if not impossible, to go stalking on the hill, due to heavy rain with burns in spate, mist or snow. This means that the theoretical time available for the hind cull is dramatically reduced in practise. Many stalking enthusiasts show little interest in shooting hinds, not only because of the bad weather conditions and uncomfortable circumstances, but because hinds carry no trophies for them to bring home for display; or they may just not care for shooting females in the way that many sportsman would far prefer to shoot cock pheasants to hens, given a choice. Some estates manage to let out a little hind stalking, but on the whole the potential revenue from hinds other than the meat value is small. The result is that the great majority of hind culling is left to estate staff, who often have great difficulty in achieving the numbers required. Indeed, it is likely that most estates with large hind populations fail to meet cull targets, let alone make any contribution towards reducing the excessive numbers of deer.

Year	estate figures	Deer killed annually dealers' figures	difference*
1980	31165	35085	3920
1981	33688	37788	4100
1982	35445	38131	2686
1983	37566	39469	1903
1984	32609	31329	1280
1985	34790	35572	782
1986	36705	37500	795
1987	37619	35784	−1835
1988	41184	39784	−1400
1989	45324	46409	1085

* Some extra presumably accounted for by sales from farmers etc, not registered as estates. Shortfall perhaps due to direct retailing by estates?

A further problem is caused by certain unsophisticated and bigoted professional stalkers who like to see large numbers of deer on their ground, but seem oblivious to the detrimental effect that such numbers are having to the herd as a whole. I can think of two areas close to here where large numbers of deer are fed in winter and continue to visit the feeding areas of flat short grass in summer, lured by the application of lime or fertiliser to this. Despite attempts to put out feed blocks containing worming compounds for the deer, observation of the beasts that hang around these areas in large numbers suggests that many are in poor condition and carrying large parasite burdens in the form of internal worms, and probably liver fluke as well. Discussion of the subject in both areas revealed that management was aware of the overpopulation by deer and related problems in these areas, but was reluctant to implement the heavy cull required until after the impending retirement of the resident stalker, since both of these men liked to see large numbers of deer and had resisted attempts to increase culls.

Quite naturally, professional stalkers and estate employees, if not owners, may be reticent, if not reluctant, about recruiting assistance for the hind cull, especially if that assistance is in the form of stalkers unwilling or unable to pay handsome sums and tips for the supposed privilege. Although perhaps understandable to a degree, this reaction is unfortunate, for the well-being of the deer herd and the standard of its management must be of paramount importance and have due effect on long-term financial implications. Failure to keep hind numbers to reasonable levels must eventually lead either to outside official influence being brought to bear on it or to deterioration in the herd, both to the substantial disadvantage of the owner. There is undoubtedly a significant reservoir of keen stalkers in this country who are fit, sensible, competent shots and responsible stalkers, who cannot afford the high prices charged for stag stalking, or even to pay for stalking at all, but who would willingly grasp the opportunity of a week on the hill in winter culling hinds. Use of these to assist in the attainment of a responsible hind cull would at least increase the venison revenue of the estate to compensate to some degree for the disastrous fall in the price paid for wild venison as a result of the German market being flooded with deer meat from Eastern Europe. I am sure that there are plenty of problems with the logistics of such an increased volume of manpower on the hill, and only individual forests can judge conditions on their own ground to best advantage, but I cannot accept that a major increase in the cull of hinds is not feasible given the will of the estates to carry it out.

Excess stag numbers can be a complete waste to an estate, too. It may be nice at stalking time to be able to go on the hill and choose a stag to shoot from a party, and to be sure of the opportunity of a shot, but this view can be, and clearly is, carried to extremes. I know of one estate carrying a very large number of deer, far in excess of what the poor nature of the rocky ground would suggest. The stags, and indeed the deer as a whole, appear to be of very indifferent quality. Admirable as the views of the conservation minded management may be, the result is not only that the stags, indicative of overall herd quality, are poor, particularly in comparison with those on a neighbouring estate, but in winter large numbers of stags, driven by bad weather and low food availability, move down the valley to other more amenable ground, raiding crops. These beasts are then shot as marauders, either by the farmers whose crops they are devastating or by the estates upon which they have taken up residence. Although the original estate might have to look a little harder for stags at stalking time, or have less choice of what to shoot, it would seem to be beneficial to them as well as to their neighbours if the numbers of deer on their ground in summer were low enough to be largely sustainable on their own land throughout much of the rest of the year, with less competition for food and better quality animals.

Year	Stags killed (estate figures) Out of season	(dealers' figures) Ex season	Total
1980	1664	3467	5131
1981	1303	2676	3979
1982	1599	2920	4519
1983	1928	2790	4718
1984	1626	2254	3880
1985	1363	2960	4323
1986	1424	3155	4579
1987	1309	2774	4083
1988	1646	2900	4546
1989	1664	3755	5419

The question of how many stags and how many hinds should be shot, or rather how many should be carried on the ground, is not answered easily, since while one can pontificate on generalised levels, all ground differs and has its own idiosyncrasies, and circumstances vary enormously. Often an equally contentious question is what age groups of deer should be shot, and of course first of all the stalker has to be able to distinguish these on the ground. This is not difficult with experience, especially in the case of stags. The problem with stags lies in their attraction as trophies and the fact that many stalkers really want to shoot a royal, if not an imperial! Most stalkers will say that they do not really mind and are quite happy to shoot indifferent stags, but man's make-up is such that faced with a superb head the heart generally beats a little faster. Mostly really good heads are left as breeding stock, of course, but the ideal would be that all the stags had superb heads so that there was the opportunity for shooting superb trophies.

Although one cannot be dogmatic about these things, especially with wild animals in a largely uncontrolled environment, generally strong large antlers on a stag are indicative of good condition and good feeding and circumstances. It is reasonable to presume that the best stags mated to the best hinds will beget the best progeny. Many people forget that two beasts are required to achieve this, and the most superb of stags may not throw good calves if mated to poor hinds. Clearly choice of breeding stock must favour the best stags to be preserved for this purpose. Identifying mature stags of good quality with fine heads is easy. Identifying young, equally good stags fully of breeding age but not yet of final maturity is less straightforward. Choosing potentially good rams or bulls is a task that even expert stockmen with ample opportunity to walk round and handle an animal find difficult. Selecting potentially good stags from among young ones in a bunch, while the observer is lying prone and hidden, or at long range, is obviously that much more difficult, and often antlers are the sole criterion on which judgement can be made.

As with the management of other animal herds, one of the first tasks must be to eliminate poor specimens. This is for two reasons. Firstly, a poor beast might serve a hind or two and beget poor progeny, if not that year then in ensuing years if he escaped a bullet; and secondly, given bad winter conditions the poor beast is less likely to survive, and so be wasted, at the same time his competition for food would be unfavourable for better animals. Unfortunately it is abundantly clear that many, if not most, deer forests place greater importance on the prestige of their present and past records than on that of their future ones. Consequently much emphasis is placed on the weights of deer shot, and most lists of the results of the stalking season show average and maximum weights of stags killed, in a clearly competitive manner. Thus the inclusion of half a dozen runt stags or poor yearlings would bring down the average, unless these were surreptitiously omitted from the record.

A number of estates, influenced by dogmatic ideas engendered by this striving for reputation by owners or stalkers, seem actually to have a policy of only shooting stags adjudged to be of a certain body size, a certain age group and head quality, irrespective of other conditions, rather than trying to achieve a balanced population of animals of good quality in the first place. Going round different forests and seeing representative groups of stags, which can be done quite easily on those estates where deer are fed in winter if one visits them at feeding time, one is invariably struck by the large number of indifferent or poor young stags present, rather than the percentage of good stags, and also by the way that in a party of observers most of these concentrate on looking at and commenting upon the few good stags in view, if any. It is also apparent that those estates that have made efforts to improve hill ground to which the deer have access for grazing have shown more noticeable improvement in the herd than those that merely throw out a few bales of hay or a bag or two of cobs to the deer.

For effective management of a deer herd with a view to improvement of the quality of the deer, and of the stags in particular, which is the objective of most professional stalkers and deer-forest owners, a determined effort should be made to take out as many poor young stags as possible. This may be more easily done when stags are still in groups in late August or early September. They are then probably in better condition in any case before the feed value of the grazing deteriorates in the autumn, so their carcases may be better quality. At the same time switches, hummels and other obvious candidates for a bullet may be culled, as they too are in the best condition, should opportunities to do this present themselves. A problem is that early in the stalking season is not always popular, apart from the rut being a traditional stag-stalking time, because many would-be stalkers and keepers are still involved with grouse shooting then, and moreover the fearsome scourge of the Highlands, *Culicoides impunctatus,* the Highland midge, is still in evidence before being banished by the cooler autumnal weather.

While the male in a herd may be the most important individual from the viewpoint that he will serve a number of females and thus influence more progeny, nevertheless in each pair the resultant calf depends at least as much, and perhaps even more, upon the hind. This is because not only does she contribute her genes to the embryo, but its survival and growth depends on her condition, and its subsequent growth and development depend upon her health and ability to give adequate milk. Thus the choice of those hinds to be culled or left for breeding probably requires more thought and better judgement than the choice of stags.

In order to make a choice of hinds to be shot one first of all has to be able to identify categories. Differentiation between young and old hinds is comparatively simple to the trained eye, but differentiation between milk hinds and yeld beasts, those without a calf at foot, is much more difficult. Deer do not have obvious udders like cattle, and in a herd it is not always easy to decide to which hinds calves might belong. One has to decide whether the policy is to take out young hinds, old beasts or those that are yeld. The choice is dictated by the requirement. This may be to reduce numbers, to maintain the herd at current levels for the future or to obtain venison. There can be no doubt that the best venison comes from a yeld hind in good condition. Without the burden of raising a calf she should carry more flesh and fat, and the best venison animals are likely to appear obviously in better condition than those with calves.

The question as to whether one should shoot yeld hinds for reasons other than obtaining the best carcase is more debated by some and depends on the situation. A hind may be yeld for several reasons. She may be just coming to maturity and not yet have conceived, in which case she could be ideal future breeding stock. She may have borne a calf but lost it for a great variety of reasons, such as accident, disease or inability to look after it properly. If the loss of her calf was not her fault then she could breed good calves in future, but equally she might be unable to conceive or to rear a good calf successfully, in which case she will continue to be yeld and make no useful contribution to the herd. The idea that a yeld hind is in good condition so more likely to conceive and bear a good calf in future is acceptable only if she is actually sound internally and able to breed; in cases where deer numbers are adequate, let alone where they are excessive, the risk should not be taken and yeld hinds should be converted into venison.

Old hinds, like old cattle, ewes and so on, lose their ability to breed, in time, for a variety of reasons. They also lose their ability to provide sufficient milk to make a strong calf, and even to survive hard weather. For this reason old hinds should be selected for culling where possible. However, it is important to be sure whether or not she has a calf at foot, for weak calves are unlikely to survive a winter without their mother. A strong calf may survive if the weather is not harsh, but a weak, orphaned calf has little chance. In this case the stalker should establish which calf belongs to the old hind and take it as well. Thus yeld hinds and old hinds with their calves should be the first choice for culling, and which of these two categories takes precedence depends much on the requirement of the herd, the environment and the demand for venison. In the unlikely event of the cull of yeld and old beasts being complete, it is then a matter of trying to choose which are the poorest hinds and which have the poorest calves and deciding on the combination of these, if the purpose of the cull is to simply maintain numbers and improve the herd. Otherwise the next and perhaps easiest choice for shooting would be young hinds that are the future breeding stock, with a view to reducing numbers of potential breeding females.

However, careful selection of hinds from a large herd may be difficult to put into practise if the purpose is to reduce numbers drastically by taking as many from the herd as possible. The stalker can then only try to do his best perhaps to pick out several shootable beasts that may be together or easily recognisable preparatory to quick

Year	Hinds killed (estate figures) Out of season	(dealers' figures) Ex season	Total
1980	373	886	1259
1981	299	908	1207
1982	473	675	1148
1983	415	1203	1618
1984	417	1462	1879
1985	503	1340	1843
1986	417	777	1194
1987	368	803	1171
1988	357	692	1049
1989	385	926	1311

shooting if the chance arises to take out several beasts at the same time. In such circumstances the presence of several rifles each with selected targets is a great help. Careful planning to take maximum advantage of suitable hinds found in a situation of easy access for a vehicle, or in a place from which removal of the carcases presents least difficulty, will help reduce pressure to achieve the cull target later in the season.

Chapter 19
The River

My marriage to Diana meant two changes to the Sutherland stalking holidays. First of all it was necessary to enlarge the house, and secondly the composition of our stalking house parties ceased to be entirely bachelor groups. In any case, two of my regular stalking companions had also got married in the previous years and rather than their having to stay at somewhat distant hotels, it would clearly be nicer if we were able to accommodate them in the house. Planning extensions to the house from several hundred miles distance was not easy, but the builder in the north had both ingenuity and practical sense, and the result achieved was very satisfactory. On to the west side of the house I added two small double bedrooms, a sitting room and small cloakroom. With windows on what used to be on the back of the house, we were now able to watch the deer coming down the hill in the evenings. They came down every night to graze in the old fields along the side of the river round the house, where the grass was sweet, and in the long May evenings one could watch them feeding around the house, mostly stags, sometimes within only a yard or two of the windows. So close did they come that we spoke in whispers inside the closed windows for fear of scaring them. I suppose that they were so used to the house being unoccupied a large part of the year that it never occurred to them to be frightened of it, though I was always surprised that they appeared to take no notice at all of the vehicle parked outside, nor of the obvious human smells that we must have left while moving around outside during the day. In the autumn, too, the deer came down and seemed to take little notice of the lights in the house. On one occasion I was able to show someone who was unfamiliar with deer, or with stags roaring, a beast lying behind the house roaring at intervals, at about ten o'clock at night in the light of a powerful torch.

Other than its water supply the house had no 'modern conveniences', of course. By this I mean that there was no electricity, and no telephone, the nearest being five miles away – and that radio operated and unreliable. Moreover, there was no prospect, even had I wanted it, which I most certainly did not, of having these services supplied to the house. Although I could have used a generator to provide electricity, I resented the idea of the noise intruding into the tranquil environment totally unpolluted by the noises and fumes of modern society. We preferred to light the house by candles, and occasionally by Tilley lamps, which gave a better light for reading, and we cooked by calor gas or on the old range. The nearest shop was half an hour's drive away, if one was able to cross the river, or an hour if one had to drive round when the river was in spate. We always had a policy of trying to ensure that we had a vehicle on both sides of the river, usually taking our own four-wheel-drive car down the rough five-mile road to the house, and arranging for guests to make the

shorter journey to the track on the opposite side of the river, from which we ferried them across by boat. In many years, only once were we completely stuck by being unable to cross the river when a guest was due to depart, because the river was in such a strong spate that we felt that it was irresponsibly dangerous to try to do so. That morning we realised the situation and so drove him all the way round, up to the sea and then down on the other side of the loch, back to his car opposite, which involved a drive of an hour to reach his car 150 yards away!

We had a number of quite anxious crossings of the river. Once, in the days before I was married, I had gone up there alone at the beginning of the holiday and had arranged for two friends to come up on the following day. The plan was that they would park their car across the river and I would fetch them in the boat. That night there was a considerable storm and the river rose almost to flood level, accompanied by a very strong wind blowing down river. Whether the river was crossable depended not only on the strength of a spate, but also on the amount of water in the loch below, since this backed up to almost opposite the house when the loch was really full, reducing the speed of the current there. On this morning the loch was high and although there was a considerable amount of water coming downstream I felt that the current was not too strong and that it was possible to cross safely in the boat.

I waited for my friends to arrive, enjoying a cup of tea in front of the warm stove, and while doing so heard what I thought was a plastic bottle dropping on to the concrete floor in the kitchen. I could not understand this and when I went through to have a look I found nothing. A minute or two later I heard a similar noise. Having searched the kitchen, mystified I went outside the front door and saw my two guests standing on the river bank opposite. Apparently, after waiting a while for me to appear they had fired a rifle shot over the top of the house, followed by another! This had been the small 'plop' that I had heard above the noise of the wind.

I crossed the river in the boat without too much trouble, but while we were all over the other side collecting luggage, the wind seemed to rise considerably, whipping spray off the water in squalls. We decided that it might be sensible to wait a few minutes to see if it died down, sitting in their car. After half an hour with the wind showing no sign of dying we decided that we should have to make a move. We had noticed, while we were sitting in the car, that the wind seemed to come in gusts at intervals, and it occurred to us that if we timed these and judged correctly we should be able to cross the river between gusts. Needless to say, this did not work out according to plan, and we were in the middle of the river when a strong gust came down the water and hit us. The boat swung, and in our effort to straighten the course the downstream oar got stuck under the boat, which drifted on to it and snapped it. Happily we were at least two-thirds of the way across the river by this time and, although a little lower downstream than anticipated, I was able to grab the other oar from its rowlock and use it as a pole to propel us into the bank, the water being sufficiently shallow at that point. I had a spare pair of oars at the house.

The speed at which the river was capable of rising was quite remarkable. Sometimes, when the storm was in the hills further inland, the river would rise without immediate warning, but if it was a local storm we could watch the water tumbling off the mountain in front of the house in white torrents and it seemed little time before it appeared to affect the river, too. Sometimes in a strong wind it was quite spectacular to see the spray from the burns in spate high up on the mountain blowing vertically in a manner almost giving the effect that the burns were flowing upwards rather than down.

One day three of us had been out stalking on the east side of the hill, having been dropped on the road by one of the party in order that we could wade across the river to climb to some deer spotted earlier. The plan was to return and rendezvous on the road in the late afternoon. The three of us managed to get up to a stag and one of my guests shot it. We dragged it down the hill to the river by early afternoon. We discovered that the river had risen considerably while we were out on the hill; it was now in spate and there was no chance that we could recross it back to the road. With a drag rope attached to the stag we simply launched the carcase into the river and rapidly followed it downstream. The neighbour's lodge and stalker's house were situated beside the road further downstream, not far from the river. One of us went downstream, discovered that they were not out on the hill that day and managed to attract the attention of the stalker, who was a good friend of ours. He came over to help, and by tying our three drag ropes together we made a long enough rope to enable us to float the stag diagonally across the river where the current flowed from our bank to close in to the other side; our friend threw a rope with a stone attached, snagged our rope, quickly drew it into his side and secured it so that the stag floated completely over to his bank. He was then able to drag it out on to the bank, though this must have been a strenuous task with the carcase thoroughly soaked. We shouted our thanks and told him that we would be back to collect the beast later in the afternoon having walked home and crossed the river by boat to a vehicle on the other side. Despite all this extra effort we were able to get back to the house, walking down the river on our side, before our companion had left to rendezvous with us and so we were able to collect the stag ourselves.

We were only cut off like this a couple of times, however, for we learned to keep a watchful eye on the weather and the river if there was any question of having to cross it. Another time two of us had crossed the river at the start of the day, having spied beasts on the east side of the hill on some 'greens' by a burn high up on the hill. It was a wet day, and we were slightly concerned about the river level, although it had not actually risen a great deal. Our stalk was unsuccessful. I forget why this was so, but we failed to get in close enough to the beasts somehow; it was probably because of a wind eddy, for the wind had a tiresome tendency to blow up some of the little burns when the main wind was apparently blowing down the hill. We came down the hill again fairly early in the day, with the checking of the river much in mind. It had risen, but not greatly, and recrossing presented no difficulty.

Once over the other side and back on to the road, we could spy our hill again, this being impossible when close under the foot of it. We spotted a couple of stags a little further on, not far up the hill and quite close to the river. We decided that my companion, who was keen to have a go, should try to stalk these and that I should remain on the road partly so that I could signal to him if they moved, and partly so that if he got something and the river rose I could assist getting over to the road side. The beasts were on a steep part where getting one down to the river would not be arduous.

The operation did not take very long – both stags moved off for some reason, and I was able to signal to the other fellow to abort the stalk and return. By the time that he did so we were disconcerted to find that the river had already risen several inches and was continuing to rise rapidly. My companion could no longer wade where we had crossed earlier, and though there was another place lower down where he might still cross safely, a place where I often saw deer crossing, this involved walking across at a certain point diagonally upstream and a person would be unlikely to find it unless he knew the spot; moreover, we were some way from this. I felt that even if this ford was still crossable by the time that we got there it would involve both of us in a long walk downstream to show him precisely where to enter the river. The afternoon was now getting on and we began to think of remaining daylight. We felt that it would be quicker, and more certain, if he walked back to the house diagonally across the end of the ground, involving a short climb away from the river to cut off a corner, while I waited at the agreed rendezvous for the other member of the party to pick me up. On our return to the house we would walk back out on that side to check that he was all right and on course. His walk on the higher ground would be much easier than trying to follow the river bank the whole way back.

All turned out well in the end, except for it being a blank day, but in retrospect it was foolhardy to have attempted a second stalk at that time of day, and my companion finished his walk back to the house in semi-darkness, having at one stage, as he came down off the hill, found himself confronted with a short but steep drop in the gloaming that might have been dangerous half an hour later.

I had a marker board at the edge of the river opposite the house with six inch levels shown and a mark indicating the level at which I knew that wading across where the ford used to be became impossible. At the end of one holiday Diana and I remained in the house alone for the last night in order to shut the place up for the winter, our guests having departed the previous day. During the night I could hear the rain beating down on the roof of the house and I was concerned since our vehicle was on the other side of the river to save the extra hour's drive the following day. Although I could ferry Diana and the luggage across in the boat, I had to bring the boat back to lock it in the deer larder and then wade back to the car. By the time that we had had breakfast, drained the water from the hot water system and prepared the house for winter with the wooden outside shutters in place, the river had risen from a low level the previous evening to rather close to the wading mark, but still below it.

I ferried Diana over and dumped the luggage on the far side, so that I could get the boat put away before returning to pack up the car. I pulled the boat, with the aid of the Gnat, back up to the deer larder and was starting to lock these inside when I noticed Diana signalling from the other bank. I went down to find out the problem, to be told that our vehicle had a puncture. I dared not leave dealing with this until I tried wading across in case I could not do so and Diana was stranded with the punctured tyre on one side and me on the other, so back I went with Gnat and boat and crossed to change wheels, glad that the car was not packed to the brim with luggage.

In retrospect, with the benefit of that wonderful but irritating hindsight, I should have left changing the wheel until I put the Gnat and the boat away, because the time wasted lost me the opportunity to wade back to the car, the river having risen by this time to well over the mark. I put this unwise decision down to the fact that I had contracted influenza and was running quite a high temperature and not thinking so clearly as perhaps I might otherwise have done. Anyway, by the time that Gnat and boat were securely locked away until next spring it was clear that wading opposite the house was quite out of the question. The two alternatives were for Diana to drive up to the coast and back down again round the loch to collect me, which double journey would waste two hours and mean that we were almost certain to fail to reach Perth in time to catch the motor rail train south, or for me to walk up the river, over a mile, to the deer crossing that I mentioned earlier, which I hoped would still be passable provided that the water did not rise too high in the time that it took me to walk up there. I shouted to Diana to drive south to opposite this crossing, where the river was actually some distance from the road but visible from it, and wait for me in the car there. I walked as quickly as I could and happily found the place, which I knew well from watching the deer, but which I had never crossed personally before. The water was already deeper than I had anticipated – well above my knees – and I had to take off my trousers and tie these round my shoulders. I could just about make out the shallows running diagonally upstream, and doubtless being slightly comatosed by the high temperature helped stem any fear that all might not go well. My rather deep paddling actually presented no problem, and I emerged on the far bank with relief, to face a chilly half mile walk to the car, which certainly dried me off, but did not assist the fact that I was feeling distinctly ill.

Such calamities and hardships are the stuff of memories, and all part of the experience of stalking holidays upon which one can look back later in life with some amusement.

Chapter 20
Deer and Vegetation, Warbles and Midges

Wildlife on the open hill in the far north of Scotland is not so varied as in more southern woods, and the plant life available for deer food provides them with less choice, though red deer in any case are primarily grazers, rather than browsers like roe. Red deer will browse given the opportunity, however, as will cattle and sheep, for a variation in diet. The result of this is that alternative food plants, being scarce, become more attractive to deer, which means that in areas of heavy deer concentration seedlings, especially those of self-generating trees and bushes, stand little chance of reaching sizeable growth, due to being constantly eaten down or destroyed altogether. The all-important factor here is balance. This is easily said, but difficult to achieve or to estimate the appropriate emphases. Indeed, this ecological balance is often on a constantly moving scale and cannot be static.

A good example of this was quoted to me recently by the head keeper of a nearby estate. This same account also offers a classic example of the extreme difficulty of population assessment of woodland deer on any but a very long term and exhaustive basis. The property contains some fine examples of so-called natural woodland. I use the adjective advisedly, for almost no area in Britain is natural and uninfluenced by the hand of man, and the following is an excellent example of the consequences of man's interference. A national conservation body decided that an area of sixty acres of such woodland should be conserved or preserved. To achieve this objective they erected a high fence round the area and installed a locked gate. The keeper was asked to clear the area of rabbits and deer. He knew that a roebuck had been enclosed within the fence, so he positioned a rifle at the far end of the wood, while he proceeded with rabbit clearance at the other end, in the belief that the disturbance would move the deer to the rifle. Later he heard five shots fairly close to each other, and was angry that something had gone wrong and the buck had been missed or wounded. On going to investigate he found five deer lying dead, all shot perfectly! Now, uncontrolled by limited browsing of deer and rabbits that enclosed woodland is a mess of undergrowth of 'undesirable' kinds blotting out hope of natural regeneration and perpetuation.

Similar instances can be seen on many small islands in lochs and lakes inaccessible to browsing animals, where little havens of natural trees and vegetation thrive. Frequent examples can be seen along river banks in the north of Scotland, which are often the only areas where trees can grow, usually resulting from inaccessible seedlings of willow and alder taking hold and growing away from hungry mouths until they mature, in the later stages growth being able to compensate for browsing. However, as these trees mature and verge on senescence in the presence of a large and growing deer population, damage reaches a stage where recovery is no longer possible, with shoots nibbled and particularly with stags fraying and thrashing branches. With no further seedling regeneration possible, the area becomes bare and further shelter and food alternative for the deer are lost. As one might expect, an ecological imbalance leads to undesirable results.

Fraying and thrashing trees and saplings is a natural part of the behaviour of male deer, both for cleaning their antlers of velvet and in territory marking from glands on the head. In some areas devoid of trees stags will use telephone poles as fraying stocks, though these cannot be as satisfactory for them as the pliant saplings they usually use. Often young trees with a strong scent, such as that from the resin of conifers, are chosen as fraying stocks; and in the same way that rabbits pick out planted rather than natural trees, especially non-indigenous ones, for gnawing, so deer pick out the same targets. Even when all the trees in an area are planted, deer will often concentrate their attention upon any odd trees of differing species. Foresters can sometimes use this to their advantage by either deliberately planting a few trees of different species as fraying stocks to divert the attention of bucks away from the main crop, or leaving some young saplings deliberately for this purpose round the edge of a planting. Wallowing in mud-holes in hot weather and at rutting time in particular is also part of the lifestyle of red deer, and these factors should be born in mind by those engaged in the newly emergent business of deer farming. The difficulty is that suitable trees in an enclosure, unless very extensive, soon get destroyed, so careful planning to allow for this needs to be considered, as well as provision of suitable water-holes and wallowing areas.

One of the natural irritations, if not parasites, of deer, as stalkers that have suffered its attentions know only too well, is the midge. Flies and midges bother all deer, whether in woods or on the hill. Stalking in some areas can be tiresome in the extreme because of these pests. Even the small bracken or birch flies that do not bite can be desperately irritating, and while appropriate coating with a layer of chemical can discourage them from settling, trying to stalk quietly through a wood can be intolerable and distracting with their constant buzzing interfering with the stalker's ability to hear all-important small woodland sounds, even without the temptation to make an aggressive, all too obvious movement to dissuade them. The constant ear-flicking and other movements of deer show that they, too, while perhaps necessarily more tolerant than humans, are bothered by flies and in warm weather usually retreat to places where they are pestered less. The woodland deer retire deep into the cover and sleep, and the hill deer seek the breezy cooler tops of the hills, returning to the better grazing lower down only when the temperature drops sufficiently to reduce the activity of flies and midges.

Deer are troubled by various flying pests in the same way that cattle are also attacked. One has only to watch cattle in midsummer in muggy weather and see one or two put their tails vertically in the air and stampede across the field, sometimes taking the whole herd, to appreciate the real fear in which these animals hold some flying parasites such as the bot flies and warble flies, the former being one of the fastest flying of all insects. These unattractive pests lay their eggs on the unfortunate victim and the maggots hatch and enter the body. Some bot fly maggots almost totally block the noses of the victim, and the warble fly lays its eggs on the legs of cattle and deer – hence its other name of heel fly in some areas. The grubs subsequently hatch and burrow into the skin, and then migrate over a long period through the animal's body to end finally as large maggots about 3 cm long and 8 mm thick in boil-like lumps under the skin of the beast's back. They arrive there in late winter and early spring, and make a breathing hole. They stay there for a month or so, then finally wriggle out and fall to the ground, where in due course they pupate. Anyone who has shot and skinned hinds in late winter will probably be familiar with the sight of a deer skin looking from the underside as though it has been blasted with a shotgun; it is ruined as a hide, to say nothing of the obvious misery that these awful maggots must have caused the animal. Fear of these flies under such circumstances is fully understandable.

The principal biting flies are troublesome to both stalker and deer. Clegs or horseflies are more prevalent in cover or near undergrowth, but midges are ubiquitous. There are several species, and those found in woodland and in the south are different from those inhabiting peatlands and blanket bogs in the north. Those encountered by southern stalkers in woods and fields are likely to be the inappropriately named *Culicoides obsoletus,* or garden midge, or *Culicoides nubeculosus,* but the fearsome terror of the Highlands, that may well be the cause of the start of the season for red deer stags, when often they are in best condition, to be totally ignored by stalkers, is *Culicoides impunctatus,* the Highland midge, the most troublesome of the thirty-four species of biting midge found in Scotland. My own experience of a visit to our house in Sutherland in July, not for stalking, was one never likely to be forgotten. I had to attend to a blockage in the settling tank of the house water supply, and the midge attack was unlike anything I have experienced on any other occasion. Being bitten was a discomfort only secondary to the nausea of breathing in clouds of these minute monsters, and I had to dash to put my head into the comfort of the exhaust fumes of the Gnat every two minutes to enable me to complete the job. Blowing my nose on a handkerchief produced a black mass of dead midges. I swore never to venture there again after early June or before mid September!

It is little consolation for stalker or deer to know that it is the female that bites, and that she requires a meal of blood in order to breed successfully, though it is possible for a few eggs to hatch without this and so perpetuate the species in the absence of unwilling donors. The midge season is from early June to mid or late September, much depending on the weather. Midges are light- and temperature-sensitive, not liking bright sunlight nor cold, and a breeze often brings welcome relief from their attentions. Midges favour warm, muggy, moist weather, and the onset of cooler weather or early frosts in September usually heralds the end of the midge problem. Surprisingly, midges rarely entered the house even when one could see them clambering around the outside of the windows in clouds. Whether the drier atmosphere deterred them, or the darker room, I do not know, but in view of the fact that each day one could sweep up dead midges on the window sills like spilled tea leaves suggests that the former may have been the reason for their reluctance to come further into the rooms.

Chapter 21
Skulls, Skins and Cooking

Since my stalking was largely learned on my own and not sitting at the feet of some expert, or at the side of an experienced mentor, I simply did things in the way that seemed appropriate. Knowing how well boiled meat comes off a bone it never occurred to me to skin heads before boiling for trophy preparation. I simply cut the skull to the required shape with a saw, popped it into a saucepan and boiled it until the skin receded somewhat, by which time it peeled off the bone cleanly and easily. It has always amazed and amused me to hear and read of people advocating the skinning of deer heads before boiling, and whitening the skull subsequently, both of which I find completely unnecessary; indeed I find artificially whitened skulls rather unattractive. Boiling a head with the skin on, and subsequently peeling off the cooked skin and meat in one piece leaves a clean skull and a clean white finish. If the nose bones become loose with overcooking it is a simple matter to replace them and put the head carefully to dry with these in position – they will harden into place as they dry. I prefer deer skulls with the short nose cut rather than the longer one, but it is purely a matter of personal preference, in the same way that mostly I do not care for trophies mounted on shields.

The procedure of boiling unskinned heads is a useful tip for those who habitually cook rabbits for their dogs. When a friend pointed this out to me I confess that I did not much like the idea of boiling an unskinned whole rabbit. But, having followed his advice on this, some years ago, I would not now consider cooking the daily rabbit for the dogs any other way. I simply gut the rabbit, leaving the liver, heart and lungs in the animal, in true Highland gralloching fashion, and boil it in an ancient pan complete with head, feet and skin still on. When cooked, the head and feet are easily pulled off with a gentle tug, and the skin comes off with a sweep of the hand.

I have tried curing skins on several occasions, but the result has never been particularly satisfactory, and in any case I have found that the use for skins with hair on is somewhat limited, since after a few years the hairs tend to come out anyway. If I was able or prepared to cure skins into proper leather the product would be useful, but I have never done this and feel that the process is hardly justified for single skins. Dried feet, especially of roe, can make satisfactory stick handles, coat hooks and even rifle racks, but the hair still tends to come out with wear, and a good dose of moth-proofer is wisely applied. In practise, really only the antlers are of practical long term use to the unskilled amateur.

The most important part of a deer to us, unless the antlers are of exceptional interest for some reason, is the meat. I have not eaten sika, and I have only eaten the one muntjac, which was not memorable as superb eating, but we have always regarded roe as the best venison of all, especially from those better fed and larger animals from the south of England. Red deer venison would be our next choice followed by fallow a good way behind. I do not recall ever serving venison to guests without favourable comment on the quality of the meat. Butchering an animal as small as a roe is comparatively simple. I always prefer to skin and butcher an animal, be it a roe, a red deer or a sheep, hanging up. I have tried using a skinning table, but have always found this highly unsatisfactory and awkward compared to a hanging carcase, especially where one can alter the level of the carcase at will by varying this on a pulley. Again, I suppose this is a matter of personal preference and habit.

I generally hang roe for about five days, depending on the weather. I used to hang them for seven or eight days in cool weather, the same as for pheasants and ducks, but gradually I have found that I prefer them hung less long; now in the region of five to seven days at most is our choice. Often in warm summer weather I find that three days hanging is adequate. I even lost two roebucks after only three days one hot summer, and though I thought that I had managed to save some of the haunch meat, when cooked we found it revolting, inedible and definitely off. Once it starts to go off it does so very rapidly. The important thing is to bleed the animal as soon as possible after it is shot, and then to cool the carcase quickly by propping open the body cavity with a piece of stick.

In recent years the handling and hygiene of venison has improved considerably, and now EEC regulations govern larder facilities and meat conditions in respect of venison to be sold. The deer larder that I had built in Sutherland would probably not now pass the tests, but in practise it was extremely hygienic and the excellent finish on the concrete walls and floor enabled every speck of blood to be washed off. The game dealer collected carcases twice a week, so that it hung long enough to cool properly but never too long for onward transport. I am sure that poor handling of venison in the past is a major reason for its lack of popularity in this country, when it is highly regarded elsewhere in the world. With the increasing availability of farmed venison, public awareness of this excellent meat, conforming to all the modern requirements of low fat, freedom from chemicals and so on, is improving.

I hang venison in skin, with head and legs on, and if the inside of the body cavity is messy from excessive blood or stomach content I wash it out with a damp cloth. I then spray the whole carcase, especially the wound and orifices, with a fly-repellent stated to be safe near food. This chemical never touches the meat that we eat in any case, since this is protected by the skin, except the filets. These are protected by a membrane, which I am always careful to peel off and discard, since I do not care for the idea of chemicals on my food, even if they are stated to be harmless. As a result I have never had any problem with flies, and this procedure has the added satisfaction of killing any ticks and keds on the beast.

I have a number of gambrels that are ideal for hanging roe, though originally designed for sheep. They are metal with swivelling rings on top. Two or three of these I picked up at farm sales and the remainder at the auction of the contents of a butcher's shop, where I also purchased a proper chopping block and a hand operated bacon slicer, which was invaluable when I used to make my own bacon. For red deer I made my own gambrels out of wood hung on short loops of rope; these worked very well, and still do. I have even used them for cattle. One needs a fairly hefty pulley for hoisting up big stags to hang them from a beam, but I have light tackle for roe, though often the gralloched beast is easily lifted to be hung up.

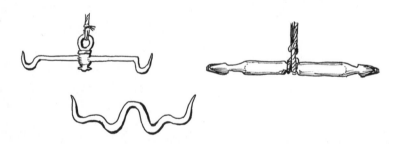

Occasionally, we retain the forelegs as a whole joint for roasting, but there is not a great deal on them and they are difficult to carve, so to save room in the freezer, we often cut off the meat to use for stew. The small amount of meat on the ribs also goes for stew. Sometimes we retain the saddle complete, cutting the whole back into two joints, one being the proper saddle, which makes a splendid roast joint, but at other times, depending on freezer availability and desired variation, we simply strip all the meat off each side of the back in a long piece and cut this into steaks, also removing the filets underneath. These 'backstraps' and the haunches are the best of the meat from a roe, or indeed from any deer. We generally use the haunches for roast venison, but occasionally use cuts from a haunch (being particular to avoid pieces with any membrane) for either barbecue meat or for venison Wiener schnitzel.

Some people go to much trouble marinading roe haunches in wine preparations and so on. This may be helpful for red deer haunches that tend to have larger fibres and be less tender, but after trying other methods we generally cook a roe haunch without such preparation, roasting it with garlic and perhaps a few herbs sprinkled on top and covered in foil to preserve moisture, usually for the same timing as one would use for beef. For barbecue meat we simply cut off small pieces of backstrap or haunch, being careful to remove all membrane, which is tough, and soak these in cooking oil, cover them well in salt and pepper and any preferred spices, and then grill them over red hot charcoal – no need for smart barbecue equipment, for a fireplace made of bricks or even a hole in the ground or old dustbin lid full of charcoal suffices – and coat in barbecue sauce.

Our favourite way of serving venison, when we are prepared to go the trouble of the preparation, is venison Wiener schnitzel, eaten hot or cold. Usually we make a good lot, cook it and eat our fill hot and then eat the remainder cold at a later date. The recipe for this, utilising say one roe haunch, would be to take perhaps half a dozen eggs, break these into a bowl and beat in parmesan cheese to make a loose paste. Add salt, pepper and garlic to taste. Cut small mouthful sized, or slightly larger, pieces of meat from the haunch, being careful to remove any membrane and use only the best quality meat, and submerge these in the mixture in a bowl. Cover this meat totally immersed in this mixture with cling film and place in a cool place or refrigerator for a couple of days. Coat these pieces in breadcrumbs and fry in a mixture of half oil and half butter until golden brown.

We adopt much the same approach to red deer, though the haunches are rather bigger and for a small family might be better cut in half before cooking to give two joints.

Smoked venison is also excellent. I have not tried smoking red deer venison, which is now sold regularly in expensive shops, mostly made from farmed deer, but smoked roe haunch is a favourite when I can make the effort to carry out the procedure, although I have to confess that it is really quite easy. For curing and smoking a roe haunch it is first of all necessary to bone the meat and trim it slightly to make it an even shape. Place this in sweet pickle for eight days, stirring daily. It may be necessary to weigh the haunch down with a plate, or some such, to stop it floating. A plastic bucket makes a good receptacle for brining. After eight days remove the meat and wash it well under the cold tap. Then place on a grid or hang up until dry, for perhaps two or three days. Next rub the meat thoroughly all over with seasoning then tie up as tightly as possible in a roll with circular bands of string. Hang the roll up in the smoker and smoke for a day or two, according to taste. Finally hang it up in the larder for a week or two before eating. Slice thinly like Parma ham.

The sweet pickle for brining the meat is made by taking a gallon of water and a pound of salt and dissolving this in the water with four ounces of sugar. Add a pinch of saltpetre (potassium nitrate) and some crushed garlic. Simmer one ounce of mixed pickling spice in half a pint of water or so for half an hour, and then filter off the solids and pour into the brine solution.

The seasoning for the cured meat consists of one tablespoon each of onion powder, garlic and paprika, and four tablespoons each of black and white pepper, all mixed up thoroughly.

Smoking food is extremely simple and there is no need to have elaborate equipment for this. I know of two people smoking commercially, one selling smoked fish and the other smoked meat and sausages, both of whom use an old wooden privy, with food hanging near the roof and a fire on the floor. I use an old wooden barrel, which necessarily can take only smaller quantities, but is adequate for personal use; I smoke bacon and hams, salmon and mackerel, and so on, as well as venison, for our own consumption. The important principles are that the smoke should be cool and that the food should be well enveloped in the smoke. My barrel, open at both ends, sits on a small hummock, or mound of earth, on a rough cement base. At the bottom of this mound I made a small fireplace about eighteen inches in diameter, very rough, with cement and bricks; it has a metal lid that goes on the top, leaving a hole at the front. At the back of the fire I placed half a dozen clay field drain pipes run up at an angle to a hole in the base on which the barrel stands. This is the 'chimney', and the six feet or so is sufficient to cool the smoke, provided that the fire in the fireplace is smouldering, not blazing. I cover the top of the barrel with an old sack, which delays the smoke somewhat to linger about the food. To start I kindle a hot fire with dry twigs, and when this is going I put dry sawdust on it and replace the metal lid. The sawdust is from our woodpile, where we have used a chainsaw or circular saw for the firewood, largely birch. The results are most satisfactory.

There can be no doubt that a principal factor in producing good quality meat is rapid bleeding and cooling of the carcase. In this context a tip that I once learned from an expatriate East European stalker that I met is to soak deer liver overnight in milk. This reduces the strong flavour and makes it far more acceptable so far as I am concerned, either for straight frying, or, as I actually prefer it, as the excellent pâté made by Diana.

The Last Will and Testament of Ian Alcock

This is the last Will and Testament of Ian Alcock of The Shannel, Aberdeenshire. Being of sound mind but weak in body it occurs to me to attend to the disposition of such that I have to leave behind me. My financial assets are insignificant and my chattels of value few, but these ephemeral trappings of our society I leave, naturally, to my wife Diana. My considerable collection of stalking paraphernalia and impedimenta I leave also to my wife, for although not a stalker as conventionally regarded, she will be able to make good use of much of it, except the rifles and knives, of which she will be able to dispose in a well thought out manner, I am sure.

Other assets, easily transferable if the recipients have a mind to receive them, are ones in which Diana is already rich and requires no addition. Although not a deerstalker as commonly defined, I submit that she has a general knowledge of deer gathered over many years – since even before the Deer Group broke away from the Mammal Society and later formed the British Deer Society – exceeded only by a handful of people in this country, perhaps. Indeed, she has that rare gift of seeing deer through an artist's eye that enables her to distinguish readily individual animals from a group just as the experienced shepherd knows the constituents of his flock.

I wish to bestow on those stalkers new to the pastime, and those that have not yet appreciated this, the early realisation that the most beautiful deer's head, or antlers, looks best on the live animal and not on a wall.

I bequeath to those stalkers who rise early in the morning to seek their quarry, my share, for which I have ever been grateful, of the enjoyment of a warm sunny summer morning after a night of rain, when in the peace and solitude of the stalking ground one is able to experience the pleasures of scents and sounds, flowers and plants, as well as the plethora of fauna of many kinds that share the environment, which opportunity is denied to the overwhelming majority of one's fellow men and women. I bequeath, too, my share of the appreciation of deer and their place in the environment. The delicate movement of the dainty roe deer, the beauty of the spotted fallow in dappled sunlight, the exhilarating whistle or shriek of a sika stag, the roar of a red deer stag or the deep hollow bark of an alerted hind, all convey to the person fortunate enough to experience these, and realise their privilege and good fortune, a thrill far beyond anything that can be created by man.

To the stalker of red deer on the open hill, who probably does not rise early enough to see magnificent sunrises, or cannot do so because of the terrain, I pass on my love of watching the rays of the setting sun on the hilltops and the comfort of enjoying these rejuvenated from a hard day on the hill by a hot bath. I pass to those that stalk on the high hills my not inconsiderable pleasure and thrill from watching an eagle soaring, and ravens playing against the rocky crags, and spying undisturbed herds of deer far below. I would like also to bequeath to those people the ability, of which sadly I have but little to hand on, to control their anger at the sight of a white woolly tail flapping down the hillside as a danger signal to all the deer in sight.

Experience and expertise I cannot pass on, for these are not hereditary and have to be earned, and in any case my own small measure would be of little value to the majority of stalkers. However, I can pass on to those keen young stalkers confident in their ability some of the realisation that comes with the passing of years as to one's lack of knowledge of the subject and eagerness to learn more at a time when powers of assimilation and retention of information have weakened.

Finally, I should like to bequeath to all those people interested in deer, and there are many of these, and perhaps even more who are not stalkers, even with a camera, the hope that viewpoints can be examined on an unbiased basis and the knowledge that both stalker and non-stalker can co-exist peacefully. It can readily be demonstrated to the non-stalker that deer need to be shot in order to control numbers and that in many places there are already far more deer than is good for the welfare of the population of these animals. Such a fact loses some of its lucidity when stated against a background of commercial interest.

Shooting Seasons

Scotland

Red Deer	stags	July 1–October 20
	hinds	October 21–February 15
Sika Deer	stags	July 1–October 20
	hinds	October 21–February 15
Fallow Deer	bucks	August 1–April 30
	does	October 21–February 15
Roe Deer	bucks	April 1–October 20
	does	October 21–March 30

England

Red Deer	stags	August 1–April 30	*
	hinds	November 1–February 28/9	*
Sika Deer	stags	August 1–April 30	*
	hinds	November 1–February 28/9	*
Fallow Deer	bucks	August 1–April 30	
	does	November 1–February 28/9	*
Roe Deer	bucks	April 1–October 30	*
	does	November 1–February 28/9	*

* Different dates between Scotland and England.

Legal Rifles for Stalking

Scotland

For Roe Deer   not less than 50-grain bullet
not less than 2450 fps muzzle velocity
not less than 1000 ft/lb muzzle energy
i.e. not less than .222 calibre.

For other Deer   not less than 100-grain bullet
not less than 2450 fps muzzle velocity
not less than 1750 ft/lb muzzle energy
i. e. not less than .243 calibre.

England

For all deer   not less than .240 calibre
not less than 1700 ft/lb muzzle energy

All bullets used on deer must be of an expanding type.

A person over seventeen years of age may borrow a rifle from the occupier of private premises and use it only in his (or his employee's) presence on those premises, provided that the occupier or employee has a relevant firearm certificate and the user conforms to its conditions. Anyone using a rifle in these circumstances may buy or acquire relevant ammunition during the period of the loan.

A firearm may not be carried in a public place without reasonable excuse if you have ammunition for it even though it is unloaded. Carrying a firearm, even without ammunition, when trespassing without reasonable excuse is defined as Armed Trespass, which is a criminal offence (as opposed to ordinary trespass, which is a civil offence).

Measurement of Deer Antlers based on CIC Scales (Conseil International de la Chasse)

Differing species are allotted differing values according to characteristics. Roe antler measurement is heavily biased towards weight and volume, with the latter able to influence up to half the score, whereas antler length may only affect ten per cent of the total. With other species antler length and spread are of importance. Hill red deer are so much smaller than continental woodland red deer that the CIC scales are inappropriate, though these can apply in the UK to park stags, and big woodland red deer stags from Norfolk, the West Country, and northern England. Most stalkers of red deer on conventional deer forests would not be concerned about points scored for red deer heads.

There is a differentiation between Japanese and Manchurian sika, the latter requiring substantially more CIC points to achieve medal standard.

Perhaps because I am unfamiliar with these deer, I regard the scoring of trophy points for muntjac heads as absurd, but I recognise that if there is to be some attempt at a yardstick for all species to be judged, they have to be included. I believe that the vast majority of red deer stalkers have little interest in the European trophy scoring system, and in most of their territories in this country fallow deer and sika would not qualify to compete with continental trophies, though fine specimens do occur in the New Forest area and elsewhere.

Roebuck antlers in many areas of Britain compare very favourably with those elsewhere in Europe, and comparison on a points system may be of more interest. To qualify for medals awarded by international hunting committees, or by the Game Conservancy and British Deer Society in Britain, roe antlers have to achieve 105 points for a bronze award, 115 points for a silver award and 130 points for gold medal standard, as adjudicated by an officially appointed referee on the basis of the following measurements.

Antler length in cm left + right/2 x 0. 5	points
Weight (gms, allowing for skull cut, etc) x 0. 1	points
Volume (wt in air – wt in water) in cm³ x 0.3	points
Spread of antlers/Av length x100 = % Max 4 points	points
(under 30% = 0; 30-35% = 1; 35.1-40% = 2;	
40.1-45% = 3; 45.1-75% = 4; over 75% = 0)	

Colour of antlers max 4 points   points
Pearling of antlers max 4 points   points
Coronets max 4 points   points
Tine ends max 2 points   points
Appearance max 5 points   points
Deductions for various unspecified abnormalities max 5 points   points

Total   points scored

Points awarded for the antlers of other deer species are based upon differing formulae, though these follow the same rough pattern of measurement.

Index